PRAISE FOR NANCY ROMMELMANN

"'How do you understand the not understandable and forgive the unforgivable?' So asks one of the characters in this clear-eyed investigation into something we all turn away from. *To the Bridge* is a tour-de-force of both journalism and compassion, in the lineage of such masterpieces as *In Cold Blood* and *The Executioner's Song*. Word by word, sentence by sentence, Rommelmann's writing is that good. And so is her heart."

—Nick Flynn, PEN/Martha Albrand Award–winning author of *Another Bullshit Night in Suck City*

"In *To the Bridge*, Nancy Rommelmann takes what many consider the most unforgivable of crimes—a mother set on murdering her own children—and delivers something thoughtful and provocative: a deeply reported, sensitively told, all-too-relevant tragedy of addiction and codependency, toxic masculinity, and capricious justice. You won't be able to look away—nor should any of us."

—Robert Kolker, *New York Times* bestselling author of *Lost Girls: An Unsolved American Mystery*

W9-BOB-760

TO THE
BRIDGE

TO THE

BRIDGE

A TRUE STORY
OF MOTHERHOOD AND MURDER

NANCY
ROMMELMANN

Published by Little A, New York

We gratefully acknowledge permission from the following:

Excerpt from *Day Out of Days: Stories*, by Sam Shepard, copyright © 2010 by Sam Shepard. Used by permission of Alfred A. Knopf, an imprint of the Knopf Doubleday Publishing Group, a division of Penguin Random House LLC. All rights reserved.

Excerpt from *Netherland: A Novel*, by Joseph O'Neill, copyright © 2008 by Joseph O'Neill. Used by permission of Alfred A. Knopf, an imprint of the Knopf Doubleday Publishing Group, a division of Penguin Random House LLC. All rights reserved.

Excerpt from *Iphigenia in Forest Hills*, by Janet Malcolm, copyright © 2011 by Janet Malcolm. Used by permission of Yale University Press.

Excerpt from *Down City*, by Leah Carroll, copyright © 2017 by Leah Carroll. Used by permission of Hachette Book Group USA.

www.apub.com

Amazon, the Amazon logo, and Little A are trademarks of Amazon.com, Inc., or its affiliates.

ISBN-13: 9781542048422 (hardcover)
ISBN-10: 1542048427 (hardcover)
ISBN-13: 9781542048415 (paperback)
ISBN-10: 1542048419 (paperback)

Cover design by Angela Moody

Printed in the United States of America

First edition

To Gavin, Trinity, and Eldon, for what they did and did not live through

To Din, for everything

It is easy—terribly easy—to shake a man's faith in himself. To take advantage of that to break a man's spirit is devil's work.

—George Bernard Shaw, *Candida*

How did fear and respect become synonymous? Whenever there's a murder here, the suspect always says, "Maybe now they'll show a little respect."

—Sam Shepard, *Day Out of Days*

Who has the courage to set right those misperceptions that bring us love?

—Joseph O'Neill, *Netherland*

AUTHOR'S NOTE

This is a work of reported nonfiction. All scenes are reconstructed from interviews, published reports, court documents, police and correctional facility files, witnessed accounts, or my own experience. Dialogue has been taken from audio recordings, handwritten notes, interviews, emails, phone calls, and other direct forms of contact. I have consulted Amanda Stott-Smith's own writing, as well as the letters, emails, and documentation of family members, friends, legal teams, and others. People in this book are called by their real names, with the exceptions of two who did not wish to be identified, one of whom is given the pseudonym "Molly," as noted in the text.

PROLOGUE

The breakup of Amanda Stott-Smith and Jason Smith's seven-year marriage did not seem out of the ordinary. They were arguing about money and stressed about the kids. Jason moved out of the family home in Tualatin, Oregon—thirteen miles southwest of Portland—in June 2008. Amanda stayed in the house, which one of her college classmates later described as "the color of throw-up," with the couple's nearly four-year-old son, Eldon; six-year-old daughter, Trinity; and Gavin, Amanda's eleven-year-old son from a previous relationship. Jason moved in with a buddy for the summer, and by fall he was living in one of his mother's rental properties in Eugene. As he had throughout his marriage to Amanda, Jason relied on his mother, Christine Duncan, to pay for what he could not. She helped with the rent on the Tualatin house and made sure the children were cared for when they visited their father. She took the family to Southern California for Thanksgiving. She saw her daughter-in-law's increasingly poor mothering skills as reason why Jason should pursue custody of the two younger children in the divorce.

It was also not out of the ordinary, at the start of the new American century, when following her arrest for dropping Eldon and Trinity from a Portland bridge just after one o'clock on the morning of May 23, 2009, Amanda would tell detectives, several times, that she did not want to be on television.

The request for anonymity proved impossible to honor. Amanda's picture ran on the front pages of the *Portland Tribune* and *Oregonian* newspapers. Advocates for capital punishment argued that mothers who kill their children are the reason the state has the death penalty. Those who saw mental illness as a factor called for more funding of social programs, and a city councilman told fellow council members that he became committed to finding money in the budget for a new rescue boat after he "listened to the 911 tapes, [and] could hear the little girl screaming, 'Don't, Mommy, don't.'" That this was not what Trinity or any child had screamed on tape did not stop the *Oregonian* from running the quote.

Most people found what Amanda had done unfathomable. Unpacking the reasons why a mother kills her children can scare people, and spectators at Amanda's sentencing in April 2010 may have felt the burden lifted when the judge called Amanda's actions "truly incomprehensible." It was a sentiment echoed by Jason. During sentencing, he told Amanda, who would not meet his eye, "The nature of this crime will never be known to me, and no thoughts of the murder will ever make sense to anyone."

If Amanda briefly cried that day in court, she for the most part maintained the half smile I had seen her wear at previous court dates, one that could be described as placid, or bemused, or frozen, or as a latent tell of the criminal mind. The smile might have been locked in place by the antidepressants she both had and had not been taking since Jason left, or by bewilderment. It made sense that Amanda would be bewildered by where she found herself, at the defense table during her conviction for the murder of her son and attempted murder of her daughter, her ex-husband sitting beside the woman he had married earlier that week, giving him the opportunity to say, for the TV cameras and thus posterity, that Trinity now had "a new mother she can love." Amanda Stott-Smith's identity had been pinned to being her children's mother, to being Jason's wife. Hearing how she had lost it all and would pay for that loss would have been stultifying, and in addition to whatever else it was, the half smile seemed like a way for Amanda to cover her mortification.

Whether Amanda had lost her identity before or after she dropped the children from the bridge was not addressed that day in court. "Truly incomprehensible . . ." put a period on curiosity. If the judge declared examination futile, if Jason believed the murder of his son would never make sense to anyone, then spectators could reasonably conclude they were off the hook, that incuriosity was perhaps kindlier, safer for all involved. When given the opportunity to stand and tell Amanda how her actions had undone their lives, only Jason and two of the perhaps seventy other people in the courtroom chose to do so. Jason's mother read a poem written by Eldon's preschool teacher; Gavin's stepmother, through tears, said, "I pray now that this part of the story is completed."

Amanda herself kept it short, saying she was "deeply sorry" for what she had done and hoped that people would someday find it in their hearts to forgive her. And then she was led away, and the case was closed, and anyone with questions about why a mother who loved her children would take them to a bridge in the middle of the night and drop them over was, if informally, invited to keep quiet and let the healing begin.

Or that's how I saw it. Others saw it differently. Two days after her arrest, a commenter on the website *The Weekly Vice* with the screen name Lil Miss Sunshine posted, under a summary of the crime and Amanda's mug shot, "Stop crying you dumb bitch cuz NOBODY feels sorry for you!"

After sitting for a somewhat longer period of reflection, the poet Mary Szybist wrote "So and So Descending from the Bridge" about Amanda and the children. The poem appeared in her collection *Incarnadine*, which won the 2013 National Book Award for Poetry.

"Behavior makes sense," Jen Johnson, Amanda's college friend, told me four days after Amanda was sentenced. Also, the last time she had seen Amanda, "she was pregnant with Eldon. She was beautiful and radiant and knew she was having a boy."

During the years I looked into Amanda's story, I sometimes thought of her half smile in court and wondered how deliberate the expression had been, how much control she had over keeping her face just so. I read the John Cheever story "The Country Husband" and came across the sentence, "Her head was bent and her face was set in that empty half smile behind which the whipped soul is suspended." I wondered whether Amanda's soul was whipped or if she were sly, and also, whether looking into the murder of a child by its mother was like staring into a prism in your hand: the more you turned it, the more possibilities beamed back, anguish, rage, comprehension, and untruths refracting— whatever you wanted to see you would find there.

PART ONE

Sellwood Bridge, 2010. Photo courtesy of Zeb Andrews.

1

At 1:17 a.m. on May 23, 2009, Pati Gallagher and her husband, Dan, were having a last after-dinner drink on the patio of their waterside condo in Portland, Oregon. Their chairs were angled toward the Willamette River, not fifty feet away, when they heard something hit the water. The couple did not become alarmed. Lots of things fell from the Sellwood Bridge: shopping carts, bottles tossed by hooting teenagers.

Then they heard a child yell, "Help me!"

There was no moonlight that night and few lights onshore. The couple scrambled to the river's edge but could see nothing.

"Where are you?" Dan shouted.

Pati called 911. She told the operator someone had fallen from the bridge and was in the water yelling for help. It had been more than two minutes.

"Can you hear that?" Pati said, and she held the phone toward the river.

The voice floated north with the current, past a recreation area, past an old amusement park. It was a clear night, and had someone in the water been looking toward the river's east bank, they would have seen the outline of a Ferris wheel and a thrill ride called the Scream-N-Eagle.

The screams continued. "Help me! Help me!"

David Haag, who lived in a floating home along the river, heard the cries for help. At one thirty, he and his companion, Cheryl Robb, motored their boat onto the Willamette to find whoever was screaming. It was twenty-five minutes before they saw the partially submerged form of a young girl. Haag jumped in the water and grabbed her. He was swimming her back to the boat when Robb called out, "My god, there's another one!"

Haag went after the other child, a boy. The girl, who had been in the fifty-six-degree water for more than thirty minutes, was sobbing. The boy was not. He had been facedown in the water and was not breathing when Haag got him into the boat. The boy was still not breathing by the time Haag motored the boat to a yacht club on the river's eastern shore.

It was now 2:10 a.m. Officers were waiting. Sergeant Pete Simpson administered CPR to the boy, who was blue and cold. He was pronounced dead at the scene. The girl was rushed to the hospital. Police initiated a homicide investigation.

Authorities first had to ask, who were these children? Did they fall off a boat? Were they kidnapped? Were there others in the river still? The water beneath Portland's southernmost bridge was now cut by rescue boats, lit by searchlights, beaten by helicopters, the river's banks trampled by police and residents who could not or did not want to go back to sleep.

Two miles downriver in Milwaukie, twelve-year-old Gavin Stott could not sleep. He had decided to stay home when his mother went to pick up his two younger half siblings. At midnight, and again at twelve thirty, he woke his grandparents, asking why his mom was not back. Kathy and Mike Stott called their daughter Amanda. She did not answer their calls. Shortly after one o'clock, they called Amanda's younger sister, Chantel Gardner, and asked if she had seen Amanda. Chantel had eaten dinner with her the night before at a Mongolian barbecue restaurant but had not heard from her since. Amanda had told Chantel she would be taking the children to the downtown waterfront to see the fireworks. It was a Friday night, the start of the Memorial Day weekend, and the opening celebration of Portland's annual Rose Festival. Knowing that Amanda had previously driven drunk with her kids in the car, Chantel and her husband got out of bed and drove around looking for her.

At 1:33, Kathy Stott called Amanda's estranged husband, Jason Smith, asking if he had spoken with Amanda. Jason had not, not since he left their two children with her at around eight o'clock the previous evening. Because Jason's license was suspended, his mother, Christine Duncan, had driven them the hundred miles from Eugene, where he and the children were staying in one of Duncan's rental apartments. Amanda met them at the house on Southwest Cayuse Court in Tualatin, where she and the children had lived with Jason before he moved out the previous June. Though she was staying with her parents, the Tualatin house was where Amanda preferred to meet the children for their visitations every other weekend.

Amanda had in fact phoned Jason at 1:22 a.m. He had not picked up her call. But after speaking with Kathy Stott, he tried calling Amanda back. For more than an hour, she did not answer.

At 2:49 a.m., Amanda answered.

"Help me," she said.

"Are the kids okay?" Jason asked. "Where are the kids?"

"Why have you done this to me?" she said. "Why have you taken my joy away?"

Jason again asked where the children were. Amanda would not say.

Christine Duncan called 911 and filed a missing person report, stating she believed her son's children were in immediate danger.

At 3:25 a.m., Jason spoke with the police. He told them that he did not know where his children were, that they had been with their mother, that he had checked the Cayuse Court house and found it empty.

Around 7:00 a.m., Chantel heard a news report: two children were found in the river. She called her mother, who said Amanda and the children had not come home. Kathy Stott again phoned Jason, who again called the police. He told them the kids in the river might be his. He and his mother headed to the Portland Police Bureau. As they were speaking with detectives, they received confirmation that the children found in the river were Jason's. His daughter, Trinity Christine Kimberly Smith, age seven, was in the hospital in serious condition. His son, Eldon Jay Rebhan Smith, had drowned. He was four years old.

At 10:25 a.m., Portland police officers approached a battered blue 1991 Audi parked on the ninth floor of a downtown Portland parking garage. The car matched the description of the one they were looking for. A woman's hand, holding a cigarette, rested on the open driver's-side window. Officer Wade Greaves climbed a retaining wall to get a better look. The woman spotted him and opened her car door. She bolted. Officer Greaves ran after her. The woman made it to the garage's outer wall, climbed through an opening, and dropped. Greaves grabbed her. He and another officer hauled Amanda Jo Stott-Smith back up and placed her under arrest.

News of the incident dominated the front page of the Sunday *Oregonian*, though only the barest details were available. The children had been in the water more than thirty minutes. Because of their ages, they were not initially named. Onlookers shared disbelief and grief. A woman who lived along the river recalled a man who jumped from the Sellwood Bridge to evade police. But children thrown into the river "just makes my heart sick," she said. "And it's so close to home."

The article included Amanda's mug shot. Her forehead was creased with tension, but except for her dark hair in disarray, she looked . . . How did she look? Dazed? Spent? In surrender?

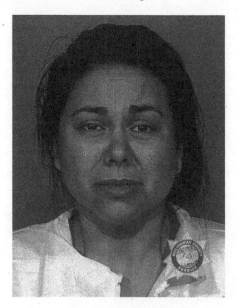

Amanda's mug shot, 2009

I could not tell, standing at my kitchen counter, holding the morning's first cup of coffee. What did I expect a mother who had just dropped her children off a bridge to look like? "Wrecked" was the best answer I could come up with.

I went online. While there was some compassion in the comments that accompanied the news stories, prayers for the children and pleas to understand mental illness, Amanda was largely vilified. People suggested that she be hanged from the Sellwood Bridge and lowered slowly so as not to break the neck right away, that "child killer" be tattooed on her forehead before releasing her to the general population. The reactions were frustrated, angry, a group censure so we might agree to move on, if to where was not specified.

I looked at the photo again. Amanda was attractive; she looked her age, thirty-one, nearly the age I was when my daughter turned four, the age Amanda had determined for her son to die. What had brought her to the bridge, to a place where she thought the right decision was to murder her children?

On Tuesday, May 26, Amanda Stott-Smith was arraigned at Justice Center in downtown Portland. Two cameramen were the only people in the gallery when I arrived. We wondered whether Amanda would appear facing forward or looking down. We talked about other parents who had murdered their children in Oregon: Christian Longo, who strangled his wife and baby, then threw his two other children off a bridge; Diane Downs, who shot her three children inside of her car.

By 2:10, the room was filled with twenty-two people on four rows of benches. I did not know whom the spectators were here for but thought maybe the young man in the back row, the one snuffling loudly and pressed between what appeared to be his mother and sister, might be related to Amanda. If he was, I wanted to speak with him.

As the female clerks and court reporters talked and laughed and booted up computers that made the Windows chime, I looked at the young man. I gave him a small, respectful smile. He gave me one back.

At 2:27, Judge Julia Philbrook entered. We all rose. The district attorney told her she would see three defendants in addition to Stott-Smith. They called the young man in the back row. My snuffling boy got up and stood before the judge. He was accused of third-degree assault. He pled not guilty. He was ordered to come back on June 3, and then he left, his tear-tracked mother looking back at me before joining her son in walking out.

The judge was informed that Stott-Smith was not yet ready to appear. Instead, a young man was called next; he wore prison blues and was tall and lanky with rocker-boy hair. He was accused of possessing heroin. The judge asked if he understood this.

"'K," he said.

He was told he could go to the STOP program. He did not appear to be listening. He asked his attorney, "Will I be released today?" She said he would be.

"Cool," he said.

Next up was another young man, charged with second-degree assault. The judge asked whether he could afford a lawyer.

"It depends on how much it costs," he said.

"Do you have a bank account?" asked the judge.

"Yes."

"And how much is in it?"

"Well, it's overdrawn," he said. The judge assigned him a lawyer.

All three were dispensed within eight minutes.

Two guards led Amanda in. She wore a padded pine-green vest, the prison-issued "turtle shell" given to those on suicide watch. She looked Native American, maybe; her skin was a creamy coffee color, her cheekbones high and wide. Her thick dark hair was loose and not untidy. She was not, as the TV cameramen had guessed, looking at the floor. She kept her face up and stared straight ahead, but her eyes landed nowhere in the room.

The judge read the charges: one count of aggravated murder, one of attempted aggravated murder. The "aggravated" designation carried heavier penalties and, in this instance, indicated that the crimes were committed intentionally. If Amanda's case went to trial, she would face the death penalty.

Amanda's attorney mentioned he was here as a courtesy to the family. It was unclear what this meant. I could not stop staring at Amanda, whose gaze remained unfixed. She looked as though standing were an effort, as though a weight on her shoulders was dragging her forward and down. The judge asked, "Do you understand the nature of the charges against you?"

Amanda did not answer. The judge asked again, "Do you understand the charges against you?"

This time, Amanda looked toward the judge. She appeared to move her lips. Everyone in the courtroom was waiting to hear what she said. What came out was, "Muh."

At this, a syllable later interpreted in editorials, by police and politicians, as "No one will ever understand how this happened" and "No one could ever have seen this coming," Judge Philbrook issued her orders: Amanda Stott-Smith would remain in custody until she reappeared on June 3.

A guard took Amanda's elbow to escort her from the room. Amanda did not appear to understand the gesture. Another guard turned her, and she moved out the door as if moving through deep water.

2

May 23, 2009, Milwaukie, Oregon

Jackie Dreiling heard the police car roll up to the house just before 7:00 p.m. Jackie had not dared leave the duplex she shared with her daughter and son-in-law, Kathy and Mike Stott, not since finding out about the children. She would not make a spectacle of herself for the news trucks idling at the curb, the reporters waiting in ambush. To her dying day—which at this point she hoped was not far off—she would not understand why such a thing had hit this family. They were law-abiding citizens!

Jackie opened her front door. Detectives Steve Ober and Jim McCausland walked past the photos in the vestibule—a four-generation shot of Jackie, Kathy, Amanda, and Trinity; another of Jackie's younger daughter, Hildy, in her police uniform—and into the living room. The officers did not make note of Jackie's walking stick, which looked like something out of *Lord of the Rings*. Jackie asked the detectives if they wanted coffee. They declined. The men looked huge perched on the edge of the couch, but at least they were battening it down. Keeping what Amanda had done out of your mind was like trying to hold back the ocean.

Jackie sat in her recliner across from the TV and answered the detectives' questions: her granddaughter Amanda had been living next door with her parents on and off all spring. She had not seen her children much the past few months. Suicide? Amanda said one time that she was going to jump off a bridge, but Jackie had not taken her seriously, and Amanda never insinuated she would hurt her children.

To that point, Jackie initially had a theory: Amanda had parked her car on a boat ramp, the brakes had failed, and the car had rolled into the river. This almost happened to Jackie fifty years earlier when she and her husband drove their children to the waterfront. They had parked nose-down on a slope, and Jackie thought she felt the brakes slip. She had said to her husband, "This scares me. This scares me," and he backed up. Maybe Amanda had not been able to back up; maybe she had been trapped while the children managed to float free. Until Amanda's arrest, Jackie believed this might have been what happened.

Detectives Ober and McCausland knew this was not what happened. As homicide investigators, they were familiar with the narratives people create to avoid the obvious answer. The Stott household was the picture of middle-class placidity, but it didn't matter how ordered your life was; murder flew in like a brick through a window and no one was ever ready. The detectives' boilerplate questions—did Amanda drink alcohol? Did she do illegal drugs?—were as much about fact-finding as measuring out for people what they were facing, introducing them to the new now.

How new, Jackie was not sure. A few weeks earlier, Amanda had left her favorite ring on Jackie's mantel. Jackie had long admired this ring, cloisonné with sapphire and green topaz. Later, she mentioned to Amanda that she'd forgotten her ring, but Amanda had simply picked it up and put it back down. Jackie had not considered at the time that people who are going to commit suicide sometimes give away their possessions. But Amanda had not killed herself; she had chosen to kill her children, and detectives may have judged Jackie capable of holding competing truths in her mind when she told them that Amanda was the number-one most self-centered and selfish person she knew.

Kathy and Mike Stott returned home shortly after 7:00 p.m. Ober and McCausland interviewed them in Jackie's living room. They were, the detectives noted, "very emotional" and apologized for what their daughter had allegedly done. Kathy Stott said Jason and Amanda had a long history of domestic violence. She said he was seeing another woman and had gained custody of the children. Amanda had been upset all spring about the dissolution of her life; at her mother's urging, Amanda had entered treatment three times for depression and an eating disorder. Still, Kathy Stott insisted Amanda had been excited to see the children this weekend. She had talked about buying their favorite cereals and made up three beds in the room where they would sleep.

Jackie did not interject that at seven that morning she had gone over to Kathy's side of the house because she saw on the news that two children had been found in the river. She had looked into the bedroom with the made-up beds, seen they had not been slept in, and thought, it couldn't be; it couldn't be.

Until May 23, 2009, the Stott family appeared close knit and unexceptional. Mike and Kathy had been sweethearts since high school. He worked for a company that made commercial paper products. She'd been a property manager when her girls were young, and she later became a registered nurse. The couple raised Amanda and Chantel in the side-by-side ranch house in Milwaukie. Jackie lived on the west side of the home. Both sides were neat and inviting, with carpeting freshly vacuumed and boxed mini-muffins on the kitchen counter. Mike could fix anything: the children's bikes, the family cars; the girls said, "Daddy, fix!" so often it became like a song. The Stotts worshipped at a small nondenominational Christian church two miles from their home; Jackie did secretarial work there for years. As the children grew and had children of their own, the families would sometimes caravan to Lincoln City on the Oregon coast. The Nordic Oceanfront Inn featured suites with efficiency kitchens, others with in-room Jacuzzis facing the sea.

Within days of the children falling from the bridge, the Stott family learned they would not be permitted to visit Trinity in the hospital. They learned they were not yet permitted to visit Amanda in jail. They received word that Christine Duncan had taken out a court order against the family, forbidding them to show up at Eldon's funeral. Authorities were granted search warrants and took into evidence computers and cell phone records belonging to Amanda's immediate family.

Before the week was out, the Stott family packed their cars and drove to the Nordic. They put ninety miles between themselves and the wreckage in Portland. They did not talk about what they began to call "the incident." They left their rooms only for meals. Jackie wondered if what Amanda had done was a form of suicide and if she was taking parts of them with her. Kathy Stott spent the days on the telephone speaking with attorneys. Jackie distracted herself with a stack of paperbacks but often wound up staring at the ocean.

3

I went to the Sellwood Bridge three days after the arraignment. I told my husband I was going to buy watermelons, but instead I drove to the bridge. I had to see where Amanda took her children and, so far as we knew, threw them over.

The Willamette River cuts Portland in half, east from west. In 2009, ten bridges spanned the river within city limits. To get to the Sellwood Bridge from the city's eastside, I drove along Tacoma Boulevard, past one-story homes with fenceless front yards. I parked across from Riverside Corral, an old sailors' bar-turned-strip club, and wondered if Amanda had, too.

I walked the long block to the bridge's entry and saw the sort of memorial spontaneously set up for children who have died in public: stuffed bunnies and teddy bears, one Mylar balloon that read, "We'll miss you," a whiteboard onto which people had written their good-byes and God blesses. Some of the writing was in a child's large wobbly script ("To the bravest girl in the world! We are sorry to hear about your brother."). Tucked amid the wilted bouquets were notes, including one that read, "I hope your new birthday life goes well."

I continued onto the bridge. The walkway was about four feet across. Approaching cyclists rang their bells; people could not easily pass one another. The bridge had one traffic lane in each direction. There was no walkway on the south side.

I thought perhaps Amanda did not park and walk. Maybe she stopped the car on the roadway. This seemed unlikely. Had she stopped the car, other cars would have jammed up behind her, and people driving from the opposite direction would have seen what was going on. Even on a dark night on the poorly lit bridge, someone would have noticed her taking children from the car and thought, what the hell?

Consider the size of four- and seven-year-old children. They are usually small. You can lift them from beneath their arms and pass them over a waist-high rail with little trouble. Two would be more trouble, especially if they were kicking and screaming. They would have been dead weight had she taken them warm and sleeping from the car.

But I did not think the children were sleeping, because I did not think Amanda could have parked, gotten them out, thrown them over, and driven away without being seen. It was too busy and too tight a roadway. There would have been little time to pause after dropping one child, then another, over the rail and into the river seventy-five feet below.

Did she look down? Did she see them in the water? Did she hear her daughter's cries? I could not know how long she waited on the bridge after she dropped her children, or if she waited at all. If she parked her car on the roadway, she could not have waited. She would have had to get back in the car and drive.

I thought she might have walked the children onto the bridge. Is it possible she made a game of the walk? This seemed an unlikely scenario, that she had the largeness or smallness of heart to tell her children, "We are going to play a game." I did not want to see the children skipping at one in the morning along that narrow walkway. It was scary enough in daytime for an adult to feel the velocity of the passing cars, your waist brushing the too-low rail. Looking at the water, you feel your groin seize with the electric jolt that comes when looking down from a dangerous height.

I did not think the children experienced this. It was dark; it was late, past most young children's bedtime. Their adrenaline would have been pumping for different reasons: How mad was Mommy? What was happening? They were too small to see over the rail, to see how far down the water was. What could they know of their fate? To be thrown off a bridge in the middle of the night was out of the purview of what four- and seven-year-olds needed to know.

Did Amanda make the children stand with their backs against the concrete railing, with its wide, church-window-shaped cutouts? Eldon was possibly small enough to crawl through one of these cutouts. The children may have stood with their backs to the rail, the breeze of passing cars pushing them against it. They must have been extremely frightened. Perhaps their mother had to wave cars on, to say, "We're okay, we're fine," and the children would have wondered, are we? Or maybe there had been no cars.

I did not know if Amanda had been ranting or silent before the children were forced off the bridge. I thought the latter would be scarier to a child. Perhaps she was in a mood so bad, a mood the children could not hope to navigate, that all was chaos. Perhaps she told them what she was going to do. Perhaps she made them stand together atop the rail and told them to hold hands. Maybe she told them, "We have to do this." While it seemed heartless to inflict this information, I preferred this scenario to seeing them tossed in their sleep. This way, they knew their fate and were, in Trinity's case, able to gird for it.

Eldon had no chance. How at four years old in a moving river in the middle of the night do you survive? You don't. You take in some water, and you take in some more. I imagined his sister would have been holding on to him. I imagined everyone who heard about the children wished they could have helped, that we all could have lined up on the banks of the river in the dark and offered Eldon one more breath. He had only his sister in the water with him. She did the best she could. She screamed.

And where was their mother? Can we imagine her standing on the bridge, watching her children drift north, wondering when they would stop crying? Was she afraid someone would hear her children? Was that what got her back in her car and gone fast, the fear of capture being broadcast with each of her daughter's screams?

Or did she sleepwalk back to her car? Or did she run? Was she crying? Was she yelling? Was she white and cold? Did she feel victorious? Was her heart pounding? Did she turn around? Did she call her children's names?

So far as we were aware, only two living people knew what happened on the bridge that night. No witnesses had come forward; no one had seen or heard anything, on or off the bridge, before the children were in the water.

On this Friday—two days after Trinity was released from the hospital in good condition, two days before her brother's funeral—the weather was glorious. There were barely ripples on the Willamette; the air was soft, and the trees on the west bank were in full leaf.

As I stood midspan beside a second, smaller memorial of bouquets tied to a lamppost, a motorboat passed beneath. It slowed. The driver turned back to look up at the bridge. He looked up for a long time. Maybe he was thinking, that's a long way for two little kids to fall. Then he looked at me, and in the seconds before he motored south, I had the impractical thought to shout to him, to connect his concern with my own.

4

Jason Smith was going to a barbecue as soon as he dropped the kids off with Amanda. He and his mother, who was driving them up Interstate 5 from Eugene, were running late. Jason called Amanda to say he'd be at the house a little after eight. She told him she wanted to spend more time with the kids, that she never got to see the kids. It was the same conversation they'd been having for months. She wanted Jason to pay for an apartment in Eugene so she could be nearer to him and the children. Jason said if she wanted to move she could get a job and pay for a place herself.

"I'm trying, but it's hard," she told him.

Jason did not know whether she had been trying. According to her mother, Amanda had been moping around and not in a state to do much of anything. He told Amanda what he always told her, that she needed to get her life back on track.

Amanda had known for months she needed to be out of the house in Tualatin by May 31, that the rent would no longer be paid. Christine

Duncan had footed much of the bill for Amanda and the children since the previous fall, when Jason entered rehab. Amanda had asked Duncan to pay for her to go to rehab as well. Amanda had read that 70 percent of marriages fail when only one partner goes through treatment, and she wanted her marriage to succeed. She thought Duncan would want this, too. Duncan believed Amanda's parents should take care of whatever help their daughter needed. Soon, none of Amanda's problems would be Duncan's to solve. Jason had provisional custody of the kids, and he had been in touch with a divorce attorney; it was time for the marriage to be over.

Trinity could hear her dad on the phone telling her mom she needed to get a job. When they all lived in the same house, she sometimes heard her parents yell in their bedroom. Her dad didn't like her mom because she smoked cigarettes. He said he paid all the bills and that her mom did not help. Trinity sometimes did not think her dad liked her either. She was crying when she asked her grandmother, her mom's mother, why her dad did not love her as much as he loved Eldon, whom he carried around all the time. But her father also sometimes told Eldon he smelled like a bowel movement. This would make Eldon mad. Sometimes he threw his Transformers down the toilet on purpose, which would make their mom really, really mad, and then she'd try to get them out with chopsticks.

Jason got off the phone and told the kids that he was going to a barbecue but they were not to tell their mother. The barbecue was at his friend Ryan's house. Did the children understand? Don't tell their mother because she was not invited. Trinity listened to what her father said. Four-year-old Eldon was beside her on the back seat. He was wearing the clothes of an American boy his age: a yellow T-shirt with a bulldog logo, a pair of Marvel Comics underwear.

5

On May 29, 2009, James Gumm took his two adopted children on a hike in a Portland-area park. The children, a boy and a girl, were ages seven and six. Gumm was recently divorced; it was his weekend with the kids. They hiked a path called the Otter March Loop before Gumm used a 9 mm handgun to shoot the children. Then he shot himself in the mouth.

"We have the second-highest unemployment in the nation. Social services are stressed to the breaking point or failing altogether," went one comment on the *Oregonian*'s website, in reaction to the Gumm murders. "People are free-falling through the cracks. Unfortunately, stuff like this is going to happen more and more. . . . We are in for a long, hot, dangerous summer."

Unlike readers insisting Amanda be hung from the Sellwood Bridge, or those who thought the right thing to do was "just hurry up and give her the needle in the arm," this commenter was searching for context, asking why these murders were happening in Portland now.

It was a valid question in the summer of 2009. While places like Las Vegas and San Diego were seeing their local economies run off the rails, Portland appeared to be hitting its stride. *Popular Science* magazine had named it America's "top green city." The restaurant scene was nonpareil. Portland was dubbed "the new Brooklyn" and was attracting, according to the *Wall Street Journal*, "college-educated, single people between the ages of 25 and 39 at a higher rate than most other cities in the country." There was editorial space available for idealized Portland stories, and the message that through some confluence of bike paths, pinot noir, and progressive politics, Portland was producing citizens with the sort of decency more cynical cities lacked.

The day classmates of the Gumm children released memorial balloons to the sky, twenty-one-year-old Heather Snively, who had moved to Portland three weeks earlier, went to the home of Korena Roberts. Roberts, who had told family and friends she was expecting twins, had responded to the ad Snively placed on Craigslist asking for used baby clothes. Snively was more than seven months pregnant when Roberts sliced through her womb and removed the baby, which was transported to the hospital and pronounced dead. Snively's body was found stuffed in a crawl space at Roberts's home. The day this story hit the papers, a migrant worker named Araceli Velasquez-Espain delivered her newborn into the waste tank of a portable toilet. She told authorities she had seen the umbilical cord and the placenta; that she "knew her baby was underneath . . . but she saw the blue water was disgusting and did not want to reach into it." An autopsy of the baby showed he had been alive as he submerged in the blue septic chemical.

If Portland's murder rate had declined over the decade, the child murders this summer nevertheless felt like a sickening trend. The local papers could barely keep up. Too many children needed attention; you could not properly take care of one before you had to look after another.

I wondered, after reading about Baby Boy Velasquez-Espain, if the press outside of Portland would take a moment to look away from the city's food carts to focus on child murder. I asked a stringer for the *New York Times* if the paper was going to devote more than the 113-word wire service item it had to Amanda's story.

"It's not what they want from Portland," he told me.

A half hour before Amanda's second arraignment on June 3, the landing outside of the second-story courtroom was mobbed. A dozen reporters and two TV crews scoped out each new arrival coming up the steps. They were waiting for Ken Hadley, Amanda's new attorney, who barely made it off the top step before he had a microphone in his face.

Hadley looked a bit like Jon Voight, with broad, flat cheekbones, no visible eyelid crease, and fine gray hair worn longish over his ears. Reporters shouted over each other: What could Hadley tell them about Stott-Smith? What was her emotional state?

Hadley appeared to give each question his full attention. He had a way with pauses, casting his eyes toward a midpoint on the floor, curling his hand in a loose fist, pressing the knuckle of his forefinger to his lips. He kept his answers brief: He had just been assigned to Stott-Smith's case so could not say much about her emotional state. He could not discuss legal particulars. He could confirm she was on suicide watch.

Hadley broke away.

The courtroom was packed, people hip to hip on benches and standing against walls. There were cameras and laptops and different people crying in the back row. If there were any family members in attendance, they were not making themselves known. An *Oregonian* crime reporter asked a cried-out woman in a flowered dress whether she knew Amanda. The woman nodded but would not say more.

Amanda's case was not first on the docket, yet she was the first brought in. Her hair was in a neat braid. She looked hyperalert, her eyes wide and the whites of her eyes very white. She wore a curious *What are we going to do today?* expression and looked more polished than I might expect a woman in her position to be.

Judge Philbrook read the indictment against her. A grand jury had convened and come back with additional charges. Amanda was now facing five counts of aggravated murder, two counts of attempted aggravated murder, and one count of assault in the second degree, this last because of bruises on the children's bodies. Hadley acknowledged the charges. The judge asked how Amanda pleaded; Hadley's cocounsel said, "Not guilty." There was no immediate reaction from anyone in the courtroom. Amanda herself had no reaction. People filed out as she was led away, this time under her own steam.

A press conference took place within the hour, on the fourteenth floor of the Justice Center in downtown Portland. TV cameras were set up behind two dozen reporters. Conversations were of layoffs and buyouts. One retirement-aged man floated the idea of going into radio. Another went through the receipts in his wallet. No one commented on the bank of windows to our right, offering a full view of the Sellwood Bridge.

A spokesperson for the Portland Police Bureau stood at the lectern and told us how it was going to go: We would get a timeline of the Stott-Smith case; detectives and the chief of police would appear. Representatives would be available to answer some questions.

Police Commissioner Dan Saltzman was up first. He had the build of a weekend basketball player and a clammy complexion. "I'm here really to express the profound regret that I feel—and all of us on the city council feel, and I think every citizen in Portland feels—the profound sense of grief over the tragic drowning of Eldon Smith. This type of death shakes us all to our core. We're here today to learn more about it and help us to try to understand something that is perhaps not capable of being understood."

He ceded the stage to Police Chief Rosie Sizer, who repeated Saltzman's sentiments and reminded us how deeply this sort of crime affected not just the public but her officers, many of them parents of young children. Later, during a discussion of whether Officer Wade Greaves had "made a heroic effort" to save Amanda, Chief Sizer said, "My reading of the reports was, she was dangling over the side [of the parking garage] and he grabbed hold of her wrist and kept her from falling to the sidewalk and dying."

Sergeant Rich Austria explained that any records pertaining to the children—before, during, or after the incident—would not be provided. He gave us the timeline of Amanda and the children's whereabouts for May 22 and May 23, offering almost nothing that had not already been reported. When asked for additional details, he said he would not comment, that the 911 tapes would not be released, that he was going to "hold off" as far as giving any information as to how Amanda had been found, though it was obvious to everyone in the room that she had been tracked by her cell phone. The press conference was pro forma, and I wondered at the point of doling out scraps and what we were expected to make from them. Then time was called and everyone was thanked and pads were folded and good-bye.

I approached Chief Sizer. I told her I wanted to interview Officer Greaves, that I thought what he had done was an incredible feat, something out of the movies, but beyond that, he must have found it psychologically tough, knowing what this woman was accused of doing to her kids and yet—of course, of course—doing his job and saving her life. It was a heroic act and a complicated one, and Sizer said yes, yes, yes, and that Greaves would be honored the following week in a ceremony, and I said, that's well deserved, but what I really wanted was to interview him, and how did the department feel about that?

"We encourage our officers to speak with the media," she said, and all I had to do was arrange it with the department's spokesperson, who did a yeoman's job of avoiding my calls and throwing up bulwarks before saying no, I could not have the interview; Officer Greaves was not interested.

The pieces in the next day's papers carried stories by reporters who had done their best with what they had. They quoted neighbors. Two articles included the declaration that Amanda had sought to hurt her husband, though the reason why she wanted to hurt him was not advanced. The narratives were dutiful but did not answer the central questions of why and how.

Hadley was not distressed by the papers providing so little information, by cops staying tight-lipped. He preferred it this way.

"I like the media. I read gossip pages, and I watch enough news that my family members get bored," he told me the next morning at Elmer's Restaurant, a diner located off the interstate. "But the media can also really hurt us because the more publicity, the more you've got the public excited about it. . . . The judge doesn't want you tried in the newspaper, and I don't, either."

Before he agreed to meet with me, Hadley said I needed to appreciate how little he could say at this time. While the police may have all but finished their investigation, he was just starting his. It was a hermetic process, the pretrial gathering of evidence, and he could not reveal anything about a client that might affect her case.

Hadley was as high profile as one could be as a public defender in the state of Oregon. For the last twenty years, each of the people he represented was charged with aggravated murder, the state's only capital offense. Hadley knew the job did not make him popular. He was used to being called "an SOB" and "a bleeding heart" and meeting people at parties who asked, "How can you do what you do?" He believed the job he did was an important one, and he did it well: out of thirty clients, only two had received the death penalty, and only one of those sentences—that of family killer Christian Longo—had stuck. I had seen a photo of Longo as the guilty verdict was read. Hadley stands beside him, head hinged toward his chest, eyes closed, thumb and fingers gripping the bridge of his nose.

Longo, against Hadley's advice, had pleaded not guilty to aggravated murder in two of the four killings, implying that his wife had killed their two older children before Longo killed her and their baby. Hadley did not think the jury would buy Longo's half-truth. The jury had not.

Amanda, too, had pleaded not guilty. If her case went to trial, the death penalty would be on the table. Hadley seemed unperturbed by this possibility, sunny even, as our breakfasts arrived, as though having a person's life in his hands was as much a part of the day as eggs and toast.

6

Ryan Barron was totally stoked to see Jason. It had been a crazy, crazy couple of years, last summer particularly; man, he didn't even want to think about it. Jason said he would be over as soon as he dropped off the kids; his mom was driving him. They'd swing by Ryan's around eight. Jason got there a little late, but that was normal.

Ryan gave his buddy a man hug. He hadn't seen the guy in two months. They were getting to be two middle-aged white dudes. Each had less hair and more gut than when they met in 2001, but today Jason looked good, not all freaked and scraggly like he'd been the summer before, when he was living with Ryan and his fiancée, Sara. Maybe "living" was a little strong; Jason had been staying with Ryan. It had been bad, just bad news. Too much junkie business. Seeing Jason looking all sharp, dressed preppy like he liked, even Sara commented on how he had filled out. It was refreshing to see him looking clean and healthy.

Ryan and Jason took off for Whole Foods. Ryan was an amateur chef, something he planned to capitalize on, since he'd been canned from his job. Jason loved good food, too. He had a thing for French cheese, the kind that was as big as your thumb and cost $25. At the store, they went wild buying things for the grill: rock shrimp, halibut, flanken ribs, and sweet corn; they were going to make a giant feast. Man, it was good to see his friend, especially considering how last summer had ended, with Ryan ratting Jason out, having to tell their boss, listen, Jason's got a serious drug problem.

That had been in September. Ryan knew some of what had happened to Jason since then, was pretty sure the guy had stayed clean and that his marriage was over. It was hard to know a lot more. Jason could be sort of calculating; he would gravitate to people weaker than he was because, as Ryan saw it, Jason was addicted to being in charge. Whatever. Tonight Jason was totally chill. They drank beers and grilled, didn't start eating until nine, ten o'clock. It was a nice night, clear and warm, and Ryan decided to tease his buddy, to ask, "Bro, when are we going to head back out to the desert?" It was something they used to do—take off and look for arrowheads. Then one time, maybe five years ago, Jason said he'd brought along some coke, said he'd never tried it but maybe they should do some. Ryan had never done coke, either. He totally loved it, becoming so focused he could hunt artifacts for days. It had been a fun, fun trip, and when Jason said they should do it again sometime, Ryan was down for it, though he did kind of wonder. Jason was superorganized; he had a binder with a piece of glass and all this stuff tucked in, razor blades and cards and some snooters. It seemed like he knew way more than a dude doing blow for the second time would know.

They started heading out to the woods a lot, camping and rock hounding in the Columbia Basin, out at Burns in eastern Oregon. Vancouver Lake was less than twenty miles from Portland; they'd head out there for the day and swim and hunt for agates when they were supposed to be working. Ryan knew he shouldn't have been screwing up like that or doing so much coke with Jason, but hell, Ryan was enjoying himself. Even when it got hairy, he kept at it, staying up all night, sleeping in his car during the day when he was supposedly on the clock. The job he and Jason did, running mail room operations for Ricoh, wasn't hard. It was easy to bullshit your way through—until it wasn't, until the mistakes piled up.

That was all over now. Ryan had stopped doing drugs completely, Jason had gone through rehab, and here they were, full bellies under a night sky. The only interruption was Amanda calling and calling Jason's phone. Jason ignored her calls and suggested to Ryan, as far as camping, how about they go tomorrow? Jason was staying overnight at his aunt's a few blocks away; he and Ryan could meet up in the morning and head to Kalama, explore this old Indian encampment Jason knew about. Ryan was totally down for it, though he was sort of surprised when Jason said, yeah, I got all my stuff with me. Ryan knew Jason had pawned or sold anything he could the summer before, and he knew because sometimes he went with the guy.

One time, they went by the Tualatin house when Amanda and the kids were still living there—what a disaster that place was; every house Jason and Amanda lived in turned into a shithole. Jason took all the DVDs that time, so many that the guy at the pawnshop said it would take a while to tally up, that Jason and Ryan should come back later. When they returned, the guy said he couldn't give Jason any money because there were no DVDs in the boxes. Ryan thought Amanda was a certifiable nutjob on top of being an alcoholic—he had once seen her wing a fifteen-pound tub of laundry detergent at Jason's head—but he had to give it to her: she knew Jason was stealing their stuff and took the DVDs before he could.

If Jason had all his camping gear, Ryan figured Jason's mom had helped get it back. She'd bailed him out thousands of times. So, cool, they'd go in the morning. They planned until about eleven, and then Jason took off, saying he'd call Ryan by seven thirty.

Sara was grateful to see Jason looking so healthy, to see how genuinely excited both he and Ryan were about getting back to the woods, this time without alcohol and whatever else. They were going to drink water and bring a picnic and eat real food and go arrowhead hunting like normal people. A relief. Sara worked with special-needs kids, and there was no way she could be associated with what had been going on the summer before. Sara could see Ryan was relieved, too; as they cleaned up the dinner dishes, he kept saying, "I have my friend back, my normal, healthy, good friend. This is going to be normal like before all the crap happened, and we're going to get back to being normal people."

Jason walked a mile to his aunt's house on Southwest Coquille Drive. She and his mom were still up watching TV. Jason talked with the sisters and then headed upstairs. He turned on the History Channel. He did not check his phone messages. Amanda had gotten in the habit of calling him late at night to say he had ruined her life or whatever she was upset about; that or she hung up, called, and hung up. If she called tonight, he was not going to answer.

Christine Duncan looked in on her son a little after midnight, saw he was asleep, and turned off the TV.

Ryan had set his alarm and was ready to go in the morning. But there was no call from Jason. Ryan tried his friend a bunch of times. Jason's voice mail was full, as it always was. It seemed weird, though, that he wasn't answering; Jason had been so excited the night before. Sara had seen it too, right? Sara assured Ryan that Jason had seemed ready to go, that Ryan had not misunderstood the plan.

Ryan's anxiety ramped up as he called and called Jason's phone—still to voice mail. Maybe he was falling back into the pattern of taking part in his friend's crises, but Ryan felt there was really something wrong. He kept saying to Sara, "This is not normal. This is not right."

Jason called just before eleven.

Sara heard Ryan in the hallway saying, "What are you talking about?" He was holding on to the wall, and then he was sliding down the wall, saying, "No, no, no, no, no."

Sara reached for him, and the first thing she thought was, it's Amanda. She's done something; it was only a matter of time.

7

A scrum of people waited outside the Multnomah County Courthouse at 8:30 a.m. This was not the courthouse where Amanda had been arraigned the week before. That building, across the street, had a glass-faced lobby and the antiseptic feel of a corporate hotel. County court, by contrast, was a pile-on. News vans hogged the curb. Lawyers talked on their phones as they pulled open the heavy wood doors. Inside the entrance, a man in a Panama hat auctioned tax-foreclosed properties, and people waiting to go through security dumped backpacks and diaper bags onto the x-ray machine's conveyor belt as though being here was a casual chore, like checking out at the grocery store. Matters as small as parking fines were settled here at circuit court, but so were death penalty cases.

The records room on the first floor looked like it had not changed much since the courthouse opened in 1914. A stack of paper slips waited to be filled out with half pencils, while young female clerks fetched files and made copies.

The file I requested was insubstantial. Its start date was May 23. Amanda's intake papers included her birth date, 06-05-77, that she was female, and that she was white; she was in fact part Filipino, from her father's side. The sections for Housing, Relationship, Alcohol/Drugs, Employment, and Mental Health were diagonally slashed and noted with the word "Refused." Under Victim Relationship, it said, "vic's are Δ's children." Amanda was Δ. A summary in full read, "Δ refused interview. Δ stated she did not want media attention and did not want the information to be public information. Δ has no prior criminal convictions." The intake papers listed the eight charges against Amanda and the respective amounts of security: "NO BAIL + NO BAIL + NO BAIL + NO BAIL + NO BAIL + $250,000 + $250,000 + $250,000." She was five feet five inches tall and weighed 120 pounds.

If Amanda had refused an interview, if "Δ stated she did not want media attention and did not want the information to be public information," her actions spoke otherwise. Killing children in public said "spectacle." Amanda made sure, whether she would live to see it or not, that she would be acknowledged.

The adjacent room, where I read Amanda's intake file and made notes, was the size of a janitor's closet, with a cafeteria table that took up most of the space and a copy machine that took quarters and which I had been told I could not use. A blonde in what looked like a homemade blouse moved from table to copy machine, apparently under no such constraints.

"Because I'm a paralegal," she answered when I asked why she was allowed to make her own copies. I asked if additional records were housed elsewhere in the courthouse. She said there might be some on the second floor.

There were no additional records on the second floor, and the file I had covered only the events of the past week. Earlier records of Amanda and Jason's separation and custody issues regarding Gavin were available at courthouses in neighboring counties. These and other documents showed the spiral of the past year. Jason moved out in June 2008. Amanda was left without resources. Jason and his mother suggested Amanda go on welfare. Jason began to take Eldon and Trinity to Eugene on weekends; on February 14, 2009, he did not bring them back as planned. On February 27, Amanda awarded sole custody of Gavin to his biological father, Nathan Beck. On March 2, Jason enrolled Trinity in school in Eugene. On March 20, Amanda filed for legal separation from Jason, citing irreconcilable differences. She also filed a temporary protective order of restraint, stating that "on or around February 10, 2009, Respondent [Jason Smith] and his mother took the children from my home down to Eugene to his mother's home. The children have been there since that time. I did not give Respondent or his mother [permission] to move the children." On March 23, in response to Amanda's filing, a judge ruled that "until custody or visitation is determined by mediation or further order of the court," the children's schedules and living arrangements were not to be disturbed by either parent; they would stay with their father for now. On April 6, Amanda, her sister, and a police officer brought a court order to Trinity's new school, took the girl, and registered her in a school near Amanda's parents' home, telling an administrator the "enrollment was to be kept confidential and her father was not to know where she was." On April 21, a judge granted a temporary order of custody of both children to Jason. Amanda was given every-other-weekend visitation and permission to speak to her children by phone each night. She was not to see the children without Jason's permission.

The progression showed children pulled from their home, from their half brother, from their mother; it showed Amanda losing ground and her retaliatory moves backfiring. Was it strategy or coincidence that Jason left her on her birthday, that the children were not brought home on Valentine's Day? Why did she give up custody of her oldest child? As recently as August 2008, Amanda had gone to court to deny Nathan Beck additional time with his son. She had represented herself, countering family members who testified against her: her brother-in-law, who said she had a history of drinking and driving with the kids in the car; her grandmother, who said of Amanda, "She used to be a really good mother, and I'm sure she could be a good one again, but she's going through problems and she's drinking on a steady basis." Amanda dismissed their concerns as "rubbish."

"I think a glass of wine is good for the heart on occasion," she had told the judge. "There's nothing wrong with having that, just like Jesus did."

This incident suggested an out-of-control woman, as did what appeared in the *Oregonian* on June 3, eleven days after Amanda's arrest. An article titled "Police release timeline in the Amanda Jo Stott-Smith case" stated, "Interviews, public documents and timelines released by two city agencies reveal what investigators say was a fatal act of revenge against Stott-Smith's estranged husband."

Revenge made as much sense as anything else. It was neat, it had fire; we could roll it around in our mouths and feel the shape of it. Whether the families believed revenge was the whole story, part of the story, or not helpful in understanding the story, the public would not know. Through a third party, Jason released only a statement thanking the rescuers and saying, "His daughter is doing very well and he considers her recovery to be a miracle." Nathan Beck's attorney quoted Nathan as saying, "We are all saddened and shocked by the events that have taken place. Our prayers are with all the families involved in this tragedy." Amanda's family said nothing; there were no photos of them avoiding or confronting news cameras. None of Amanda's friends came forward to express shock or condemnation. As to the kind of parent she was, we had only Amanda speaking on her own behalf from the court filing on March 20, 2009, nine weeks before Trinity and Eldon were dropped from the bridge.

"I am a stay-at-home mother," she wrote. "In the afternoons I fed Eldon lunch, and played with him until it was time to pick his sister up. Many afternoons the three of us would go to the library together. I cared for my children 24 hours a day."

8

May 26, 2009, Tualatin, Oregon

Sabrina Trembley pulled her car to the end of the car line for Living Savior Lutheran Preschool. If the car line had always bugged her—these were preschoolers, for goodness' sake, so why in the world should parents not be allowed to walk their four-year-olds to class?—today she was especially annoyed. It had been only two days since Eldon was killed; were they expected to stay honeycombed in their cars and interact as little as possible?

Sabrina couldn't do it. She couldn't drive up like everything was normal and drop off her son. She swung the car around and parked in the church parking lot. It was a beautiful clear morning. She opened the car doors and sat there with Max. The car line looked longer than usual because the school doors had not opened on time. Sabrina was under the impression that teachers came early to pray together before school started. What could that have been like this morning, absorbing the news about Eldon while planning how to keep the kids happy all day?

When the doors opened, Sabrina saw how strained things were. The teachers wore grim half smiles while trying to sound ordinary: "Hi, Daphne. Oh, here's Athena." Their former classmate had been murdered by his mother, and yes, what Amanda had done was unspeakable, but did that mean they were supposed to act as though it had not happened?

Sabrina thought the email the school sent over the weekend, essentially a "we regret to inform you" note, had been vastly inadequate. Any sentient parent knew what happened. Amanda's mug shot had been in every newspaper and on television. What disturbed Sabrina about the email, and again watching the children being escorted inside, was the sense that the murder was not going to be talked about. Did the faculty think that just because Eldon had been taken out of school in February—Sabrina was not sure why; something about his father taking him to Eugene—the children would forget him?

Max would not forget, and though Sabrina could not know as much in the car that morning, he never would. Six years later, he would cry in the back of a different car after being reminded of Eldon, of whom he would say, "He will always be four."

Eldon had just turned four when the boys met at the start of the school year. There were seventeen children in the class at Living Savior. All the boys were rambunctious, grabbing each other and making loud noises, except for Max and Eldon. Both boys were on the small side, blond, quiet, and rules oriented. After a week or two at school, it became clear to Sabrina that her son had found his first best friend. Max came home jabbering about Eldon, how he had "the coolest lunchbox *ever*," and could Sabrina ask Eldon's mom where she got it? It had an alien on it. Sabrina had once watched the boys during chapel time; they took their spots on the little carpet squares the teachers laid out, while the boy next to them threw himself all over the floor. Sabrina had a photo of Max and Eldon in the Christmas pageant, standing over a cradle holding the baby Jesus, a Cabbage Patch doll in this incarnation.

Sabrina kept the preschool class photo on the refrigerator at home. Eldon, she thought, was the most adorable of the whole class, a cherub with big, round dark eyes and the apple cheeks of a young child. He looked a lot like his mother. Sabrina did not know Amanda well, only what she had gathered by attending class meetings with her. Amanda was striking, with a Native American or Hawaiian or Polynesian look and that beautiful hair. The first time Sabrina spoke with Eldon, she ran her hands over his hair; it was clipped very short, prickly, and soft. She was so happy to meet this boy her son was taken with, and she said, "You're Eldon, hi!" And he had been sweet and quiet, very quiet.

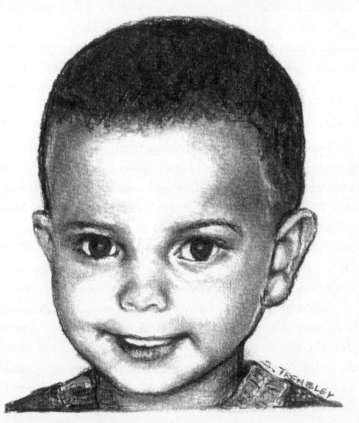

Sketch courtesy of Sabrina Trembley

Only later would Sabrina think he was perhaps too quiet. Eldon had been so rules oriented, it made her wonder if he wasn't a classic example of a child who was being hit. Sabrina had never seen any marks on him, but she knew about being silent, about trying to be invisible. Her own mother had been a teenager when Sabrina was born, had been immature and violent and used Sabrina as a pawn during a bitter divorce. Growing up with a volatile parent made you walk a tight and narrow path and read people quickly, and Sabrina wondered now whether every time Eldon had seen his mother, he'd had to read her in an instant to know if it was going to be a good moment or a bad moment. Or maybe there were issues with the father, whom Sabrina had never seen at school. The thought that Eldon might have been navigating abuse, without Sabrina keying into telltale signs, ran inside her like a hot river. If the school, or the other parents dropping off their kids this morning, did not feel compelled to memorialize him, she did.

The email from the school informing class parents of Eldon's tragic death had arrived a half hour before Sabrina's husband was leaving on a business trip for Europe. They had little time to discuss how they would tell Max. Sabrina waited until her husband got in the Town Car and drove off, and then she sat Max down. She made it as simple as she could. She said, "I have some bad news." He asked her if that was why she was crying. She said yes and that she wanted to let Max know that Eldon had died. He was up in heaven, and he could not come back.

Max started to cry and asked what happened. She said that Eldon had drowned in the river. She did not go further than that; it just seemed pointless. Max was crying in a way she had never heard, and she realized her five-year-old was in mourning. Everything about this was wrong. Then he said, "Can we write a letter to his mother? I want her to know how much I liked Eldon."

Sabrina let this sink in and said yes, and did Max know that people could get mail in heaven? She was winging it—she sent Max to a church school out of convenience, not conviction—but what could she say?

The next day they bought three balloons and drove to the Sellwood Bridge. It was not fun being there. The walkway was stupidly narrow, and Sabrina could not see Amanda walking there at night with her children. It was a long enough slog in the daytime, holding her son by one hand, the balloons in another. She could not imagine this walk if Max had been tired or resisting, and she flashed on an image of Amanda on the phone with her husband: Amanda screaming, and in a snap, stopping the car . . .

Max stopped. It was time to let the balloons go; he had tied his letter to the strings. He released the balloons, and they flew straight up, as though they had been plucked into the sky.

"My sadness," he said, "flew away with the balloons."

But Sabrina knew he was angry, too, because he said to her later, "Why did his mom let him swim in the river? Why wasn't she watching him?" He was asking Sabrina why Eldon's mother had not been doing her job. What could she say? That this will never happen to you? Sabrina could not fathom that Amanda thought this would happen to her children. Unlike the class mother who later wrote that she "got an immediate gut feeling that she [Amanda] was a very bizarre woman— her behavior was very strange," Sabrina did not see Amanda as strange. She saw her as a broken person, someone who did not believe anybody loved her; someone who threw everything she loved off the bridge in order to punish herself, to punish her soon-to-be ex-husband, to punish life.

Six days after Eldon's murder, there was a graduation ceremony for the preschool class. Sabrina could see not announcing Eldon's death, but not even a subtle honoring of the fact that he had been their classmate? No. Eldon's name had been taken off the list. When the pastor spoke, he made no mention of the loss of a child, no "let us remember those who aren't with us," nothing.

After the ceremony, Sabrina went to the classroom, to a wall of more than two hundred photos of the children. At the end of the year, parents could take any they wanted. Sabrina knew there were pictures of Eldon; she had seen them throughout the year, including one of him sitting in Amanda's lap the first day of school. What she found was that all the photos of Eldon had been removed.

9

An estimated five hundred children are killed by their parents each year in the United States, according to homicide data compiled by the Federal Bureau of Investigation. This number has been static for decades. It is also unreliable and certainly low. The picture of parents killing their children is anathema to most people and makes us susceptible to seeing even the suspicious death of a child explained away: the infant died in her sleep, the child struck his head falling off the coffee table, and who are you to say it did not happen this way? Unless a filicide, the killing of a child by a parent or stepparent, is committed in public, we may not hear about it at all, the circumstances of anonymous people killing their kids too tawdry, too sad, too somehow private to report on. The news you read this week is unlikely to include ten children being murdered by their parents.

But ten were murdered, at least ten. The murdered children of the last week of June 2017 included a six-month-old in Fresno (June 23); a two-month-old in Hanford, CA (June 23); a two-year-old in Houston (June 24); a one-month-old in Terra Bella, CA (June 24); a two-month-old in Valdosta, GA (June 24); a four-year-old in Tullahoma, TN (June 28); a two-year-old and a six-month-old in Paron, AR (June 28); a three-year-old in Rancho Cordova, CA (June 28); and a three-year-old in Chandler, AZ (June 30).

Taking this in requires some measure of calm and, lest we immediately be laid low, logic. Here we hesitate, since there is nothing innately logical about children being murdered by their parents. We operate, if we operate at all, from emotion, conjuring images of stringing up the killers or intervening in the dead children's lives, maybe putting your arms around them and telling them how sorry you are for what they went through. This does nothing for them. It does not affect the fate of any other child moving forward, but I understand if you do it, because I do it, too.

The next hesitation involves looking squarely at the issue. Reading case studies about filicide is difficult, and I do not recommend it unless you want to sit in a coffee shop and cry after reading about a four-year-old boy in Finland whom social services suspected of being serially abused. A public health nurse visited the boy at his home. She took him onto her lap, where he rested his head on her shoulder for an hour and a half. The nurse saw this behavior as a call for protection. Three days later, the boy was beaten to death. I can never not see the image of the Finnish boy with his head resting on the nurse's shoulder.

But I do not look away, because there is logic here—twisted logic, to be sure, but in the eyes of the perpetrators, logic nonetheless. We know this because they killed their children. At some point, whether a year prior or a minute before, these parents looked at what they perceived to be their options and decided their children would be better off dead.

Filicide is divided into three classifications: neonaticide, for children killed within the first twenty-four hours of birth; infanticide, children killed during their first year of life; and filicide, a child from age one to any age. Younger children are killed most often, with 70 percent of filicide victims younger than six years old.

Each category of filicidal parent displays certain patterns. Those who commit neonaticide tend to be young, in their teens or early twenties. It is nearly always the birth mother who does the killing. Often, she has hidden the pregnancy or claims to be unaware she was pregnant. She gives birth in secret, usually at home. She usually kills the child immediately. Neonates are often smothered or strangled; sometimes they are drowned. The mother then hides the body—in a dumpster, in a coffee can under the sink—and carries on as though nothing has happened. The pattern of denial and dissociation she had throughout her pregnancy continues; she was passive and made no plans for the child, and perceives now she will not need to. While newborns comprise 33 percent of all victims of filicide, the true number of neonates can never be known. We cannot account for the murder of a human we do not know exists.

Infanticide accounts for another 14 percent of murders. While these youngest children still tend to be killed by their mothers, fathers are gaining, with the overall percentage of filicidal parents evenly split between the sexes. This seems like a remarkable number in a country where men commit nearly 90 percent of all violent crime, until you take into account that young children are primarily cared for by their mothers. The idea that an infant can abet his or her own murder is ludicrous; nonetheless, in one study 58 percent of killers said the child's crying precipitated the murder. Men becoming involved in the murder of their children raises the level of violence. According to *Why Mothers Kill* by Geoffrey R. McKee, mothers tend to kill with hands-on methods: children are smothered in their beds, drowned in the bathtub, their bodies sometimes swaddled and hidden inside or close to the home. These methods can be seen as a way for the mother to figuratively put the child back in the womb, though it is also the case that many women who kill their children are poor and kill with what is available. Fathers are three times more likely to use a firearm, according to a report in *Forensic Science International* in 2013. Men also engage in higher rates of assault; children are beaten or thrown or stabbed, their bodies disposed of far from where they lived, in some cases driven hundreds of miles.

Victims of filicide are four years old on average. Boys are killed very slightly more often than girls. The average age of a filicidal parent is thirty-one. All races and nationalities kill their children. Ideology can play a part. China's one-child policy, which ended in 2016, all but assured the use of neonaticide as a form of birth control. War and famine have, and will continue to, put parents in the position of deciding whether it is viable to keep all their children alive, and if not, they may kill the weakest or youngest. This is categorized as altruistic filicide, a designation both common and controversial.

In 1969, Dr. Philip Resnick developed five categories of motives to explain why mothers kill their children. In altruistic filicide, a suicidal mother feels it will be too cruel to leave the child in the world without her, or she feels the child has a disability, real or imagined, that will make the child's life intolerable moving forward. Acutely psychotic filicide is the result of a psychosis: the mother kills the child with no rational motive. Unwanted child filicide, while most often involving neonaticide, can also include the murder of a child who is seen as a burden. Accidental filicide occurs when a child is unintentionally killed as a result of abuse; these include deaths as the result of Munchausen syndrome by proxy, a psychological disorder that compels caretakers, usually women, to exaggerate or fabricate medical conditions in those they care for in order to get attention for themselves. Most rare, according to Resnick, is spouse revenge filicide, wherein the child is killed to punish a partner.

That Resnick classified 49 percent of the maternal filicides he studied as altruistic reflects the belief that parents, mothers especially, are hardwired to protect the child. Seen this way, her actions are an extension of motherly love, protecting the child despite possible consequences to herself. If a woman kills someone else's daughter, she can face charges of criminal homicide. If she kills her own daughter, the system is more likely to take a measure of pity, to say she could not have been in her right mind at the time and charge her with a lesser crime.

The laws in a number of countries support this belief. The British Infanticide Act allows a mother to be charged with manslaughter rather than murder for killing her infant, on the grounds that she has not fully recovered from giving birth; she is then more often referred for mental health treatment than remanded to jail. More than twenty other nations have similar laws. In New Zealand, the law covers a murder of a child up to the age of ten. These exceptions are made only for mothers, not fathers.

Though the United States has no such law, our bias toward mothers is clear in the ways we punish filicidal parents. Resnick found that mothers were sent to mental institutions 68 percent of the time and to prison 27 percent of the time, whereas fathers went to prison 72 percent of the time and to hospitals 14 percent.

"We still view children as the mother's property," wrote Dahlia Lithwick in a 2002 *Slate* article about filicidal parents. "Since destroying one's own property is considered crazy while destroying someone else's property is criminal, women who murder their own children are sent to hospitals, whereas their husbands are criminals who go to jail."

A default determination of "crazy" can feel like security, a fence between mothers who kill their children and the rest of us, so long as we maintain our marbles. But it also removes a person's will from the situation. As Lithwick further wrote, "The destruction and control of something deemed to be a woman's sole property sends a powerful message about who's *really* in charge, and this message hasn't changed since the time of Jason and Medea."

Medea, who after murdering her two children to punish Jason's infidelity flies away in a golden chariot driven by dragons, and does so without remorse. Her rational choice to sacrifice her children has made Medea one of the great pariahs of literature. If we have no trouble seeing her act as one of unmitigated revenge, we have a harder time ascribing the same intention to real filicides. Mothers who mean to commit suicide after killing their children rarely succeed, scholars argue, because they have already killed what is most important to them. Their suicide, in other words, becomes redundant.

Five decades after Resnick's seminal work, the motives for filicide have grown to eleven, to seventeen, depending on current perceptions and psychological diagnoses. A 2012 study of fatal child abuse, for instance, found that perpetrators in more than 90 percent of filicide cases suffered from a personality disorder, including borderline, narcissistic, dependent, and immature; that 38 percent abused alcohol; and that 46 percent were perpetrators or victims of domestic violence.

Risk factors for those who kill their children include social isolation, mental illness, a pattern of unemployment or underemployment, and psychological stresses, such as financial hardship, housing problems, marital difficulties, and a lack of family and community support. Amanda's eroding circumstances—the loss of her marriage, her home, losing custody of her children—are all factors that can move a mother closer to killing her child.

It is unlikely anyone looked at the coordinates of Amanda's increasingly disordered life and calculated how she was at risk for killing her children. If Kathy Stott checked her daughter into treatment three times in the spring of 2009, it was for depression and an eating disorder. If Christine Duncan thought Jason should file for custody of the children, it was because Amanda had become an irresponsible mother. If Chantel Gardner knew her sister had previous mental health and alcohol issues, she nevertheless told police, who asked whether she thought Amanda capable of harming the kids, "I didn't believe she could."

Of course she didn't. The eventuality was unthinkable to Amanda's family. But they did see it coming; they just didn't know what it was.

10

Easter 2003, Oak Grove, Oregon

Chelsea Errington had been dating Nathan Beck for a month when he told her he wanted her to meet his son. Chelsea knew little about Gavin, who lived with his mother somewhere near Portland. She knew Gavin had just turned six and that Nathan saw him as often as he could. But Chelsea was vague on the relationship with Gavin's mother, or more precisely, it seemed something Nathan did not want to talk about. He and Amanda had been casual friends, a friendship that progressed to a brief intimacy around June 1996.

Nathan did not talk about that time. What was there to talk about? Amanda's getting pregnant was not something he had planned for. He barely knew her; they were both nineteen and trying to decide what to do. Mike Stott wanted Nathan to marry his daughter. Instead, Nathan and Amanda decided to give the baby up for adoption. They picked a family. It was all set. Six months into the pregnancy, Amanda changed her mind; she wanted to keep the child. Nathan needed to figure out how to make this work. He assessed the situation and accepted his duties: he would join the navy. The navy would provide a secure future and steady pay. By January 1997, he was in boot camp, in Great Lakes, Illinois. His son, Gavin Michael Nathan Stott, was born in March. Nathan began making monthly child support payments soon after and never stopped. Later based in Washington State, he tried to see Gavin whenever he was in port.

Amanda had called Nathan a few days before Easter 2003 to say Gavin would appear in an Easter play at her parents' church, and why didn't Nathan come? Nathan said he would come earlier and take Gavin to dinner the Friday before.

"Hi, Nathan," said the little boy with the glossy black hair by way of greeting. Chelsea thought it odd Gavin called his father by his first name. She knew that Gavin had lived with Amanda and her husband, Jason, for several years; perhaps he was accustomed to calling Jason "Dad." Still, Gavin repeatedly saying Nathan's name had a practiced tone, as though he'd only ever heard his father referred to by his first name or perhaps had been coached to use it.

They were eating dinner at McDonald's when Nathan's phone rang. It was Amanda, saying maybe it would be better if Nathan did not come to the Easter service, that Jason would not be comfortable with it. If Chelsea thought this a strange request, it became increasingly bizarre when Amanda called again and again—it seemed like she called fifty times—saying please don't come; she knew Jason was being silly about the whole thing, but still, it would be better if Nathan did not show up.

Nathan and Chelsea showed up anyway.

The church was plain and did not look to Chelsea to hold more than a hundred people. The small sanctuary had chairs rather than pews. If Chelsea expected Nathan might get a big greeting from Amanda's family, she was disappointed. Only Amanda came up to them before the service. She reminded Chelsea of an '80s Hawaiian girl, with long, long hair and frosted blue eye shadow. Amanda was talking in a ditzy voice, saying it would have been better if Nathan and Chelsea had not come, but they were here now so, oh well!

The parishioners filed into the sanctuary. Jason, Amanda, baby Trinity, and Gavin sat toward the front. Jackie Dreiling was seated several rows behind them, on the aisle. She thought Jason was probably furious that Gavin's father had come. Amanda had told her mother that Jason hated Nathan. Jackie thought this was because Jason was insecure, the reason, too, that Amanda used her children like gifts: she gave them to Jason to appease his insecurity. Jason wanted to be Gavin's father? Here, I give him to you; you are his father.

But he was not Gavin's father. Nathan was his father, and when Jackie saw Nathan take a seat in the back, she motioned to Gavin to come to her. She took him on her lap and whispered, "Daddy's here." She pointed at Nathan.

Gavin jumped off her lap and ran up the aisle and threw himself on Nathan. He knew exactly, Jackie thought, who his father was. From separate rows, the families watched the Easter production. They watched the children sing songs, Gavin dressed in a hat with little lamb ears.

Afterward in the lobby, Amanda again went up to Nathan and Chelsea. She nodded at Jason. That's my husband, she said. She tried to wave Jason over, to get him to come say hello. He would not come their way; he did not say anything to Nathan or Chelsea that day. Weird for sure, Chelsea thought, as was Amanda trying to make light of it, repeating, oh, he's just a goose this way. Later that year, after Nathan and Chelsea married, Amanda would tell Chelsea she was so pleased because now she could talk to Chelsea about Gavin rather than speaking directly with Nathan, thus avoiding jealousy on Jason's part. And Chelsea would think, what the hell is this?

11

The late intellectual Christopher Hitchens sat across from me in a window booth at Jake's Grill in downtown Portland. The faux-historic watering hole did brisk business at lunch, mostly businessmen at four-tops or alone at the bar. Hitchens was drinking Johnny Walker Black. Michael Totten, our mutual friend and fellow reporter, stuck to beer. There was no reason for me to be at this lunch other than Totten thinking I would enjoy meeting Hitchens, who was in Portland for an event for his latest book, *God is Not Great*.

I did enjoy meeting Hitchens. I enjoyed watching him silence the chattering buffoon at the next table without the man realizing how it had happened. I enjoyed catching the breathless "I love you . . ." from a woman who passed behind Hitchens's chair and ran a finger along the shoulders of his suit jacket.

"I had it made in Vietnam," he said when I told him the suit was beautiful. I asked if I might get him a proper fork so he did not have to keep eating his entrée with his oyster fork. I told him about Amanda and the children.

"Did she think the children would be going to heaven?" Hitchens asked. I told him that I believed she did. I appreciated how quickly he saw that the existence of heaven, something he actively did not believe existed, might matter to Amanda, that her thinking heaven was where she was sending her children might be a factor here.

***

"Do you really believe that?" asked my husband, Din.

We were finishing a bottle of wine in the living room when I suggested that Amanda had done what she had to protect the children; that maybe she thought they would be better off dead than in whatever situation they had been in. Din found this idea a serious reach. He thought Amanda was a coward.

"If things were so bad, why didn't she jump in the river?" he asked.

He did not see the benefit of trafficking in maybes. Wasn't the shortest distance between two points a straight line?

The year had made me consider what we make of people who kill and try to kill children. Two months after Eldon was killed and Trinity nearly killed, a girl who had gone to grade school with my daughter was murdered. She was seventeen. To protect her family's privacy, I will call this girl Helen. She was on an errand for her mother when a man approached her and asked for money. Surveillance cameras at an ATM showed Helen unsuccessfully trying to withdraw cash with a credit card her parents had given her for contingencies. What happened during the several hours between when Helen was captured on camera and when the man was picked up for drinking in public and possessing a crack pipe is unknown. Upon his arrest, the man was found to have the keys to Helen's Volvo and her cell phone. The following morning, Helen was discovered in her car in a parking lot. Her throat had been cut.

I lay in bed for two nights trying to come up with what I wanted to do with this man. I settled on taking him up in a small plane and flying him over the ocean ten or twenty miles, opening the door, and pushing him out. He would not survive the fall, but if for some reason he did, I imagined his terror in knowing he had no chance to get back to shore. He would be there alone. Maybe he would cry. Shortly, he would drown. Eventually, he would be eaten.

I mentioned my plane-drop solution to an acquaintance, an attorney. He disagreed with the revenge fantasy, not because he thought Helen's killer might be innocent but because he thought the man could not help doing what he had done. The man had mental health issues, as did, in the attorney's opinion, anyone who committed murder. He was extending the exemption we make for mothers who murder their children to everyone who murders anyone; he saw the act axiomatically as one done by the mentally ill, and thus, it must be forgiven.

His explanation made me uncomfortable. Summer 2009 was forcing me to consider what we make of the people who kill children. You might think such consideration would galvanize a position. This was not the case. The more I looked, the more each position had some legitimacy. Mikal Gilmore, brother of executed murderer Gary Gilmore, explored this condition in his memoir, *Shot in the Heart*. "Individual murders could be solved or punished, but murder itself, of course, could never be solved," he wrote. "That could not be done without solving the human heart, and without solving the history that has rendered the heart so dark and desolate."

I did not see a paradox in wanting to understand why Amanda had killed yet condemning Helen's killer to death. I thought people had the right to as many views as the human heart could summon. I also wondered at the idea of meting out justice, whether only the murderers could do this for themselves.

In the film *I've Loved You So Long*, the protagonist has served a fifteen-year sentence for killing her terminally ill young son. Leaving prison, she hears birdsong. The recognition of it brings a flicker of a smile, which she instantly loses. Smiles are no longer allowed. They are for the world before. She lives in the after world, the world in which your child is dead. Later, she expresses how she had wanted to go to prison; she did not want to live in the outside world. It held nothing for her.

Amanda had seemed unmoored in court. Had anyone allowed her to express her grief? Were mothers who killed their children allowed to grieve? Did their culpability render it grief qua grief, and if so, how did they go on?

In July 2001, *Newsweek* ran a piece entitled "Anna Quindlen on Every Mother's Struggle." Quindlen was writing about Andrea Yates, the Texas mother who had drowned her five young children in a bathtub the previous month: "Every mother I've asked about the Yates case has the same reaction. She's appalled; she's aghast. And then she gets this look. And the look says that at some forbidden level, she understands."

I did not think this statement was true, and not just because I did not detect in myself, as every mother (how many?) Quindlen asked evidently did, the aforementioned forbidden level on which I could see myself murdering my daughter. Quindlen seemed in the essay to be tossing one tarp over all mothers in order to make a point about agency or lack thereof: motherhood can be a terrible trial, one only other mothers can understand and acknowledge only via forbidden levels. That I thought the statement glib, if not syrupy, was not the (only) problem; the problem was that it made motherhood a syndrome, a handicap, with a hazard that most of us thankfully avoid. But who knew? It could happen to you.

In fact, what Andrea Yates did was exceedingly rare, so rare that she landed in the national consciousness and stayed there. We would struggle to understand how she could commit an act so horrific. We would learn her mind had been struggling for a long time, about her firm diagnosis of postpartum psychosis, of depression that had rendered her catatonic, of her multiple suicide attempts and hospitalizations in the years before she killed her children. We would learn that she was deeply religious and believed her children were not developing correctly according to God's law.

"My children were not righteous. I let them stumble. They were doomed to perish in the fires of hell," Yates told a prison psychiatrist the day after the murders. Later, she would say she had been planning to kill her children for several months. The latter would seem to imply premeditation, and in 2002, a jury judged Yates responsible for her actions and sentenced her to life in prison.

Dr. Phillip Resnick, sometimes referred to as the father of maternal filicide, disagreed. On a 2013 CNN program, "Crimes of the Century: Andrea Yates," he spoke of what Yates told him during an interview a month after she killed her children.

"She believed that one son would become a serial killer. One son was going to become a mute homosexual prostitute, and she had these fantastic beliefs that each of her children was going to end up in some evil way and would literally go to hell," he said. "She did not show remorse. She did not show regret. She believed that she had arranged for her children to go to heaven."

He went on: "I find her quite sympathetic. And not only do I think that she is not criminally responsible, but the fact that she has to live with what she has done and live childless and so forth, that's the tragedy in its own right."

Resnick had advocated to have Yates's sentence overturned, and in 2006, a second jury decided she was insane at the time of the killings, a decision that sent her from prison to a mental hospital, where, as of this writing, she spends some of her time making greeting cards and aprons and giving the proceeds to a fund started in her dead children's names.

12

Baker City, Oregon, is three hundred miles from Portland. The high-desert town, established in 1870, is close enough to the Idaho border that those arriving by air often fly to Boise. Not many do fly in. The population in 2009 was less than ten thousand, and while the Old West storefronts along Main Street had a bygone charm, many were vacant. The town's riches lay in its scenery. Baker City sits in a valley, with the Wallowa Mountains to the northeast and the Elkhorn Mountains to the west. The Powder River runs through the center of downtown. On a Friday afternoon in mid-August, downtown was ninety-one degrees and pedestrian-free. There was little to occupy the visitor, so I headed to my air-conditioned motel to wait for Hadley's call, which came a little before five. Before we talked about Amanda, he said, we were going to take a drive.

Hadley revved the Chevy Avalanche up a narrow rural road.

"What's the definition of a three-time loser?" he half shouted as the brush outside slapped my window. "A pregnant nun driving an Edsel with a Nixon sticker!"

We were on our way to the town of Elgin. On July 24, 2009, children trying to catch goldfish in a pond outside of town had instead found a human hand. Authorities later recovered the body of a woman. She was missing her head and feet. Several days later, the remains of two men were found in the woods north of Elgin. Gregory Cook was arrested for the killings on August 3.

"I did it," a handcuffed, shirtless Cook, age forty-two, confessed on camera. "Methamphetamines were largely responsible."

Hadley had been appointed Cook's defense attorney, another case where guilt was beside the point. While he was not conducting business today in Elgin, there was something in town Hadley thought I might like to see. He parked across from the Elgin Opera House. A two-story brick Colonial built in 1911, the opera house was an unexpected refinement in a town whose businesses ran to auto repair shops and livestock feed, but the building was not why Hadley had brought me here. Greg Cook, he said as we walked the two blocks that constituted downtown Elgin, wanted his story written. Unlike Amanda, Cook craved media attention, so much that he had asked Hadley if he knew a writer. Or, Hadley said, it might have been that he told Cook about me. Or, I thought, pretending to look through the plate-glass window of another out-of-business-looking business, having me on a story other than Amanda's might be a relief for Hadley. I told him I appreciated the courtesy. I did not say that I was not writing about Amanda and the children because I relished murder per se.

We drove back to Baker City, no jokes this time. We stopped for a drink at the formerly grand Geyser Grand Hotel, on Main Street. The place was so empty I felt as though we were entering the bar from *The Shining*. I had a pad but did not take it out. Hadley said I was not to take out my money, either. It was nine o'clock, not yet dark.

"High desert here," he said. "Plenty of quail and deer around."

And hot, I said, so hot.

Sure, he said, but in winter it could drop to twenty below; that's when he liked to hunt and fish.

We had a second drink. He told me about his kids, his grandson. I told him about my daughter. We talked about how Portland's new Democratic mayor had flown back from DC on the day of President

Obama's inauguration to face questions about having had a sexual affair with a then-underage legislative intern with the made-to-order name of Beau Breedlove. We might have ordered a third drink, but the bartender had disappeared. Hadley put some money on the counter and had me walk out ahead of him. I drove to my motel with the windows down and thought how we had spent an hour not talking about murder.

Back in my room, I looked up Cook's case. He had been charged with three counts of aggravated murder. His on-camera testimony left small doubt that despite entering an initial plea of not guilty, he would eventually change his plea to guilty and accept whatever sentence Hadley was able to strike with the prosecution, thereby avoiding a trial and a possible sentence of death. Amanda had pleaded not guilty to five counts of aggravated murder. If her case went to trial, the jury would have the option of imposing the death penalty. The chance of this happening was low. There were thirty-five people on Oregon's death row in 2009, none of them women. The state had never executed a woman and had sentenced only one to death: In 1961, nineteen-year-old Jeannace Freeman and her lover, Gertrude Mae Jackson, had thrown Jackson's son and daughter, ages six and four, off the Crooked River Canyon Bridge into a three-hundred-foot gorge. Jackson had testified against Freeman, who was sentenced to death, a sentence commuted to life in prison when the state's death penalty law was repealed in 1964. Voters reinstated the law in 1978.

Hadley had represented women up against the death penalty, if none for killing their own children. None had been condemned to death. Hadley worked inside what I was coming to think of as the murder machine. I had followed him inside the machine earlier in the summer, to the postconviction relief trial for an inmate on death row for fatally shooting a security guard in 1992. The proceeding, in the state capital of Salem, featured a half dozen "expert witnesses" for the defense, testimony countered by the prosecution, and nearly seven hours of opinion, which resulted in the judge deciding nothing beyond that there would be another hearing six months hence. The whole thing seemed like a jurisdictional circle jerk with no climax, a questionable use of time and money, and a frustrating experience for the inmate, who had been locked inside this machine for seventeen years and could expect to stay there until he died or was put to death. Amanda had now entered this machine, was just starting down whatever years-long path the system would create for her. I had heard that she was off suicide watch. That she was a model prisoner. That she was a bossy prisoner, yelling after guards that she wanted more cake. That she told police revenge was her motive. That she told police nothing. The stories could be true, or they could be conjecture; people stuck stories to her like wet plaster. Into what position would they set?

Hadley lived a few miles outside of Baker City, in a triple-wide manu-factured home with what were once stunning views of the mountains.

"Of course, none of these houses were here when I bought," he said, waving at a neighbor backing out of his driveway. "They let me go over and look at the view once in a while."

Hadley walked up his own driveway, most of it taken up by a twenty-seven-foot RV, and into the cool of the house. From the thresh-old, I could see into several empty rooms. Hadley had, until recently, lived here with his fourth wife, a Mormon he met on the Internet. When she left, she took the furniture.

Hadley was a bachelor again, which meant he could paint the walls in colors he liked. If the ochre he had chosen looked "a little too much like baby poop," he didn't much care. There was rarely anyone here to see it, to tell him he might move the cases of Diet Orange Crush within arm's reach of the lounger to the kitchen, or to stop him from bringing dogs home from the pound, including the chocolate Lab slobbering in the driveway.

"I don't even like to see a dog put to death," he said. Then, "I think we understand each other. I just cannot talk about any specific case."

We were just going to talk about him, I said.

"Oh, that's even worse." He looked at the room's other furnishing, a TV on mute, and spoke about his time in college and the air force, his respect and affection for his late father, who had been a policeman before going into the motel business. His father was one of the people Hadley had looked to early in his legal career for reassurance.

"I said, 'You know, Dad, I don't think you've ever had an enemy, and I wish sometimes I could say that,'" he recalled. "He said, 'Son, I thought about what you said. Running motels, we treat people different than you do, so don't feel bad about it. You got a job to do.'"

Hadley had to take off his glasses for a moment. "Anyway, I know what I do is right," he said. "I'm proud of what I do."

And if some people heard "meth addict murders three people" or "mother throws children from bridge" and thought, get rid of them, and then voted for the death penalty?

"But that just isn't justice," he said, later emphasizing, "It's a pendulum swing. I still don't quite understand why the United States wants that kind of vengeance, and that's all it is."

It was not that Hadley did not appreciate swift justice. He had cheered several months earlier when US Navy snipers shot and killed pirates holding hostages on a cargo ship off Somalia. And he vigorously defended people's rights to own guns.

"But self-defense has nothing to do with executing people," he said. "It's not just an easy one-liner. The state can't seem to keep the roads paved; you think we should trust them with life-and-death decisions?"

There were aggravated murder cases he was not eager to take on. He was grateful, for instance, that he had not been assigned "the woman who cut the baby out of the womb," if only because defending her and Amanda at the same time risked attracting attention that benefited neither client. But he believed there could never be someone whose crimes could not be understood.

"There have to be reasons. Just a normal person doesn't walk down the street and start wanting to kill people," he said. "One of the things that happens when I start working with a client, and the things we do with a jury, is called humanizing. We show them it's not just this monster. You've got to start showing how they were raised, the problems that came up, if they had fetal alcohol syndrome. It's sure not their fault if their mother was drinking John Barleycorn while they were in the womb. That doesn't *excuse* them; that doesn't get them off. That doesn't send them home."

Hadley stared at the TV, preseason college football.

"If you watch people, get to know them, you realize . . ." He paused. "I don't know that anybody is just one hundred percent bad. I just don't believe that."

Hadley had said he did not think Amanda's defense would be ready for a year, and that he was looking at a possible October 1, 2010, start date for the trial.

"It takes time to get acquainted and time to build trust and confidence," he said. "You can't just walk in and say, 'I'm your lawyer; I need to know everything about your life.'"

Hadley would of course not ask Amanda to tell him everything. He would approach her as a craftsman. He would observe and assess and build a story meant to save her life. She was fully in the machine now, both cosseted and at its mercy. Maybe she felt safer there. Maybe she did not want to be understood. Hadley would not, as I did, write letters to Amanda that came back marked "Undeliverable."

13

Summer 2008, Tualatin, Oregon

Amanda's husband left her on June 5, 2008, her thirty-first birthday. There was no plan for when Jason would see the children. She was to care for Gavin, Eldon, and Trinity by herself in the Tualatin house, a split-level ranch on the corner of a street of tall pines and homes flying American flags.

Amanda's house had no flag. It also had no VCR, no computer, and no grown-up bicycles, all of which Jason had hocked or sold. Soon Amanda would not have a working car. The Honda Odyssey her mother-in-law bought the family needed repairs. Amanda asked her permission to get it serviced. The answer was no. Mike Stott offered to fix the brakes for free. The answer was still no; Jason and his mother said they would have it towed and fixed professionally; they asked Amanda for the keys, including the spare, but the car just sat in the driveway, never going anywhere.

Amanda was able to use her old car from college, the beat-up 1991 Audi. She spent time with her folks and with her sister. That was a nice change; Jason had not liked her family being around the kids. Still, she couldn't concentrate when she was away from the house; she wanted to be there in case Jason came by, and never knowing when he would was making her jittery. Amanda knew her husband was probably using drugs, if not what kind. Sometimes he would show up just to take Eldon; he would not tell her where they were going or when they'd be back. Eldon would come home in clothes belonging to the son of Jason's drug friends. Amanda washed and dried the clothes and put them in a separate pile so Jason could return them. He told her not to do that. She suggested they could have them over to dinner; she could return the clothes then. Jason didn't want her meddling. He told her Eldon was his son, and he would take the boy when he wanted, or Amanda could face legal action.

And then he'd be gone again, telling her his being away was probably temporary and that if she stopped smoking, stopped drinking, lost weight, and got a job, he would come home. She wanted to do what he wanted her to do, but it was hard. Jason and his mother demanded contradictory things: she needed to stay home with the kids, she needed to get a job, she needed to let Jason keep control of the finances, she needed to take control of her own life. She wanted to get a stop-smoking patch but missed the appointment, and anyway, her medical records were all screwed up from the times Jason had her go to the doctor—for a low-bone-density test for a cracked tailbone—and get pain pills that he would take. She knew her husband had been stuck in the world of narcotics for as long as she had known him, maybe longer. A few times, she hid his car keys so he couldn't go meet drug people or bad company, but he would get angry. She thought the children were mostly oblivious to the problems, though one time Eldon did see Jason throw a chair at her. It broke against the wall.

If all Amanda had to do was get Trinity and Eldon to swim lessons at the Sellwood Pool, or sit on the floor and play with Eldon, the summer went fine, but other things kept piling up. They ran out of milk and groceries. They lost electricity, then water and garbage collection. Nathan and his wife, Chelsea, wanted more time with Gavin; they were going to take Amanda to court. More and more, she was getting the flutter in her chest and throat, like she was going to have a panic attack. Too many people were telling her what to do: Jason telling her to fit into tiny clothes, her parents' church teaching that she needed to be an obedient wife, and her mother-in-law complaining about her spending habits.

June became July. The family's possessions kept disappearing: ski gear, Gavin's PlayStation, a very nice canoe. The furniture had been cheap or secondhand to begin with; the house was at once empty and cluttered. Grandma Chris kept buying the children toys, Polly Pockets and a million tiny toy sets. Amanda thought her mother-in-law was deliberately trying to drive her crazy, complaining that Amanda was OCD, accusing her of using too much Spray 'n Wash, and buying more and more tiny toys.

Amanda would sometimes sit on the strip of lawn next to the conked-out Odyssey and watch her younger children play. She would drink a beer, smoke a clove cigarette, and try to figure out what she needed to do to get her husband to come home. There was a lot to figure out. Was she a wife, or wasn't she? Why was Jason nice to her in private but mean to her in front of everybody else? He lied, and he was good at it, with a steel-trap memory that allowed him to convince anybody of anything and that nothing was his fault, but until now she did not think he had lied to her. They had been unified in the stories they told others, and Jason had promised Amanda before God that he would never divorce her. What did Amanda have to do to make this true? Maybe the right thing was to be perfect before God and not sin or make any mistakes to make every action of hers reflect well on Jason, to make sure everyone knew how wonderful Daddy was.

***

Everything went to crap after Jason left. It was not that Gavin minded his stepfather being gone, but his mother was falling apart. Jason had done things out of obligation, but at least he bought groceries and stuff. His mother didn't do anything anymore. She slept until noon and no longer cooked. Later, when Gavin learned how to make an egg in the microwave, he was sorry he had not known how to do so earlier; he could have given Eldon and Trinity more than cereal and milk, more than ants on a log.

That had been his job since he was eight: making sure Trinity and Eldon were okay. He made them breakfast. He made up games and watched *Shrek* with them over and over. He took the blame when he didn't need to, like when he told the lady from child services he was pretty sure the bruises on his arms were from roughhousing with his friends, and that maybe his mother had locked him out of the house by accident. He was eleven. He could take care of himself.

Eldon and Trinity could not take care of themselves. Eldon wouldn't turn four until August, Trinity was six and a half, and if Gavin had told the lady about the bruises and then made Gavin live with his father full-time, then who would take care of them? He wished his mother would just try. She said she was trying but it was hard. After Jason told her he would come home if she found a job, his mother had taken him, Eldon, and Trinity to the library for two hours so she could use the computer and make a résumé. Gavin did not think she really made one, but she did, showing her last job to have been eight years earlier and listing five references, including her mother, her aunt, her pastor, and "Jason Smith, MGR."

14

The Juvenile Justice Center on the John Serbu Youth Campus in Eugene kept its doors locked from noon to one. Those who arrived early for court dates did what they could to pass the time. A young couple made out, a teenage boy wearing an ankle monitor and oversized everything stood apart from his mother and grandmother, and a man of about thirty in a white dress shirt and cantaloupe-colored tie paced. The scene played out in the full sun on the first day of October 2009, until the pacing man asked a woman with a silver swoop of hair, a woman to whom he had not been speaking, whether he should call Laura to be let inside.

I wondered whether this man was Jason Smith. His photo had not appeared in any newspaper or on television, and he had not granted interviews. In answer to my emails, his lawyer, Laura Schantz, had been courteous, if brief, and said essentially the same things she had told the press five days after Eldon and Trinity were found in the river. Standing before the cameras in a city park, in a cornflower-blue jacket and navy skirt, her long dark hair in loose waves, Schantz had explained that Jason would now "dedicate his life to make sure his daughter has the most normal, happy childhood she can have." Further, that Jason was "drawing his faith from God." The blue-on-blue ensemble had something of the air hostess to it, as did Schantz's bright smile. A family law attorney who had been representing Jason in his divorce from Amanda, she had not spoken publicly about the case since that appearance on May 27.

But here she was now, an attractive brunette in a skirt and suit jacket opening the double-glass door for the man I thought might be Jason. She gave me a smile. I had received a last-minute tip from a newsroom friend, with no more detail than that some aspect of Amanda's case was being decided today, and the smile, mixed with my pleasure at being the only reporter in attendance, made me hope I might speak with the Smith family.

Meanwhile, in the same building but unbeknownst to me, negotiations were about to move forward. Amanda's son Gavin, age twelve; his father, Nathan; and stepmother, Chelsea, were in the Lane County district attorney's office. They had each been subpoenaed to appear. Chelsea was not opposed to being here. She had information she thought the DA should know. She felt the information crucial to the outcome of today's hearing, which would consider terminating Amanda's custodial rights to Trinity and granting Jason full custody of his surviving child. Chelsea knew if this were to happen, Gavin would not be allowed to see his half sister again. One of the reasons she knew this was that since the incident, she and Nathan had been contacted only once by the Smith family. Christine Duncan, Jason's mother, had called to say they were not welcome at Eldon's funeral. Duncan later amended this prohibition, saying Gavin could come if Nathan and Chelsea agreed to drive him to Eugene and leave the boy with her.

Chelsea had been involved with Nathan long enough to sense this was not only Duncan's grief talking. Chelsea did not doubt Duncan's grief. She did not doubt that Jason would rely on his mother to organize the funeral, as he often relied on her to handle family matters. But Chelsea did see the edict as another of the demands the Smith family had made over the years. Though it would mean Gavin would miss his brother's funeral, Nathan and Chelsea had chosen not to drive Gavin to Eugene and leave him with the Smith family. They chose not to because they did not believe the boy would be safe there.

Nathan and Chelsea had been embroiled for years in court dates and arguments with Jason and Amanda, who did not want Nathan to see Gavin. The reluctance to let father and son see each other on its face made little sense. Nathan provided financially for Gavin. An active member of the navy, stationed on a nuclear submarine until 2004, Nathan had tried to see Gavin whenever he had shore leave. Amanda and Jason had made this difficult. They cited Nathan's variable schedule as too much of an impediment to work around. Chelsea thought a more telling reason was that Amanda wanted Gavin to be a Smith; she often said so and sometimes enrolled the boy, named Gavin Stott on his birth certificate, in school as Gavin Smith. Christine Duncan had gone so far as to tell Chelsea, "Gavin will always be a Smith, not a Beck."

Nathan was reliable and even tempered. Thanks to these qualities, he had been able to interact with six hundred servicepeople during his eight years on the submarine and dislike only one person. Chelsea was more reactive. A devout Christian, as was her husband, she had no problem calling people on their bad behavior and fighting for what she thought was right. For the past six years, this had included fighting for Gavin.

Hadley arrived at the courthouse with several members of his team. He was not representing Amanda with regard to her custody rights to Trinity and was here today mostly to take in the proceedings. I thought the Smith family would not be happy to see Amanda's defense team here and told Hadley maybe he and I should not appear so friendly.

"Good plan," he said. "They won't want to talk to you if they see you talking to me."

The courthouse doors opened at one o'clock. A staircase led to a wide second-floor gallery. I caught up with Jason's attorney, Laura Schantz, heading at a clip down a corridor.

"Ms. Schantz?" I asked. She nodded. We had emailed, I said, and handed her my card.

She looked at it. "I don't think so," she said. "I would have remembered your name."

I reminded her that it was a few months ago, regarding Jason Smith and, later, Trinity. This did not jog her memory. I said, "You're Laura Schantz."

"No, I'm the DA," she said, and handed me the card back. "But I'll tell her you're here."

The district attorney disappeared down a corridor. I assumed she misheard me but still felt foolish that I'd mistaken her for Schantz.

Several dozen people had by now assembled in the gallery. They were dressed casually for the warm fall day. A relaxed conversation filled the room until a message ran through the crowd that the proceedings would be delayed.

Today was supposed to have been simple. Amanda would give up her custodial rights to Trinity, allowing Jason to assume full custody. Instead, Jason had been let into the courthouse early in order to sit in the DA's office and negotiate with Nathan and Chelsea. He had not seen the Becks in more than a year. He had not reached out to Gavin after Eldon's death and had not permitted Trinity any contact with her older brother. Nathan and Chelsea did not wish to debate Jason as to why, only to set some rules moving forward. Specifically, they wanted Jason to accept Department of Human Services oversight as a contingency of his taking custody of Trinity and pledge that he would not prevent future contact between the children. If Jason did not accede to these demands, and sign papers stating as much, Nathan, Chelsea, and Gavin would testify against him today in open court.

After the crowd learned the delay would be no more than a half hour, conversation in the gallery resumed. The echoing acoustics and marble floor made the gathering feel like a museum gala. I saw a different silver-haired woman by a balustrade smiling at me.

"We met last time, right?" she said. She was with a man whose height and girth made her look even tinier than she was. I told her I did not think we had met. She introduced herself as Kim Smith.

"I'm Jason's stepmother, and this is his father," she said of Jay Smith. The big man shook my hand. I told Kim I was writing about what had happened to their family. The couple seemed amenable to this. Jay Smith told me he worked for Western Pneumatics, a company that made equipment "that helps keep the environment clean." He talked about the Oregon Ducks, the University of Oregon football team whose gold-on-green logo sweatshirt he was wearing. He explained Eldon's unusual third name, Rebhan, was part of "a really silly family tradition" whereby babies were given, as a middle name, the last name of their delivery doctor.

"One time we had a doctor whose last name was Martini!" he said, and laughed.

Kim gave me their email addresses and, when I said I would like to visit with them, said, "We might be able to do that."

"That's Jason's mother," she said of the silver-haired woman I had seen outside.

I introduced myself to Christine Duncan. She handed me a tract written by Eldon's preschool teacher detailing how he was full of grace and walked the path of the Lord. Duncan was a tall woman with a strong voice that did not seem so much directed at the person she was speaking with as to the room. She talked nonstop about Eldon: how inquisitive he was, how loved he was, how he had been learning to write. The whites of Duncan's eyes went from pink to rose as she talked about how smart Eldon had been. He wanted to know how the big cranes working on the U of O campus got out of the holes they dug, and the last time they had gone to the Olive Garden restaurant, Eldon had taken a peppermint on the way out and asked, "Grandma, how do they get peppermint?"

"What child in the world has ever asked where peppermint comes from?" Duncan said. She abruptly stopped talking. A buzz came off her. It was like standing next to a transformer. I told Duncan I wanted to hear more about Eldon. She took my card but said she was not sure we could talk anymore and that the family had chosen to not speak to the media, which had "gotten everything wrong." I watched her move into the crowd and start telling her story to the next person from the exact point she left off with me.

It was not hard to see how Jason and the Smith family would resent the contingencies being presented in the DA's office. They had lost a son, a grandson. They were left to care for Trinity and deal with whatever emotional hurdles the girl would now face. Amanda had wrecked so many lives, and her influence even now was turning what should have been a simple matter—Jason being allowed to take custody of his daughter—into an ordeal. That Nathan and Chelsea were stalling a matter as crucial and sensitive as a child's welfare must have seemed selfish, if not insufferable.

As it happened, the welfare of Jason and Amanda's children was the reason Nathan and Chelsea were making their demands. Chelsea felt little but rancor for Jason, whom she saw as having brought devastation to Gavin's life. In 2003, when Gavin was six years old, someone in the Stott family, and very likely Amanda, had called the Oregon Department of Human Services to say the boy showed signs of abuse.

On the phone with a Child Protective Services worker, Jason admitted to spanking Gavin three days earlier. CPS visited the Smith home. The worker took note of "significant bruising" on the back of the boy's legs. Photographs were taken. The CPS worker determined the injuries "could have been the result of excessive discipline," and the case was closed. Asking today for DHS oversight of Jason's custody of Trinity was the only way the Becks saw to safeguard the girl and allow her to see her brother.

There was also the matter of Chelsea not believing anything Jason said.

In January 2005, Amanda had called Nathan and said the family was moving to Oahu. She did not consult Nathan about moving his son across the ocean. Nathan had just been released from service aboard the USS *Parche*, a Cold War–era nuclear submarine, most of whose missions remain classified despite its decommission in 2004. He and Chelsea were living in Bremerton, Washington. They made the three-hour drive to Portland to work out a parenting plan with Jason and Amanda.

"You know what?" Chelsea recalled Jason saying once they were seated at the kitchen table. "There's an Indy car race on once a year and it's on now. Can you wait?"

Nathan and Chelsea waited in the kitchen while Jason watched TV in another room. Once that was done, they hashed out a plan. Nathan and Chelsea had a lawyer draw it up. Amanda refused to sign. The family left for Oahu in March. The lawyer sent the papers there. There was no response. Each time they inquired, Jason or Amanda would say the papers had been lost or they never arrived. It went on and on, until Nathan filed for an emergency custody hearing if the papers were not signed.

The threat brought a response. Jason claimed he and Amanda were the better parents and that he was concerned about Nathan. Further, that Gavin was in a secure and stable home, and that he, Jason, was worried about Gavin not being close to his siblings, and that he believed those relationships were important.

Chelsea did not then believe Jason thought those relationships important, and she believed it less now. After Eldon was murdered, Jason had told her, let's get together, for the kids. Yes, Jason. Sounds great; good idea. Never happened.

Most people in the gallery had grown restless during the hour-long wait, except for a woman who'd been standing still and alone against the far wall. She wore glasses and a calf-length skirt, her long auburn hair in braids.

"I wouldn't approach her," said Hadley, and he confirmed that the woman was Kathy Stott. In any case there was no time to approach, as the courtroom doors were opening and the crowd migrating over, except for the DA, who was marching my way.

"Laura Schantz wants you to leave the building," she said.

Excuse me?

"I told her you'd come here to interview her, and she says she wants you to leave," she said. "And that she won't talk to you."

I told the DA I had not asked to interview Schantz, and as for my leaving, did she mean the whole building?

"Well, the building is public, so I can't ask you to leave here, but it's a closed courtroom," she said, and walked away.

"It's not a closed courtroom," Hadley whispered.

"Court is open!" the bailiff called.

I slid onto a bench in the back. Amanda's mother sat at the other end. The judge said he would have Amanda on the speakerphone from jail. He announced that the parties—the attorney representing Amanda, Jason and his attorney, the DA, and a representative from DHS—had reached a resolution and that any allegations against the father had been dismissed.

"As far as the mother's portion of the case," the judge continued, "she is incarcerated and unable to care for Trinity." The court would not rule on whether Amanda's parental rights to Trinity would be terminated in the future, only who would take or share custody of Trinity today.

"Do you understand?" asked the judge.

"I think so," said Amanda. Her voice on speakerphone—breathless, halting—took the room by surprise. We had not realized she was already on the line. This created a feeling of being exposed, as if we'd been Peeping Toms, only to discover someone was watching us.

The judge asked if Amanda needed additional time to understand.

"I think that's fine," she said with a hesitation that made it sound as if she had no idea what she was agreeing to.

The judge asked, "Do you need additional time to confer with your attorney?"

There was silence. Then, "I think so. Yes."

We were instructed to leave the courtroom. People stood more soberly now. Kathy Stott was collapsed in Kim Smith's arms and sobbing so loudly the sounds rang off the ceiling. No one else in the Smith family acknowledged them. The Stott and Smith families were estranged. The separation had started long before Eldon's murder. Watching Kim hold up Amanda's mother to keep her from sinking to the floor might have left people confused, or moved. Mostly, it was heartbreaking.

The rest of the Smith family formed a huddle outside the closed courtroom doors. They spoke a prayer aloud. Schantz stood with them but was looking at me. I approached and handed her my card. She refused it. I apologized for any misunderstanding and reminded her we had previously emailed, to which she said only, "Yes."

"What was that about?" Hadley asked.

We filed back into court. The judge asked Amanda if "termination" had been sufficiently explained. She said it had.

"Has anyone threatened you or forced you to this resolution of the case?" the judge asked.

"No," Amanda said.

"Are you currently incarcerated?"

"Yes."

"Are you taking medication that would impair your ability to make a decision?"

"No."

"Do you understand what's happening here today?"

Again there was a pause. Then, "I think so."

If Amanda had more than these three words to say about having her parental rights to Trinity taken away, we would not hear them. A woman from DHS was sworn in. She said she was assigned to Trinity Smith and that "the mother is unable to care for the child." Her testimony took less than a minute. The judge said that Jason agreed to participate with DHS. The order of the court was that Trinity would be a ward of the court, placed with Jason for now. The child was to have no contact with Amanda, nor was she allowed contact with Amanda's family without DHS approval. This second part, whether by design or not, would have an irrevocable effect on many lives. Amanda's state-appointed attorney agreed to the decision, and court was adjourned.

We exited the courtroom. The Smith family came together again in prayer. I stood with Hadley and his associates. All were courteous and, from what Hadley had told me, excellent at their jobs and making the right connections. I had been critical of the machine in which they worked, did not see how it could capture the vagaries of human behavior. Now I envied them their working within a framework that permitted them to productively move forward, whereas I was fumbling, unintentionally making enemies.

I walked down to the lobby, hoping to intersect with the Smith family on their way out. Kim and Jay Smith came down first. He shook my hand, and she gave me a hug. Next came Jason with his mother and

Laura Schantz. There was a light victorious ring to their voices. Schantz left. Jason lingered. He gave me a small wave from the waist and headed for the door. His mother followed, then stopped.

"I'll be right out," she told Jason, and came back to me.

"I must respectfully ask that you give me back that paper," she said, meaning the tract Eldon's teacher had written. I handed it back. I said I was not sure what I had done to get everyone so angry.

"I'm not either," she said. "But you have everybody up in arms."

Nathan, Chelsea, and Gavin had left the courthouse immediately after the papers were signed. Chelsea did not feel the satisfaction of things having gone their way. The best predictor of the future is the past, and their history with Jason, with Amanda, had ranged from frustrating to disastrous. What she had wanted seemed so simple: to ensure that two innocent kids be able to talk on the phone, to see each other every few months. But even with the signed legal documents in hand, Chelsea was apprehensive. She sensed Gavin would never be allowed to see Trinity and that the letters he had been writing to his sister had not reached her. For Trinity to think her big brother had abandoned her added a new misery to what was already the tragedy of these children's lives. As Nathan drove them back to Portland, where their two-year-old daughter waited, Chelsea had the feeling they had just been outfoxed.

15

May 24, 2009, Gorge Amphitheater, George, Washington

It was eight on Sunday morning, and April Anson was already drinking mimosas. She and her friends were at the second day of the Sasquatch Music Festival, getting ready to watch Nine Inch Nails and Jane's Addiction, when her boyfriend brought over her cell phone and said, you better call Tiffany; she's texted like a million times. April was in the middle of a field when she reached Tiffany Gray, a long-time best friend, who told her what Amanda, their other best friend from college, had done to her kids; it was all over the news.

April made her way to her car and cried for two hours. She knew those kids; she'd halfway raised Gavin when she and Tiffany and Amanda were in school together. April kept pictures of the children on her laptop: Trinity squealing at the ocean's edge in Oahu; Eldon sifting sand on the beach; Amanda, with eye shadow the color of pink soda above thick lines of black eyeliner, pressed cheek to cheek with baby Trinity.

That was standard, the MAC eyeliner. Amanda had been wearing it since the girls met at George Fox University. A superconservative Quaker college less than an hour from Portland in the town of Newberg, George Fox was the kind of small school students went to if they were raised Christian and their parents, or the students themselves, felt it a more wholesome environment than the nearby state schools with their tens of thousands of students; the University of Oregon especially had a reputation for raucousness and drug use. George Fox felt safe. It also felt claustrophobic. April and Tiffany and Amanda liked getting out of Newberg, liked going up to Portland, to the U of O campus in Eugene. They were good students but also partiers; they smoked a lot of weed and dated a lot of guys. The dating part had been ridiculously easy—April with titian hair to her waist and the build of a tomboy from snowboarding, and Tiffany with a way of flirting that was like a game of cards; she always had the better play, always liked the spotlight on her. Together with Amanda, with her up-tilt eyes and a breathless singsong voice that sounded like Marilyn Monroe doing Marilyn Monroe, they made the boys stand up, made them say, "My god, you're killing me." The girls pushed the campus's modest dress code, Amanda in miniskirts and platform shoes, April and Tiffany all '90s grunge, artfully ripped jeans and ratty, baggy sweaters. They joked that the day they graduated, they'd get a six-pack of beer and a pack of cigarettes, sit on the clocktower lawn, and flip everybody off.

Amanda got pregnant with Gavin the first time she had sex—at least that's what she told April. April did not know much about Nathan. She had met him a few times, and he seemed like a stand-up guy, serious, quiet, especially compared to Amanda, who was like a bubble machine, superbubbly and fun. And spacey! That voice made April think, the first time they met, that Amanda might be drunk. Tiffany said otherwise, that Amanda was just very la-di-la; she never let anything get under her skin. Amanda had been a good student in high school, but whether she cared much about college was a question: Tiffany rarely saw her study, and she never spoke about what she would do with her degree in communications. When April and Tiffany stressed about their grades, Amanda would say, "Don't worry, it's all going to work out."

And it did, mostly. April thought Amanda handled being a single mom well. She got on food stamps to keep Gavin fed and healthy. Though April and Tiffany could have relied on their parents in a similar situation, Amanda did not have a lot of financial resources. But the girls loved helping with Gavin; he was a good baby, a beautiful baby. They would push him around Pioneer Courthouse Square in his stroller, and people would stop them to remark on how gorgeous he was, how much he looked like his mother. The girls scheduled their classes so there was always someone to watch him, and they stayed with him at night when Amanda wanted to go out. Having ready babysitters gave Amanda the freedom she wanted, freedom she did not have with her own strictly religious parents. April had met them a few times and thought their faith veered toward an "Eve is responsible" sort of thing.

Amanda could take advantage of the arrangement. While April and Tiffany liked to decompress by smoking weed and listening to a little Jimi Hendrix, Amanda would make the forty-five-minute drive to Portland and get into techno clubs using a fake ID. Sometimes she didn't come home, including once when Gavin had an ear infection. April ripped into Amanda the next day, told her it sucked that she had stayed out while April and Tiffany were up all night with a screaming baby. Amanda started in on some cockamamy explanation of how she'd gotten back earlier but did not want to wake them up and so had slept in April's dorm room. What?

April tried to put this down to Amanda's being spacey. But she also knew that Amanda liked to see what she could get away with. Amanda would go to the mall, shove things she wanted in Gavin's stroller, and walk out. She had been caught or warned at least once at Nordstrom's, and security had told her not to come back. This did not seem like a very big deal—teenagers shoplift—but Amanda had not been a teenager anymore. The girls were juniors in college, and actions were starting to have consequences. Tiffany and April both got in trouble for missing chapel too many times; Tiffany moved to another school. The girls did not wind up sitting on the lawn at graduation. Amanda graduated with barely enough credits for her degree. If she had weathered being a single mother and losing the company and support of her best friends, these two events her senior year seemed, in hindsight, to change an essential piece of Amanda's psyche.

In the months after Eldon was murdered, April wondered about that change, whether a part of Amanda had been broken or activated. Had Amanda shown signs April had missed, some "evil mother waiting in the wings" thing? April had never seen Amanda treat Gavin or any of her children harshly. To April, Amanda was the twenty-year-old girl she met in 1998: voluptuous, lighthearted, a girl who trusted people. April saw herself, Tiffany, and Amanda taking turns carrying Gavin around the Oregon Country Fair, wearing their Steve Madden platforms and Amanda, a crocheted bikini top.

In 1997, Jason Smith was twenty-two. He had finished a stint in rehab, his third since age sixteen, and was waiting to hear whether he would be admitted to Nugen's Ranch, an addiction treatment program in Wasilla, Alaska. Jason's criminal history from 1994 to 1996 included arrests for drug possession, probation violations, and theft in the first and second degrees. He was a Class C felon, according to the legal definition. The theft had taken place in 1994, when Jason was nineteen. He had robbed the home of his mother and stepfather, Christine and Richard Duncan, while they were on vacation. Among the items he stole were his mother's jewelry, some of which he pawned to buy pot. His mother had him arrested.

"Jason chose to steal from our home to support his drug habit," she wrote in a letter to the judge. "I was literally sick to my stomach to think he had misused my trust." If she knew which drugs constituted this habit, she did not elaborate, saying only, via Jason's attorney, that her son's latest relapse was due to his decision to "smoke marijuana occasionally." Christine Duncan nevertheless asked the judge that Jason not be sentenced to jail time. He had not finished high school and was working as an assistant manager at the Italia Roma restaurant but had "a college education waiting for him" and was "a bright person with a great future."

Jason was given probation, with the conditions that he was to remain employed, break no laws, and report for substance abuse treatment. He failed to meet these conditions, and in August 1994 began a years-long loop of arrests for parole and other violations.

Midway through her junior year, Amanda was pregnant again. This time she was engaged to the father, Shane Cook. The girls had bought pot from him a couple of times. He was a nice guy a few years older than they were. April did not really know him but thought he might have struggled with depression. Midway through Amanda's pregnancy, he drove into the woods and swallowed a bottle of horse tranquilizers. Or that's what April heard. Tiffany said it was carbon monoxide poisoning, that Shane had "hooked it up" by running a piece of tubing from the tailpipe and through the cracked window of his car, where, with the engine running, he was overcome and eventually killed by the poison gas.

April saw Amanda soon after Shane's body was found. She thought Amanda would be destroyed. Amanda was not. Her attitude seemed to be "This is happening, and I am going to handle the situation."

Immediately after finding out Shane was dead, Amanda handled the situation by paging her mother. Kathy Stott pulled off the road and into a gas station to call Amanda back. Amanda told her Shane had committed suicide and that he died in his car writing a letter to her saying she was a wonderful person and she was not the reason he was taking his life. Jackie Dreiling was in the car with Kathy Stott at the time of the call and would remember Amanda as being devastated. This though shortly before Shane's death, Amanda had told Jackie that while she really cared for Shane and knew he loved her, he didn't have any money. Jackie took this to mean Amanda had figured out that with her looks, she could get a guy with money. Jackie did not like this development in her granddaughter, who had been smart and driven in high school, was active at church, and volunteered at a crisis pregnancy hotline. But she'd also always wanted things the family could not afford. At least once Jackie had driven Amanda to Pioneer Courthouse Square to go to the city's upscale department stores. Amanda was drawn to the ready gleam of the cosmetic counters, where a teenage girl needed only to show her wrist for a saleswoman to spritz it with Yves St. Laurent's Opium or Calvin Klein's Eternity, where shell-pink eye shadow and black eyeliner could both accentuate and disguise.

Amanda gave birth on November 2, 1999. She gave the newborn up for adoption. She asked April and Tiffany not to visit her in the hospital. The girls did not. They had been seeing less of Amanda since she started dating Jason Smith. The timing of the new romance seemed more than propitious; Jason appeared in the wake of Shane's suicide, or maybe just before, like her knight in shining armor. April thought his approach, a sort of "I'll be there, I'll be your support, you're in this awful position," was fantastic and the godsend Amanda needed, but she wondered where the hell this guy had come from.

She also wondered where Jason's money was coming from and found it odd that he drove an Audi, dressed like a child of Tommy Bahama, and had all these impressive accoutrements but did not seem to have a job.

Or maybe he did have a job. Jason sold weed; at least, he sold it to them. He and Amanda would drive down to Eugene and bring back a ton of it. This was not the sort of weed the girls were used to seeing, a dime bag here and there; this was quantity. Maybe that was how Jason was making the money to take Amanda shopping. Right after the baby was born, she started dressing up in the Nordstrom's clothes Jason bought her. She told April and Tiffany how Jason had called Carl Greve Jewelers in Portland and asked them to stay open late, that he and Amanda would be coming in. She would show off a new diamond bracelet, a new diamond pendant. Space cadet that Amanda was, she would sometimes lose or misplace these pieces; she never seemed to know how, but it didn't matter because another would take its place. April could see it was fun for Amanda to finally be that girl, the one whose boyfriend bought her expensive things, but April had started to dislike Jason. She did not see him treat Amanda with any sweetness. He was good at appearing mature and responsible, but he never seemed like a nice guy.

Then there was the dinner at Couvron. The girls were just out of school, trying to make ends meet, but it was someone's birthday and Jason said they should all go out to eat. He picked the most expensive place in Portland; every plate was like seventy-five dollars. Tiffany, her boyfriend, April, and her then-fiancé kept looking at each other at the table; there was no way to order frugally, and April was terrified the bill was going to be something like $1,800. The men reached for their wallets, but Jason would not let them pay. April wondered if Jason had planned it this way, if he wanted to make everyone uncomfortable. If so, he succeeded. The dinner no longer felt like a celebration but a setup. Tiffany's boyfriend later told her he thought Jason was an ass and that he flaunted Amanda in a way that said, this is my prize; this is what my money bought me. April thought Jason and Amanda were acting like Tom and Daisy Buchanan, like the children of celebrities allowed to run wild.

Jason turned twenty-four the year he met Amanda and was given access to a fund set up by his grandparents on his mother's side. Legal and other documents do not list the value of the assets Jason originally came into in 1999 or 2000—the total value of the inheritance was likely around $240,000—only what was still available in October 2000, when Jason was twenty-five. At that time, Christine Duncan went to court to have her husband appointed conservator of Jason's remaining accounts, including 800 shares of Cisco (valued at $39,850), 800 shares of Intel ($29,700), 1,000 shares of Qualcomm ($64,375), 444 shares of Globalstar ($2,886), and $7,626 in money market funds, for a total valuation of $144,437. Jason's other assets included an account at US Bank ($29.15), a 1994 Audi sedan ($8,000), a Merlin bike frame ($6,000), a Nikon camera ($1,050), and miscellaneous personal property, including a tent, an Abercrombie & Fitch jacket, 52 CDs, and a pair of Dr. Martens shoes (estimated total value, $2,081). The recorded total assets were $167,597.15.

In her petition to the court, his mother wrote in part:

> The respondent [Jason] suffers from alcohol and drug addiction (the drug addiction goes back to age 15). As a result, the respondent is unable to manage his financial resources and is financially incapable. Respondent has a history of not paying his bills. . . . The respondent has fallen victim to an abusive relationship with a "girlfriend," which has resulted in the respondent being financially exploited, which is ongoing. The respondent's "girlfriend" continues to blackmail him into giving her large sums of money, including $8,100 given to her in the month of August 2000. "Girlfriend's" mother reported to petitioner [Duncan] that she heard her daughter blackmail respondent over the phone. Additionally, more than $5,000 was spent by respondent and "girlfriend" at Nordstrom in September 2000. The respondent has spent nearly $25,000 or more in each of the last three months. The respondent

is vulnerable to being taken advantage of financially due to his alcohol and drug addiction.

Where Amanda's friends saw her as resourceful—getting state assistance to keep Gavin fed, and bearing up under the suicide and adoption—Christine Duncan saw a woman preying on her son. She had seen scapegoats before. In her letter to the judge after the 1994 theft of jewelry from her home, Duncan cited her divorce from Jason's father when Jason was nine, how Jason "became quite angry with his father as time passed, because of his [father's] lack of interest." There was the friend Jason made in eighth grade, "a black youth, John, who was sent to Eugene to live with his grandparents to get away from the L.A. gangs. . . . It wasn't until some time later that I learned John had introduced Jason to marijuana, and that the group of friends that John eventually introduced Jason to were regular users."

Jason was sensitive, in other words. He was swayable; others might share the blame for his addiction and its consequences. That other was now Amanda, who merited neither a name nor a straightforward appellation, always mentioned as "girlfriend" in quotes. Amanda's influence had triggered Jason's latest downfall.

Maybe they were triggering each other. Between May 2000 and May 2001, police were called at least three times to intervene between Jason and Amanda. On May 21, Jason was arrested and charged with assault IV, menacing, and interfering with making a 911 call after Amanda told police he had "held her by the wrists to prevent her from leaving." On June 14, Jason claimed Amanda vandalized her own car by puncturing its right front tire. A police report further indicated Jason was seeking a restraining order against Amanda. On July 6, Jason again called police and said he was "having problems getting his ex-girlfriend to leave" his apartment. He told police that Amanda "had been violent" on several occasions and showed them a bite mark on his left torso and two large bruises on his upper arm. Amanda told police one of the reasons for the fight was that "in the past [Jason] had caused her emotional pain." Amanda was arrested that night and charged with domestic assault IV. Eighteen days later, she was arrested for shoplifting at a suburban mall.

A Department of Human Services report in August 2000 "indicated that J.S. strangled A.S. in front of the child. When A.S. was finally released, she attempted to call police from a pay phone, but J.S. hung up the phone and took her money. A.S. managed to get inside a store with her child where she called the police. When police arrived, they found the tires of her vehicle had been punctured, and J.S. had left the area on foot. . . . One of the witnesses who was interviewed reported seeing J.S. puncture the tires with a knife."

In January 2001, Amanda called police to say that Jason had thrown her car keys, pushed her to the ground, and then locked himself in his apartment. Police documented scrapes on Amanda's elbow, hands, and knees. They made "numerous attempts to contact Mr. Smith, but he refused to answer the door." Whether police had more than Amanda's word that Jason was inside the apartment was not specified.

In May 2001, DHS received a report that Jason had left Gavin, who had recently turned four, unattended in a vehicle. Paramedics responded. A report stated that "when the child was removed from the car he was reported to be in poor condition—sweating, lethargic, and confused" and at one point "collapsed to the ground." Jason was cited by police and allowed to leave with Gavin. Many of these incidents occurred while Jason and Amanda were spending $25,000 a month, before Jason's mother stepped in and tried to stop her son's latest slide, in which Amanda was seen as complicit.

Amanda might at the time have seemed an easy mark: two pregnancies out of wedlock; shoplifting; the willingness to be treated like a princess. I wondered whether Jason chose Amanda for these reasons and how cognizant each was of exploiting the other's needs and fantasies.

The conservatorship ended in December 2001. There was nothing left to conserve. Of the $167,597.15, nearly all had been used to pay debts and taxes (more than $60,000) and to subsidize Jason's living expenses. Of his personal property, only the Audi and $2,020.34 remained. By this time, Jason had a job in the mail room of a copier company, and Amanda was expecting their first child.

April dug out her wedding video. She had not seen it since shortly after the wedding in 2002. Christian music welcomed guests to the outdoor ceremony. There was April, swaddled in yards of bridal puff, and five-year-old Gavin, wearing a tiny tuxedo and holding the rings aloft on a satin pillow. Later, the camera moved among tables, asking guests to offer best wishes. Amanda and Jason were last to speak. She wore a clingy low-cut hostess gown in a tropical print. Her skin glowed, and her hair shone. She took the microphone and in her sing-song voice said, "Thank you so much. Happy wedding! Weddings are lovely. We're going to be a married couple hanging out so, yay! To the married couples hanging out."

Jason did not glow. His hair was thin on top, and he spoke without conviction as he offered congratulations. He came off as more uncomfortable than parsimonious. If you were to assess the couple from this tableau, you would say he was in thrall to Amanda, that she was the one with the power. Trinity had been born five months earlier. Jason was running mail rooms for the company that would become Ricoh; maybe he was tired, or maybe he didn't like April. He had told Amanda he did not want April and Tiffany coming over or hanging out with Amanda.

The married couples did not hang out, either. April quickly divorced. She started teaching high school and studying for the first of what would be two graduate degrees, in English and education, on her way to a PhD. She still saw Amanda, in one or another of the cheap apartments she, Jason, and the kids moved to. Amanda always seemed cheerful, never mentioned anything was wrong. She was still la-di-la, the kind of mother who nursed Eldon for fourteen months and slept nuzzled up with him, as she once had with Gavin.

Then the family moved to Hawaii for a couple of years, for Jason's job. April and Amanda barely stayed in touch, though April did tell a good friend of hers to look up Amanda when she went to Oahu. The friend had done so and found Amanda to be more than gracious. She insisted the friend stay with her, Jason, and the kids. The friend wound up leaving after a few days. She couldn't take the situation in the house, Jason berating Amanda, Amanda trying to keep a smile pasted on. The friend went on excursions with Amanda and the children to the International Market Place in Waikiki and to the beach; she took photos of the children, tanned and smiling. Eldon had just turned two; his baby hair was fine and blond and nearly to his shoulders.

The last time April visited Amanda was spring 2008. Ricoh had transferred Jason back to Portland, and the family was living in Tualatin. Besides Jason's pot, which he had lined up neatly in jars, the house was chaotic and really, really messy. Eldon was running around in his underpants. Trinity was yelling, there's no toilet paper! Jason shouted that she knew where it was. Gavin was in a corner reading; he no longer remembered April.

How's your walk with Jesus? Amanda asked.

April gave a noncommittal answer to the Jesus question. Amanda sounded like a robot or as though all the air had gone out of her. She did not look well; she was too thin, her lushness gone. April did not know what to say, especially with Jason one room away. The tension in the house was such that she was afraid anything she said might set off a confrontation. She bought some pot from Jason and left. Amanda called her not long after to ask whether April had any friends in Eugene she and the kids could stay with. It was an odd request, and it wasn't. April had always known Amanda to be spontaneous, to put her kids in the car and go. But that was ten years ago; there were three kids now, and April did not feel comfortable calling her friends and asking if this woman they didn't know and who was frankly acting a little strange could stay with them.

April stopped returning Amanda's calls, including the last call in early May 2009, when Amanda left a message saying, "I really wish I would hear from you. Things aren't going so well."

16

By November 2009, the flow of details from Hadley about Amanda's case had more or less stopped. Whether she would change her plea to guilty, if the case would go to trial, if the prosecutor would ask for the death penalty—everything was up in the air. But was I interested, Hadley asked, in meeting someone who had escaped execution? Greg Cook's case would not be going to trial; Hadley had convinced him to accept a plea bargain. His sentencing for the triple murder of three meth buddies in mid-July would take place this month.

I wasn't sure I wanted to meet Cook. There seemed to me no mystery in what he had done or the brutality with which he killed. Maybe it was that I wasn't willing to unpack that mystery. Hadley had told me several times how Cook was determined to turn his mistakes, if you could call murder and dismemberment mistakes, into a cautionary tale, to talk about his meth problem in hopes of helping people not do what he did. This sounded to me like Cook shoveling garbage in order to save his own ass, or as Hadley had once put it, "They call convicts 'cons' for a reason." Nevertheless, Cook's ass had been saved by Hadley, who was tasked with doing the same for Amanda.

"You have to get inside the heads of some very disturbed individuals; you have to find the humanity and bond with the humanity," Hadley's sometime cocounsel Steve Krasik had told me about the job of the capital defense attorney. "And you can never lose sight of the pain of the victims, 90 percent of whom think you're prolonging their agony and that the accused should be taken outside and shot with a dirty bullet."

There were ice crystals in the air when I pulled into the eastern Oregon town of La Grande, where Cook's sentencing would take place November 9. La Grande had a wide main street and not much going on. The Royal Motor Inn was central and looked less depressing than the Super 8. I pressed zero on the front-desk phone. A curtain behind the desk parted. The woman's nameplate said Rudy. She had an accent I could not place.

"Let me see if it's available," she said when I asked for a room. There was only one car in the lot besides mine. I would interview Greg Cook's mother later in the day. If Kathy Stott had not responded to the letters I sent asking to speak about Amanda's life, about her own life, Cook, Hadley told me, was enthusiastic about having his mother speak for him.

Edith Mitts had a white streak in her fluffy copper hair. She was seventy-one, but if she had told me sixty, I would not have questioned it. Her kitchen had a low ceiling and several cases of Campbell's soup stacked against one wall. A Jack Russell and a miniature schnauzer made a loop of sliding on the linoleum floor and into Mitts's ankle.

"You better get getting," she said, hitting at them with a flyswatter. When she wasn't swatting the dogs, Mitts kept her hands atop several hundred letters and handmade cards from her son, Greg Cook. She spent two hours reading aloud from the correspondence he had sent her since age thirteen, when she put him in a boys' home near Baker City. She did not want many details of those early days on record, not more than that she'd been twenty-seven with five kids when she met Cook's dad, who was seventeen at the time. The family had been poor, moving "sometimes two, three times during the school year," living in the woods in winter, living in tents. Cook had no friends other than his dogs. He did not do well in school. At times, his dad had been violent with him. On top of this was her drinking.

Mitts turned over and over the cards, with colored drawings of bears and birds, but mostly of roses, dozens of roses. She kept reading words of love from Cook: he could have no finer mother, and he was so proud of her. She was proud of him, too—proud that he'd told police where he hid the bodies, proud that he'd told her in detail what he'd done. He'd walked Shannon McKillop into the woods and made her take off her shoes so she could not run. When she said her feet hurt, he squatted down and had her get on his shoulders because he did not, he told his mother, "want her to have to walk with her feet sore." This, before he cut off her feet, head, and hands. He also told his mother how he'd had the two other victims dig their own grave and said a prayer with them before he shot them.

"I'm not angry at all," Mitts said when I asked whether she was angry with her son. "He's sorry that he did what he done, that he can't undo it."

It was past 9:00 p.m. when we finished talking. I encouraged Mitts to eat a can of soup—she had nearly fainted when she stood up from the table. She went through the motions of heating it but did not eat; she wanted to show me family photos in the entryway. She explained how she had once gotten drunk on beer and "shot the head off a rooster because it crowed too much." She told me to be careful on the drive back to La Grande; it was elk season, and sometimes they wandered onto the road, out of the forest. That's where Cook's dad was now, in the woods, hunting.

The temperature outside was in the thirties, and the two-lane road to La Grande was unlit. I worried that a drunk driver, or a driver high on meth, would cross the yellow line. I thought about the advice that if a car (or an elk) is heading toward you, you do not look at it; you look where you want to go, and that is where you will go. Mitts saw her son as semiheroic for telling the police what he had done; his telling her he was sorry served as proof that he was. She wasn't going to change lanes now.

Back at the motel, I ate takeout and watched the last minutes of a movie called *The Green Mile*, where a good man is sent to the electric chair. There were a lot of tears and violins. I slept badly, dreaming all night of spinal columns, freshly removed, small ones and long ones, one of them framed.

Men's voices woke me at dawn. Three feet from my window, two men in camouflage loaded rifles into a pickup. Every parking spot in the lot was filled this morning, nearly all with trucks being readied for the hunt.

By 8:40 a.m., at least forty people were waiting on the steps of the Union County Courthouse. Men were dressed mostly in dun-colored clothing. Some mentioned they had taken the morning off from work. We were let into the courthouse just before nine. We moved in a mass down the narrow hall and were let into the courtroom one by one. The room was overly warm. People shed their coats and looked like hell, trembling or blotched from crying. A broad-shouldered man on the bench next to me sat as rigid as if his spine had been made of rebar.

Hadley spoke to a bailiff near the front of the courtroom. He looked relaxed. In the months leading to today's sentencing, he had convinced Cook to change his plea to guilty and accept a sentence set by the judge rather than face a trial for triple murder. It was a smart move. While it was unlikely Amanda would be sentenced to death should her case go to trial, given the state's history of being loath to impose the death penalty on female killers, juries had no such qualms about men: nearly three dozen awaited execution in Oregon in November 2009. Next to Hadley, on the DA's table, was a binder thick with papers. On its cover were four mug shots, one of Cook and one each of those he had murdered. Many of the people in the courtroom today were related to one of the victims.

At nine thirty, word came that Hadley's cocounsel had suffered an attack of vertigo on the drive in. A ten-minute recess was called. Most people headed outside to smoke. A few went to the ladies' room. A heavyset woman with curly hair leaned against the wall by the hand dryer. She was panting. I asked if she was going to be sick.

"No. I don't know," she said. "Maybe sick on the other end."

Cook was led into court at 9:40. His feet were manacled, his hands chained to his waist. Edith had told me three stories of different women finding her son attractive. I did not see it. He had sunken cheeks, prominent front teeth, a long forehead, and forearms corded with muscle. The charges against Cook were read, including three counts of aggravated murder, one count of abuse of a corpse, and one count of felony possession of a firearm. The district attorney acknowledged that Cook had supplied them with information "several times," including where to find the backpack containing Shannon McKillop's head. The woman from the bathroom made a heaving sound. The DA elaborated on the other two victims' deaths, how Cook had convinced the men to dig a grave and lie in it "like Siamese twins."

The judge announced it was time for families of the victims to speak. McKillop's oldest daughter said that despite her mother's "illness and addiction," she was a good person. She kept her house spotless and taught her children to grow things "just from a bean or a piece of popcorn." Cook nodded thoughtfully as she spoke. He let us see his tears as she said she could not rid herself of the image of her mother gasping for air and Cook "hacking into her flesh."

McKillop's younger daughter needed help to get to the microphone. She told the court she'd had a baby girl two weeks before her mother was murdered. Her mom had been her "biggest support," and she still wanted to call her.

"She was beautiful, and you brutalized her and threw her away like a piece of trash," she told Cook. "And she wasn't trash. She was my mom."

The moans and sniffling were loud enough that the girl needed to speak up. "I have just one more thing to say. Our Father, who art in heaven . . ."

The room recited the prayer with her.

Four hours had been allocated, but few others chose to speak. At ten fifteen, it was Hadley's turn. He spoke of Cook's willingness to confess, perhaps more than any client Hadley had seen in his many years of practice. If Hadley's heart was in what he was saying, I did not hear it, or maybe I did not want to hear it. Amanda's case, how she got to the bridge and what would befall her for doing so, was on my mind nearly all of the time. I did not think of her as something to be dispatched, and I did not think Hadley did, either. I thought about what Steve Krasik said, how the capital defense attorney needs to get inside the heads of deeply disturbed individuals. I did not see Hadley getting inside Cook's head. I saw him doing his job under rough conditions, working to cast butchery and showboating in a sympathetic light. It was ugly to watch. Not that it mattered—Hadley had already saved his client's life. But I expected him to do more for Amanda, and I expected him to as much out of concern for her as for the rest of us. I thought we deserved answers and not just results.

"At least we got a new police boat out of it," District Attorney Josh Marquis had mentioned to me the month before with regard to Amanda's case. One of Oregon's more vocal proponents of capital punishment, Marquis had been referring to a plan recently approved by the Portland City Council. It was a hopeful idea: that a high-speed fire-rescue boat might have saved Eldon's life. Who could be against it? Council member Dan Saltzman for one. Though he had told the press conference I attended on June 3, "the city council feel[s], and I think every citizen in Portland feels, the profound sense of grief over the tragic drowning of Eldon Smith," he had nevertheless voted against the rescue boat, claiming the city did not have the funds and should not dip into reserves "based on an emotional reaction to one incident." But what else but emotion attended every aspect of a child's murder? Was there anything with as much fuel? We hitched ourselves to it, and we made policy; we debated laws that said we value *this* life but this other one not so much. But even the meth addict who kills is someone's child. Edith Mitts would not attend her son's sentencing, she told me, because she did not think she could physically take it.

The judge today asked if Cook had anything to say. Cook nodded. He was asked to stand and did. He did not speak for a good twenty seconds. The judge asked Cook if he wanted Hadley to read his statement. Again, Cook said nothing. Then, "No, I have to be able to do this."

He turned to the room. "I don't blame you guys at all for how you feel about it," he said, his eyes lingering on one face, then another. He had been "so ashamed" after the killings that he drove to Seattle and bought "really strong heroin" and shot a lot of it "in order to die," but he didn't die. "It was not," he said, "God's desire."

"I'd give my life right now to bring your family back," he continued. But it wasn't him that killed, he said. "It was me under the influence of meth."

Cook rambled on in this vein, enjoying the sound of his own voice, an actor unaware he has lost the audience. "I will cry every day until I die an old man in prison," he concluded, and sat down. The judge sentenced Cook to three life sentences without the possibility of parole, plus fifteen years. The room broke into applause. As Cook was led away, the broad-shouldered man beside me, who had not altered his posture during the proceedings, got to his feet and shouted, "Rot in hell!"

I stood at the counselor's table with Hadley and the DA after the courtroom emptied. What no one could figure out, the DA said, was how Cook had the power to make two grown men dig their own graves. Cook's version painted them as docile, with Cook saying a prayer for men who must have been begging for their lives. The DA thought the whole prayer thing sounded dubious. Who would believe it?

I mentioned I had met the night before with Mitts.

"She was a terrible alcoholic who didn't stop drinking until last year," Hadley said. Did I know her other kids testified she had had a sexual relationship with Cook, starting when he was a teenager? The DA nodded and pointed to his binder; he had their transcripts in there.

A mother and her child live on the border of protection and destruction. This border, theirs alone, is not axiomatically fraught. Mothering came easily to me, and I had an easy daughter. But I had seen the conjuring a child can do: the child who does not feel she gets attention for being good and so is very bad; the child who feeds the mother lies until the mother determines any fault is the fault of others. This was what I sensed Mitts was doing, what Christine Duncan had historically done, what Kathy Stott by her silence about Amanda was doing now.

I had just driven into Portland when my phone rang. Mitts was calling, wanting me to tell her what happened in court. She was "just feeling sick about it."

I pulled to the curb. What could I say to her? That from what I saw, everyone hated her son? That he seemed wholly untrustworthy? In the months to come, Mitts would encourage me several times to visit Cook, including a short plea made from stuck-together Post-it notes, again giving me his address, his inmate number. The envelope the note arrived in was decorated with stickers of roses.

17

July 4, 2007, Portland, Oregon

Sara had heard about Jason ever since she and Ryan got together earlier in the year. His best friend, he said, had been living in Oahu, running mail rooms for Ricoh over there. But Jason was coming back; the company had arranged to put him and his family up in a swank high-rise in Portland's West Hills, near downtown.

Sara was excited to meet Jason and his wife, Amanda, whom Ryan had not said very nice things about; he mentioned something about her drinking. Sara worked as an early-childhood development specialist, mostly with young children with special needs. She did family and parent training and had many times seen parents not at their best. If Ryan was concerned Sara might be critical of Amanda's parenting style, Sara was fairly sure that she could handle what problems there might be.

Jason invited Ryan and Sara over for the Fourth of July. The condo had an enormous patio with a bang-on view of the river; they could watch the fireworks from there. Sara brought a salad, a pie, and, as a hostess gift, a plant. She knew how important Jason was to Ryan and wanted to make a good impression.

The apartment was open and modern. The family had just moved in. Things were a bit of a jumble, and there was a big, big turtle Jason had brought back from Hawaii. Jason was very nice and welcoming to Sara. He'd laid out some expensive cheeses and was playing host on the patio. Still, the turtle was a little weird, and the two younger kids were running around unsupervised.

Amanda floated between the living room and the kitchen. Her "hello" had a slow quality that made Sara think Amanda might already be tipsy. Sara saw a big piece of raw meat on the counter. Amanda did not seem to be making moves to do anything with it. Sara brought the salad fixings and pie into the kitchen.

I want salad! I want salad!

This was Eldon, at Sara's hip. What two-year-old, she wondered, clamored for salad? But she also noticed his language skills were advanced; he was a well-spoken child. Sara fed him crackers as she mixed the salad. She asked Amanda if it was okay to give Eldon some before the rest of the meal was ready. Amanda said to give him whatever he wanted and refilled her glass from a plastic half gallon of vodka.

Sara gave Eldon a big bowl of salad. He mowed through it and wanted more. It was odd to see a little kid scarfing down salad, and the educator in Sara knew something was off here, that little kids are not usually this hungry for vegetables.

Amanda announced she was going to the store because she needed some ingredient. She had her car keys in her hand, and Sara thought there is no way she should be driving.

"I'll drive," Sara said.

No, no, I'm driving, said Amanda, and she told Eldon and Trinity they were coming with her. Sara was dumbfounded. She went to the patio and told Jason that Amanda was leaving and that it might really be a better idea if she, Sara, drove them all to the store.

Good luck with that, he told her; Amanda did this all the time.

Sara caught up with Amanda and repeated her offer to drive. Amanda kept saying no. Sara was just over five feet tall, a head smaller than Amanda. She did not think she could get the keys from Amanda's hand, and how insane was it to be contemplating this at all? Not knowing what else to do, she got in the passenger seat, telling herself she could grab the steering wheel and have some control over this car if she needed to.

Sara kept her eyes on Amanda as she drove through downtown. The *pi-pi-pop!* of firecrackers and the whistle of bottle rockets did not make Sara any calmer. She had met the kids less than an hour before and somehow felt charged with keeping them alive.

Amanda pulled up to the Safeway supermarket near the Portland State campus, a store that attracted the homeless and crazies in the area and was nicknamed Psycho Safeway. Amanda did not help the kids out of the car. Sara would have helped Eldon, but he seemed to have no trouble getting out himself.

The supermarket was huge and bright inside, and for some reason almost empty. Maybe everybody had already bought what beer and hot dog buns they needed. Sara had no idea what Amanda needed. The kids followed their mother as she brushed around the aisles. They seemed content, stopping to touch eye-level items, Eldon especially, who struck Sara as a very bright boy.

Eldon, get over here! Amanda yelled. Her voice was sharp in the empty store, and Sara thought, I just want to give her a little advice. Was that inappropriate? What could she do, standing in the middle of Psycho Safeway with a woman who seemed half-unhinged?

"You seem like you're having a hard time with Eldon," Sara said to Amanda. "I'd be happy to offer some advice, if that's something you'd be interested in."

Amanda stopped near the end of the aisle. Her demeanor changed instantly. Her face softened and bloomed, and she said to Sara, that's so nice of you.

It seemed to Sara that Amanda had become fascinated with her, had gone from screaming to Zen and mellow, super-tuned-in.

Sara said she had a book called *Positive Discipline*. She would bring it to Amanda, and the next time they met after that, they could talk about it.

I would love that, Amanda said. Eldon could be a really hard kid sometimes, she said; she tried so hard, and she knew she was a good mom; all Sara had to do was look at how great Trinity was.

When they got back to the apartment, Sara saw Ryan and Jason were on the patio with Gavin. Gavin seemed like a quiet boy, polite, and devoted to his brother and sister. Trinity, especially, stayed close to him. If anyone aside from Sara noticed Amanda was now drinking directly from the bottle, no one brought it up. Sara looked to Jason to gauge his concern. He rolled his eyes and said this is what she does every once in a while.

The fireworks started at dusk. They all went up to the rooftop deck. The kids gathered at the edge of the deck as the cityscape lit up. Barges on the Willamette River pumped the sky full of reds, whites, and blues. Embers rained down and were extinguished by the river. Sara saw little of it. She was watching the children; they were so close to the railing. She saw Ryan watching the children, too. He would later tell her he'd been doing this for years, and tonight they gave each other secret looks that said, *You on this? Yes, I'm on it.* Sara was reassured by how close Trinity stuck to Gavin; it meant Sara could keep an eye on Eldon. He would turn three in a month. As the night became darker and the hour a child his age might be getting ready for bed approached, Sara took Eldon downstairs and read to him in his room.

Amanda appeared in the doorway. Despite consuming what seemed like a god-awful amount of vodka, she did not look a mess. She was stunning, really beautiful, if made up sort of crazily, with bright blue, green, and lavender eye shadows.

Come with me, Amanda said, and had Sara follow her into the bathroom. Amanda showed Sara her very fancy makeup, tiny shiny bottles of lotions and potions and powders, none of which Sara had much interest in, despite Amanda urging her to try some, to fancy herself up, too. Sara told Amanda she was not really into all that stuff, and she and Ryan left soon after, Sara with the feeling of being scared to death for the children.

Sara saw the Smith family many times over the summer. The scene was sometimes the same, with Sara keeping one eye on Amanda, one eye on the kids. It was like double babysitting. Amanda accepted the parenting book, which included lesson plans. Sara could not be sure whether Amanda followed the plans, but they did talk about them and she seemed genuinely grateful, at one point telling Sara, God, I just love you, and it's so nice that you care so much.

Sara felt as though she was exerting some good influence, and also, maybe, that she was developing a positive relationship with Amanda herself. Sara wanted this to be the case. Jason was Ryan's best friend, and the kids were essentially Ryan's godchildren. It wasn't as though Amanda was always terrible. She could be affectionate with the children and they with her, Trinity especially. She was a buoyant little girl, demonstrative, goofy. Eldon was more sensitive, fragile even; he followed Jason around like a puppy, waiting for his father to pay attention to him. So, yes, there was love in the family, between Amanda and the kids, but there was also dangerous neglect.

Sara saw less and less of the attentive mom as the summer wore on. She tried to court that part of Amanda. She invited her and the kids over to Ryan's apartment one day. There was a pool, and they could all keep cool. Amanda arrived wearing a bikini that revealed everything. The kids swam as Amanda sunned herself on a chaise. She chattered away to Sara, sipping from a bottle of water, which, as the afternoon wore on, Sara became convinced was not water. Amanda became increasingly hard to understand and not once, so far as Sara could see, did she look the kids' way. Eldon was not yet three years old, and as Sara stayed near him in the pool, she thought, regarding Amanda, I basically just met you, and I am solely responsible for your child?

Sara called social services. She called more than once that summer. There never seemed to be enough tangible evidence for them to move forward. One time, she called after she and Ryan had found Amanda passed out in the hall. The kids had been taking care of themselves and told Sara they had not eaten that day. She and Ryan began to bring prepared food each time they went to the condo. Jason did not seem to grasp the situation. It would be six o'clock with no dinner in sight, and Sara would ask, "Have these kids eaten?" And he'd say, well, Amanda was home with them all day, so I assume so.

Sara was at a loss over what to make of Jason. He and Ryan worked together, went camping together, and except for the pot smoking—Sara had never seen Jason or Ryan with any drugs other than pot—Jason seemed stable. He had a good job and was supporting his family. But the relationship with Amanda was not good, not at all. The couples sometimes dined at Lemongrass, a Thai restaurant they all liked. Jason always insisted on ordering everything on the menu there. Ryan would say, "We don't need leftovers for three weeks. There's no reason to spend hundreds of dollars." Amanda would be telling Jason she wanted everything with hot chiles, the kind where if you eat half of one, you're choking and sweating. Amanda would eat them by the dozen because she thought they burned calories. As soon as they ordered, Jason would start to put down Amanda. The restaurant was tiny, on the parlor floor of an old house; everyone could hear him say, Wife, do this! Wife, do that! Wife, shut your mouth! He seemed incapable of addressing Amanda any other way in public, and any affection Sara saw pass between them seemed faked, as though someone had given them a script. It was like a teenage relationship where they broke up every ten minutes and got back together.

If the food at Lemongrass was outstanding, the dinners usually ended on a gross note, with Amanda in the bathroom barfing up what she'd just eaten. Sara did not think it possible that Jason did not realize his wife was bulimic, or if he did know, he did not seem to care.

Sara found it hard to tell what Jason cared about. He would insist one thing was true while his actions spoke the opposite, like the time he explained to Sara that when he met Amanda, she was pregnant by a man who had just killed himself. This man, Jason said, had been very bad to Amanda; he had torn her down until her self-esteem was horrible and she didn't believe in herself. Jason told Sara that Amanda was the most beautiful thing he had ever seen. He just fell so in love with her so hard. Right away she was his queen, and he set about building her up, building her up.

And Sara thought, yes, so you can tear her back down.

18

"Why are you always writing about dead children?" my mother asked. I told her it seemed important.

In truth, it was not Eldon's murder, nor Trinity's survival, that preoccupied me at the time. In January 2010, the work, as yet, was about keeping an eye on their mother. The idea that I was looking out for Amanda might have been seen as private delusion, perhaps despicable. Nothing I did would affect her fate, not that I wanted to. I felt more like a sentry, as though I had to stay at my post or else.

Or else what? What was it that I was trying to understand? What could I pass on to others about something so painful? I had almost been flip with my mother, had almost said, "Well, Mom, there are enough people writing about Paris Hilton's panties." Later on, I thought that staying on the story was about sitting with a certain despair. We have all seen the interviews about the loss that cannot be gotten over: the mother explaining how her daughter had been right there in the street, riding her bike, the mother had looked away for a terrible moment, and that was twelve years ago.

To not know where your child is, to lose her, did not seem to me survivable. I once lost track of my eight-year-old for less than ten minutes at an outdoor flea market. As I ran through the kiosks, screaming her name, the floor of my world dropped out; the free fall did not stop until I found her. I might have told my mother that I thought we needed to bear witness to the loss when it happened, to recognize it, whether it was one murder or a thousand murders, the child ripped from her mother's arms at the death camp, the child thrown from the bridge.

Early 2010 and still no word from Amanda, to whom I wrote letters I hoped were not heavy. I told her that if she agreed to place me on her visitors list, we could talk about anything she wanted; we could talk about cooking or clothes, or we could sit in silence. I sent her subscriptions—the *Oprah Magazine*, *Vanity Fair*, periodicals that the penal system mandated come directly from the subscription service. She would not know whom they were from, but I did not care. Amanda did not write back. Her parents, to whom I wrote an extremely careful letter, had not written back. I did receive one letter, sent to my home with no return address. It was respectful but clear: the rest of the media had gone away but I had stayed and continued "to pour salt into a wound that so very badly needs to be healed." The sender did not think anything I wrote about Amanda could have value, only its opposite, and that it would "continue to hurt many people but will hurt Gavin and Trinity throughout their long lives." It was signed "Mandy's aunt."

In March, I was one of two people in a room at the Multnomah County Courthouse for Amanda's third or fourth settlement hearing. It was 8:20 in the morning, still dark out, a cold rain ticking the windows. The other person and I sat on opposite ends of the front bench. She was tall and very fair, with pale-red hair. She wore glasses. She did not look my way. We sat in silence for maybe fifteen minutes, the room so quiet I could hear the gears of a truck shifting five stories below.

John Casalino, the prosecutor in Amanda's case, came from judge's chambers. I knew Casalino specialized in prosecuting those who harm and kill children. He shook my hand and asked whether I had spoken with Amanda. I told him not yet. He said it would not happen today, either, not until the case was settled. The defense and prosecution had not been able to reach a plea agreement. Anything that happened today would happen in judge's chambers, and no, Casalino said, I would not be allowed inside.

The woman stood. She was nearly Casalino's height. She introduced herself as Amanda's Aunt Hildy.

"I wish you could have known her before," she said.

Casalino nodded. "I don't know if the judge will want to speak with you today, but she appreciates you're here," he told her, and went again into chambers.

"I have nothing to say to you," Hildy said when I asked if we might speak in the hall. We went back to our spots on the bench, back to waiting. And then two sheriff's deputies walked Amanda into court. She wore blue pants and top, like doctor's scrubs. A bit of coral shirt peeped at her collar. Her hair lay in a thick braid down her back. She was perhaps thirty pounds heavier than she had been in June and chained, wrists to waist, ankle to ankle. The deputies seated her at the defense table and left the room. Amanda looked at her aunt and began to cry; she cried with her mouth open as Hildy strained without speaking to tell her that it was going to be okay. Amanda calmed. She slumped. After a few minutes she cut her eyes at me, sharp enough that she might have been asking, *Who are you, and are you here to further destroy me?*

Hadley came from judge's chambers to collect Amanda. Hildy followed them inside. Twenty minutes later, Hadley came back alone. Amanda, he said, had left by a back way. I would not see her again today.

In *The Suspicions of Mr. Whicher*, Kate Summerscale wrote of the murder of a boy Eldon's age, "Perhaps this is the purpose of detective investigations, real and fictional—to transform sensation, horror and grief into a puzzle, and then to solve the puzzle, to make it go away."

This seemed exactly right. The murder of Eldon Smith and the attempted murder of his sister by their mother were puzzles. Lawyers, detectives, and the medical personnel who cared for Trinity when she was rushed to the hospital with hypothermia and a broken sternum were all charged with putting the pieces together. Hildy, who was retired from the sheriff's department, believed what peace could be found would come from these sectors, whereas my writing could "only cause more pain." I questioned how I could make things worse than what was before us: a murdered child, two more children traumatized, a mother in prison, and families blown apart. Was tragedy compounded or relieved by not speaking of it? Was it possible to hold open the wound with one hand and stitch with the other? I thought it was more than possible. I thought it was necessary.

"I guess you heard Amanda has decided to change her plea."

This was Hadley the morning of April 13. I told him I had not heard. There had been nothing in the newspaper, and my Google Alert had not surfaced anything.

"It's going to be a tough day in court," he said. "It's going to be a media zoo."

Amanda had agreed to plead guilty and thus avoid a jury trial, which might have sentenced her to death. What her punishment would be, per protocol, had been determined in judge's chambers; the defense and the district attorney bargained over a period of months until they reached an agreement. There had been input, as required by victim's rights laws, from Jason and his family, who I expected would be in court today.

I arrived to find reporters, still photographers, and TV crews set up to the right of the courtroom doors, lawyers and investigators to the left.

Amanda's family floated in the center. Kathy Stott wore a gray A-line skirt, and her long hair was loose. She looked like a schoolgirl. Hildy was with her, as was Amanda's sister, Chantel, who had darting dark eyes, a petite, hyperalert version of her sister. Chantel's husband, Daryl Gardner, looked as though he had not thought much of the occasion when getting dressed, or maybe a grubby shirt and trousers were his comment on the occasion. He saw me watching him and started pacing in a semicircle so close to me I could hear him breathing.

There was movement behind the legal teams: Amanda was being walked down the hall. Today she was dressed as if for a party, in a black velvet top and pants, her hair cascading down her back, a small smile turning up the corners of her mouth and eyes. These were striking differences from the hunched, bloated woman of two weeks earlier. The larger difference was the serene, even stoned look on her face. Maybe she was stoned; Hadley had told me she had been taking "a raft of pills" prescribed by doctors when she committed the crime and was now on antidepressants. Whether it was medication or the decision to change her plea, whether the suppleness of her features was for protection or for show, Amanda looked remarkably at peace.

The bailiff told us in what order we would enter the courtroom: cameras first, then family, then press. The legal teams took their respective tables. Reporters had settled on a bench behind the defense table when four late arrivals took seats immediately behind us.

Jason Smith was wearing the same cantaloupe-colored tie he had worn the last time I had seen him in court. His divorce attorney, Laura Schantz, was with him, as were two women with highlighted blond hair, one around thirty years old, the other maybe twice that. Jason had not seen Amanda since he left their children with her for the weekend visitation in 2009. Now he was sitting three strides from her, leaning forward with his elbows on his knees. The muscles along his jaw did not relax.

When he leaned back, I heard him mention to the two women some plans he had for the weekend, and that he had washed his hair that morning. The casualness with which he said these things felt like a slap, considering the reason we were here. How could he be concerned with how clean his hair was? I looked at the reporter on my left, to see whether she was startled by the comment. She was texting with her newsroom and had not become distracted by what might have been deemed an offhand comment, an attempt to impose some equilibrium on an otherwise horrible day. It did not register to me this way; it said that despite the grave reasons for being here, Jason was bored.

Circuit Judge Julie E. Frantz took her seat. District Attorney John Casalino explained that Amanda was changing her plea to guilty on count one, aggravated murder, and on count six, attempted aggravated murder. There would be a judgment of dismissal on counts two through five, seven, and eight. The sentence would be life with the possibility of parole in thirty-five years. Casalino said that he, Jason, and two detectives in attendance supported this sentence.

Judge Frantz spoke directly to Amanda: Had she read the petition against her?

"Yes," said Amanda.

Was that her signature on it?

"Yes."

Had her attorneys explained the implications?

"Yes."

Did her taking the prescription medication Abilify in any way hamper her ability to proceed?

"No," she said.

Judge Frantz determined that Amanda was making a "clear-headed, reasoned decision." She asked Amanda to rise. How did she plead to count one?

"I am guilty," Amanda said.

How did she plead to count six?

"I am guilty."

Her voice did not crack, she remained composed, and because she was facing away from the room, I did not until the next day see, on video, that she kept her eyes closed as the judge recounted the date of the incident, the children's names, their ages. It was only when the judge asked, in conclusion, whether Amanda had done these things that she opened her eyes and said, "Yeah."

In the run-up to Amanda's settlement hearing, Hadley had drawn a gruesome case. Angela McAnulty was accused of systematically torturing, beating, and starving to death her fifteen-year-old daughter, Jeanette Maples.

"That case," Hadley told me, "is not going well."

No matter how much his team looked into the mother's background—and he knew her upbringing was "hellish, something out of *Deliverance*"—they could find nothing that might mitigate what she had done.

"I saw photos of Jeanette," he said. "They are about the worst I've ever seen."

They had taken a toll. Hadley had recently gone to the emergency room with chest pains. And Amanda—whom he felt, without elaborating why, was "a very good person"; whose family members he respected and thought were kind—would be going away essentially for life. Her final sentencing would be next week.

As it would turn out, Angela McAnulty would be sentenced to death in 2011. This was highly unusual. No other woman was on death row in the state of Oregon. Only sixty-one women faced execution in the United States at the time, fifteen for killing their children. The reasons why McAnulty might have received the sentence undoubtedly included the duration and severity with which she tortured and murdered Jeanette, but there might also have been something else at work. At forty-three, McAnulty was more than a decade older than the average mother who kills her child, two decades older than the average perpetrator of neonaticide. She did not fit in the narrow window of conventional beauty and was not seen smiling in any photo taken after her arrest.

Contrast this with Diane Downs, Oregon's most infamous filicidal mother, who shot her three children in 1983. During trial, Downs swanned and made doe eyes for the cameras, and her attractiveness was often cited when discussing her crimes against her children. A jury did not sentence Downs to death but to life in prison plus fifty years. Farrah Fawcett played her in a TV movie about the case.

Further, contrast McAnulty with Casey Anthony. During her 2011 trial for the murder of her two-year-old daughter, Caylee, Anthony often came to court in makeup, her long hair nicely styled. Despite overwhelming evidence of her guilt, Anthony was cleared of all murder charges. She was twenty-two and, during and just after her trial, appeared on the cover of *People* magazine five times.

While we assume it is the primacy of the mother-child bond that makes us go easier on mothers who kill their children, McAnulty's sentence made me consider how looks might come into play, as they do in nearly every other aspect of American life in the twenty-first century, perhaps in any country during any century. While we might believe that pretty is as pretty does, on some level we want to see youth and beauty as signs of goodness, of innocence. The attractive woman is given a pass. The ugly one gets the chair.

Court was not a zoo on April 22, 2010. One still photographer, one TV camera, the gallery half-filled. Amanda's family took seats in rows closest to the door; reporters sat where we had last time. Space was made in the front row for Jason's family, who arrived carrying poster-board photos of Eldon. Deputies set the posters on easels at the front of the courtroom: Eldon close-up and smiling; Eldon pouring water into a tub of rubber ducks.

We heard Amanda approach, the chains around her ankles making a *shee-shee* sound, like a ghost dragging down a hall in an old movie. She shuffled through the door. She wore the same velvet outfit as the week before, but today it sagged. There was nothing festive about her appearance except, maybe, her handcuffs, which were red and taken off once the guards seated her beside Hadley.

The courtroom was silent but for people crying. One of those crying was Jason. He was curled in on himself. His mother, Christine Duncan, rubbed the back of his neck. His grandmother leaned from one row behind and said in Jason's ear, "Be strong; be strong." The Smiths did not turn to look at the Stotts. The families had not seen each other except in court since before the crime.

Judge Frantz entered. The crying quieted. Casalino announced that several people wanted to speak about how Amanda's crime had undone their lives. Jason went first. He wore a button of Eldon pinned to his T-shirt. He looked at Amanda before he started speaking.

"I wanted to start by bringing in pictures of Eldon, recent pictures taken before he was murdered," he said. He voice was deep and resonant. "I wanted to bring them to show the magnitude and gravity of the situation at hand. Eldon was a human being; he lived a life of pure love. He was a bright, wonderful, happy boy. . . . I would whisper in his ear, he was my favorite person in the world. I would whisper in my daughter's ear, she was my favorite person in the world."

Amanda was crying without sound. Hadley placed his hand on her wrist. She did not respond to his quietly asking, "Are you still on your medication?"

"The nature of this crime will never be known to me, and no thoughts of the murder will ever make sense to anyone," Jason continued. "Trinity and I talk about her brother every day. She is doing better than anyone would ever have dreamed. She is a beautiful, sweet, gentle girl."

Jason looked again at Amanda. She would not meet his eyes.

"[Trinity] will be free of the bondage of having to think of the person who murdered my son," he said. "And she has a new mother she can love and put behind her the horror."

Several days earlier, Jason had married Keli Townsend, the younger of the blond women who accompanied him to court the week before. I wondered at the timing of the marriage, if telling Amanda in open court that she was disposable had been a pain Jason wanted to inflict, and if anyone would have blamed him.

Jason continued. "As the years go by and Amanda sits in prison, watching her life day by day pass on, I hope she realizes that her suffering pales in comparison to the suffering that my daughter and my son went through the night she threw them from a bridge in Portland into an icy-cold river in the middle of the night." He sat down.

Christine Duncan spoke. She remained composed. She thanked those who had come to her grandchildren's rescue, and she thanked her son "for taking the high road," which we took to mean for not pushing for a jury trial, for sparing Amanda a possible death sentence. She turned to Amanda.

"Amanda, Eldon is in a better place now," Duncan said. "It's unfortunate those of us on this earth don't have more time with him."

Chelsea Beck cried as she explained that Gavin was supposed to go with his mother that night but decided not to. He was now haunted by the idea that he could have stopped his mother from throwing his brother and sister in the river.

"Our family has been forever changed. We worry in a different way," Chelsea said. "Gavin faces a life of knowing he didn't go. If he had been there, could he have stopped her? Amanda did throw Gavin away that night, too."

I waited for other people to speak. Now was their chance. There would be no trial, no other opportunity to be part of the official record, to speak of condemnation or forgiveness. Only one person seized the moment.

Amanda stood. She looked at the posters of Eldon. She looked, and her features softened. She did not cry as she spoke.

"I just want to say to all those I've hurt, especially my children, I am deeply sorry," she said. The words had an odd, loose quality, as though the hinge of her jaw had broken. "And I'm thankful for everyone that came today, and I'm thankful for the words expressed, and I hope that someday you can all forgive me."

She sat down.

Judge Frantz called Amanda's actions "truly incomprehensible." She said Amanda's decision to plead guilty spared the ordeal of a trial and the risk of a more severe sentence. Under Oregon Revised Statutes 163.105, Amanda Jo Stott-Smith was sentenced to thirty-five years in prison before the possibility of parole, with lifetime monitoring afterward should she be paroled in 2045. Amanda would then be sixty-seven years old. I wondered who in the courtroom would be alive when she got out. There was a good chance her parents would be dead. Would her sister meet her as she walked out of prison? Unlikely as it seemed, would it be Trinity or Gavin, or both? Would the media remember her? Amanda's case had moved slowly, and now it was over. As her mother's and sister's cries reached a crescendo, as her ex-husband slipped the posters of Eldon into plastic, Amanda was handcuffed and led out the back way.

I joined Hadley in the hall.

"How did you like that?" he asked. I said it was brutal. He nodded.

"Not a good outcome," he said. "For anyone."

Hadley found Amanda's sentencing troubling for reasons that had to do with her, and those that had nothing to do with her. He believed she had been over-medicated in the months leading up to the crime.

He believed, perhaps because she told him she did, that Amanda loved her children. He thought there was something to the revenge theory, but there were mitigating circumstances, circumstances that the courts would never consider, because Amanda's family had feared she would receive death. Her parents and her aunt had been influential in convincing Amanda to change her plea. As Hadley well knew, it was never a bad idea to get death off the table.

What had replaced it is what troubled him. When Hadley started practicing law, all aggravated murders in the state of Oregon carried a life sentence, but there was no minimum sentence. Parole boards, in his experience, usually paroled murderers—if they stayed out of trouble in prison—after seven to ten years. Hadley believed in giving people a second chance. The public evidently disagreed. People thought judges and sentences were too liberal, and when given an opportunity to get tougher on crime, they took it. Measure 11 passed in 1994 and required a minimum twenty-five-year sentence for murder, with no possibility of parole prior to the full sentence being served. Hadley hated this law and knew the liberal line to be fantasy. He'd spent more than forty years looking for these liberal judges and said he had found "darn few." He believed murderers could change for the better, could become good citizens. The belief was not academic. Hadley told me several times about a client whom he'd helped to have acquitted. The man went on to get a college degree, to have a family; he and Hadley went fishing together. There would be no fishing for Amanda, or at least not until she was a senior citizen. So, yes, he had saved her life. She would not spend the next decade or two shunted through the death row legal maze, but a thirty-five-year sentence also obviated hope and canceled the future. When Hadley said Amanda's sentence was not a good outcome for anyone, he was likely including himself.

Jen Johnson was in the middle of a craft project with her young daughters, not paying attention to the TV in the background, when she heard the newscaster say, "Amanda Jo Stott-Smith." Then he said it again. The name sounded familiar. Johnson looked up and saw the mug shot.

"That's Mandy Stott!" she said.

Johnson knew Amanda in college. They'd been part of the same casual group of friends and had occasionally stayed in touch over the years. The last time Johnson saw Amanda, she had been pregnant with Eldon.

The day after Amanda was sentenced, Johnson found some old photos from George Fox University. She, Amanda, and some other friends were standing on a wide green lawn. There wasn't a murderer in any of those pictures, she thought. She disagreed with what the judge had said, that what Amanda had done was truly incomprehensible. A former social worker, Johnson stayed up late at her computer reading the DHS reports. The Smith family's troubles were like dozens of cases she had worked on, call after call logged about Jason and Amanda, and likely more instances where calls were not made. Very little had been done. Indeed, Johnson knew, there was very little the department could do. Whether people closer to the situation sensed the family sliding toward disaster, who could say? From what she read, Jason and Amanda sounded like a toxic pair.

Johnson looked again at the photos. Her life and Amanda's, at one point, had essentially been the same, and now they could hardly be more different. How does that happen?

PART TWO

Mug shot of Amanda Stott taken in July 2000, following a
domestic dispute with then-boyfriend, Jason Smith

19

Hadley was waiting, out of a hard rain, in the entryway of Elmer's Restaurant.

"Maybe we ought to buy the joint," he said.

Our first breakfast here, in June 2009, had been nearly a year ago to the day. This was our second, but there had been drinks and coffee and lunches elsewhere, including a 1960s-era Chinese restaurant whose signature feature had been gloom. That lunch happened in January 2010, three months before Amanda's sentencing, when Hadley could give me nothing but his time. It had been an awkward lunch.

Elmer's today was cheerful. Warm air venting from the kitchen made the place smell like hash browns, and retirement-age customers read newspapers and chatted at a pitch that made the place sound like a bird colony. Hadley had me angle my chair toward him, saying his hearing aids were picking up too much background noise.

It had been five weeks since Amanda was given a life sentence, five weeks during which I'd learned that a fear of influencing the outcome, maybe, had kept some people from speaking until the proceedings were over. With Amanda's fate set, I started to receive calls, texts, and emails. People sometimes contacted me late at night. I had become accustomed to standing in my home office in my nightgown and listening as disembodied voices told stories. I wanted to run some of these stories past Hadley.

I had, for instance, been told about an incident that might or might not be explained by grief. The person telling the story did not want to be identified. The person said Jason had taken leave from his job at Ricoh after Eldon was murdered. After several months, Jason returned to work, commuting from the rural home outside of Eugene he now shared with Trinity and his new wife, Keli Townsend. The place had once belonged to Keli's grandparents, and the family lived there rent-free. In May 2010, Jason's family learned that he had not, in fact, gone back to work at Ricoh—"not one day," the person said—and that the joke around the office had become, "Is Jason coming in today?" Where he had gone each weekday for several months was unknown. The deception was revealed at a Mother's Day party attended by both the Smith and Townsend families. After Jason's mother said it was not the time to discuss Jason's employment or lack thereof, the matter was dropped.

Hadley no doubt knew more than I did about what unpredictable behaviors can follow in the wake of murder. I knew some of the escapes people sought from unbearable pain: walking great distances, folding one thousand paper cranes, sleeping. But the fake commuting was something I had only ever read about, in Emmanuel Carrère's *The Adversary*, the true story of a man who pretended for years to commute to a prestigious job and who took over the financial investments for his family. About to be exposed for never having had a job and having spent the family's money, he murdered his wife, children, and parents rather than face their contempt and disappointment. He preferred murdering to being exposed as a fraud.

Hadley did not venture a guess about where Jason had gone. He did say he knew a great deal "about Jason's history, as did the judge and DA," and that if Amanda's case had gone to trial, "it all would have come out, and his family likely knew this."

"Another reason they were willing to settle. They hated Amanda," he added, though in his opinion "it was Jason who ruined Amanda's life."

Jason's mother had commended her son at sentencing for "taking the high road," for allowing a settlement to move forward rather than having Amanda stand trial. Looked at this way, the Smith family had spared Amanda the possibility of execution. Another way to look at it was that the family had been through enough and was not going to submit to the scrutiny a trial would bring.

Hadley told me he thought Amanda would have a hard time at Coffee Creek Correctional Facility, a minimum- and medium-security facility twenty miles south of Portland. There was a hierarchy in any women's prison, where, he said, "they hate mothers who have killed their children, because they need someone to hate."

I asked if he knew that the Smiths had banned the Stotts from attending Eldon's funeral. Hadley did know this. He agreed the threat that they could be arrested was a cruelty to the Stotts.

We approached the subject of how Amanda found herself on the bridge, how she determined she would kill her children. I told Hadley my thinking had gone in many directions—she was desperate, she was fragile; she wanted life as she knew it to end.

"There's something, too," he said, "to 'You took my joy; now I will take yours.'"

Hadley would not let me pay for breakfast. He suggested we keep talking in his car. We made a break for it through the rain and were half-soaked by the time we got in his Cadillac. He told me Amanda's family had sent him "lovely notes" after she was sentenced. I told him I heard they had repeatedly checked Amanda into treatment in the months before she drove the children to the bridge. Hadley said this was true and that she'd been released with at least three different medications, including some "in a black-and-orange box, with the warning that said, 'You might go out and kill someone on these, but otherwise, have fun!'" I later looked up what these pills might be. Possibilities included Prozac and Paxil; neither listed aggression as a likely side effect. Hadley agreed the media had, for the most part, not looked past what they were told by the police, and that there had been a marked lack of digging into the case.

"I don't consider you part of the media, by the way," he said.

The downpour was making the front seat of the Cadillac feel like a cocoon. Hadley and I watched as a cyclist skidded out in the flooded gutter and slid into a car door.

"When I hear them on the radio going, 'I ride my bike even though it's raining because it's ride-your-bike-to-work day,' I think, 'Get in the fucking car,'" he said.

I told him the greener-than-thou thing drove me batty, too, and I thought, we are sitting in his car because we do not want what we have been building for a year to break, not yet. He told me he would be driving five hours back to Baker City. I told him I would bring him some books on tape for the next drive. As I did, I looked at what my foot had been resting against on the floorboard. I picked up the box of shotgun shells.

"Oh, yeah, this is new," he said. He opened the console between us and took out a gun. He said that while it was a revolver, it used shotgun shells. He pointed to the barrel, to where *El Juez* was etched. He kept the gun between us. I could have held it if I wanted to, but I had never handled a gun, and the space was so enclosed I was afraid I might accidentally blow a hole in Hadley's dashboard, or his knee.

He put the gun away. It felt time to go.

"I hope we see each other again soon," I said.

He said, "Sure, sure we will."

That night I told my husband about the gun. He looked it up online.

"Maybe we'll get one," Din said. I read over his shoulder that *el juez* meant "the judge."

I emailed Hadley to say, thanks, as always, and that we might get the gun.

He wrote back, "Maybe we'll make a cowgirl out of you."

***

Seven days after Amanda was sentenced, the state of Oregon released its Critical Incident Response Team (CIRT) Final Report on Eldon Smith. The CIRT was mandated any time there was a homicide of a youth in Oregon. The twelve-page report included ten occasions on which the Oregon Department of Human Services checked on abuse or neglect incidents involving Jason Smith and Amanda Stott-Smith, starting in June 2000 when Amanda told police Jason had restrained her and his arrest for assault IV, and ending in October 2008, with Gavin telling a Child Protective Services worker that "he was pretty sure the marks on his arms were caused by his friends and not his mother." The report detailed each incident involving the children, including Amanda leaving them in a hot car when the family lived in Hawaii in 2006, as well as arriving so late to pick them up from swim lessons in Portland in August 2008 that police were at the pool when she returned. Amanda told police then she'd been "getting snacks for the children and was involved in an automobile accident which caused her to be late."

On August 30, 2010, the state released additional records, in response to a request by KGW-TV for "all DHS records" having to do with the incident and the aftermath. The records ran more than one hundred pages and included medical information about both children. Eldon's cause of death was listed as "Asphyxiation By Drowning." Other significant findings included "Blunt Head Force Trauma." Because it was hypothesized that Amanda drugged the children before dropping them, blood and urine samples were taken. Results showed there were no controlled substances, alcohol, or common pharmaceuticals present.

Trinity was admitted to Oregon Health & Science University Emergency Medicine at 2:30 a.m. on May 23, 2009. Upon arrival, she was "talking and somewhat hysterical." She was hypothermic but quickly warmed "with bear hugger, warm blankets, gastric lavage." She underwent surgery for a sternal fracture. On May 25, "Trinity was smiling and playing with dolls." On May 25 or 26, Trinity asked Detective [Lori] Smith "where her mother and younger brother, Eldon, were." The report does not note whether Trinity received an answer. On May 27, Trinity was released and sent home with Ibuprofen 100 mg/5 ml Oral Suspension for pain, and oxycodone 5 mg/5 ml Oral Solution for moderate pain as needed, a follow-up appointment in two weeks, and the instruction that it was "okay to play on playground as long as chest doesn't hurt."

The report included a summarized "verbatim account" of an interview with Trinity on May 26, conducted by a social worker and observed by several detectives:

> During her videotaped interview, Trinity indicated that she had been in the hospital because she got hurt. When Trinity was asked how she got hurt, she said that she had been sleeping in her mother's car and then she realized that she was in the water. Trinity said that she did not know how she ended up in the water and reported that earlier in the evening she and her mother and her brother, Eldon, had been trying to find a parking spot at the Rose Garden so they could watch the fireworks. Trinity said they were not able to find a parking spot and that later she fell asleep and that when she woke up she realized she was in the water. Trinity said that it was scary being in the water and that she was all alone. When asked where her mother was, she said she was in the car. When asked where Eldon was, Trinity said he was with her mother. Trinity said that when she was in the water it was really, really cold and she couldn't get close to the sidewalk on either side of the river. Trinity said some people then came in a boat and took her to the hospital.

Trinity said that she lives with her father and she had begun to visit with her mother earlier in the day. Trinity said that the first thing she did when she was visiting her mother was give her a hug. She said that [redacted] then came. Trinity said that she was at her mother's house and she and Eldon played. Trinity said that she talked to her mother about how much they missed each other and her mother told Trinity that she really, really missed her a lot. Trinity indicated that her mother was smiling when she told her this. When asked what else they talked about, Trinity said she didn't really know. Trinity said that they ate Cheesits [*sic*] and crackers and that they were probably in her mother's house for about 10 minutes before they got in the car to drive to the fireworks. When asked what they talked about in the car, Trinity said they didn't really talk because she and Eldon were kind of sleepy. Trinity states that her mother was on the phone talking with [redacted] and that she seemed happy. Trinity said that when they were driving around she saw some fireworks and the "usual" things you see at night such as a bunch of buildings and some stars. . . .

Trinity clearly states that she had fallen asleep in the car and that when she woke up she realized she was in the water. She did not make any other statements about any unusual events during the evening that provide much insight into this tragic incident.

A summary of interviews Detectives Bryan Steed and Michele Michaels conducted with Amanda was also part of the report. It was not redacted and read in full:

During the interviews, Ms. Smith indicated that after picking the children up for visitation at approximately 8:00 p.m., she was going to take them downtown to see the Rose Festival fireworks and she ended up driving around unable to find a parking place. Ms. Smith also told the detectives that the children said after their father dropped them off [at the house] in Tualatin . . . he was going to a barbecue at a friend's house but the mother wasn't supposed to go to the barbecue. Ms. Smith acknowledged being upset after the children told her this. Ms. Smith told detectives that after driving around she eventually made her way to the Sellwood Bridge where she stopped midspan where the incident took place. Ms. Smith indicated that she was familiar with the Sellwood Bridge because the children used to take swimming lessons at Sellwood Pool. Ms. Smith said the reason she put the children in the water was to "end their suffering" in an apparent reference to the mother's perception about an ongoing custody conflict with Mr. Smith impacting her children.

This record was made public on August 30, 2010. KGW-TV aired a short piece mentioning as much on September 2. The segment received no online comments. No other news outlet picked it up. "End their suffering" required effort, required that we expand what we took to be Amanda's motivation. It did not grab the attention like "revenge," a word that did not appear in Amanda's interview. If withholding "end their suffering" from the public for 464 days might be seen as lying by omission, might have ramifications, might incite or codify hate, at least the killer was already in jail. What more did people need to know?

I needed to know: What suffering?

20

May 23–25, 2009, Oregon Coast and Portland, Oregon

Tiffany Gray and her husband, Shanon, were at the Oregon Coast with another couple. The kids were asleep; the adults were playing cards and having drinks when Tiffany heard Amanda's name on the television news. She looked over. The newscaster said Amanda's name again, but it made no sense because the mug shot was not of Amanda; Tiffany did not know who was in that picture. Then she did. She started saying, "Oh my god, oh my god," and then she grabbed her phone and called April on repeat. Tiffany did not get through to her until the morning, when she told April, "You need to sit down. Something really, really, really, really awful has happened." Tiffany told April what Amanda was accused of doing. April said, "Gavin, where's Gavin?"

Tiffany and Shanon loaded their daughters into the Land Rover and barreled back to Portland. Shanon was a former DA, now in private practice. Tiffany wanted him to get to Amanda before another attorney did, not for the job so much as support, someone who could maybe protect her, from whatever additional horrors were on the way.

The cops where Amanda was being held were not interested in her having a friend stop in for a visit. Was he representing her? Shanon, whose full-sleeve tattoos were partially inked in, said he was. They let Shanon see Amanda. She recognized him, he later told Tiffany, but otherwise she was seriously out of it. Tiffany did not want details about the crime, not yet, and heard only that Amanda had turned her face to the wall and talked to Shanon for two hours.

The next day, Tiffany found the press hiding in the bushes in front of her house. She loaded her six-month-old and her eighteen-month-old into the car while reporters shouted questions at her. They had found Tiffany's name during a check of Amanda's criminal record in Multnomah County. In July 2000, Amanda and Jason got into a fight, and she was arrested. Had she thrown an air conditioner at his head? Tiffany did not remember, only that Amanda called her at two thirty in the morning needing bail money, something like $400. Tiffany had driven downtown and bailed Amanda out. She did not recall Amanda as being shaken or hurt, and her mug shot from that arrest seemed to reflect that she was not: in it, her eyes were bright, her smile relaxed, and her skin and hair as smooth as a mannequin's.

The equipoise did not surprise Tiffany, who knew Amanda as the girl at George Fox University raising a baby alone, this barefoot, pregnant mother-goddess-earth-mama, and an excellent, excellent mother to Gavin. How funny time was. Tiffany had seen Amanda as a role model, had admired her mothering to the point that when Tiffany was pregnant with her first child, it was Amanda she had confided in, telling her she loved the baby she was carrying but did not yet feel a superintense connection.

Don't worry; it will come, Amanda had said. I know you, and once you have that baby, it will come.

And she had been right. If you could get on Amanda's wavelength, it was a mostly beautiful place, where everything was rosy and there was nothing to stress about, it was all la-di-la-di-la. Which Amanda said about everything! I have to buy a can of soup, la-di-la-di-la! I have to give a PowerPoint, la-di-la-di-la! Tiffany and April would crack up, because Amanda was living in her own little world, a place where the mantra was, "Don't worry, it will all work out."

That she did not stress over her grades or when Gavin colored with crayons all over the kitchen floor meant Amanda sometimes did not appreciate the stress she was putting on others. She would drive to clubs in her rickety-rackety Audi and leave Tiffany and April watching Gavin for one day, for two days. They'd pass him off like strangers in the night, and when Tiffany tried to tell Amanda this was not okay, Amanda would act surprised and start in on a lot of excuses that did not quite make sense: I met this guy, and he lived out in Vancouver, so I went to Vancouver, and then I tried to call, but my phone was dead, and I got a busy signal from you.

Tiffany had let this go; the girls were not yet living in a world of big consequences, though if Tiffany thought about it now, Amanda should have been. She had a baby to take care of, and she did it well when she wanted to, but she also wanted the life of a girl whose responsibilities were taken care of by others, like the time they went to Tahoe for spring break. They had to change planes in Oakland. April wanted a cigarette, so they stepped outside the terminal. Amanda started looking through her stuff, looking and looking.

Guys, she said. I lost my pot.

Tiffany did not think Amanda could seriously have brought pot through security, on the plane, but Amanda said she had; it had been in her sunglasses case and must have fallen out in the terminal when she got out her glasses.

April had no idea how Tiffany didn't lose it on Amanda. Tiffany did not lose it. She corralled the situation by saying they were just going to head back to the gate, and what they definitely were not going to do was go back in the airport and look for the pot. She knew that's what Amanda would have done: gotten down on her hands and knees and looked, and if she found it, get up and say, "I found it!" She could be clueless that way. Sometimes it could be charming, but that day it definitely was not. They missed their connecting flight.

The trip did not get better. They were staying in Tahoe with a guy Tiffany was seeing. A trust-fund baby, he had a swank place and gorgeous friends, one of whom April wound up hooking up with. And then there was Amanda, getting mad, being snotty, all I don't want to go to dinner! And why don't we find me someone that I can make out with? Over the five days the girls were in Tahoe, Amanda messed around with three guys. Tiffany and April were flirts but pretty straitlaced, and they realized on that trip that Amanda was not. In the scheme of things, she wasn't wild; she was more a typical college girl, the kind that might have better liked being in South Padre Island for spring break, doing wet T-shirt contests and Jell-O shots.

On that trip, Tiffany also saw that Amanda did not feel as though she was enough on her own. One of the guys she fooled around with was no longer interested in her the next day, which, come on; who cares? But Amanda did care; she was so worked up she had an anxiety attack while they were driving down the mountain. Tiffany and April stood at the side of the road and watched Amanda hyperventilate. Then she kicked a log. It was so overreactive, like some switch had flipped, all because some random guy did not pay her attention.

Tiffany told herself it was because Amanda always felt like the underdog, that she wanted to be accepted and liked and loved and told she was okay, and the only way she knew how to do this was through hooking up with a guy, believing what he said, and doing exactly what he told her to do. Amanda would talk about what these guys had promised her, things like, "As soon as I break up with my girlfriend, we're going to go on the phatest vacation. We're going to go to Vegas for the weekend." And Tiffany or April would say, "Amanda, do you honestly believe that? He's been with this girl for like three years, and they're not going to break up because you slept with him one night and gave him a good blow job. It's not going to happen." And Amanda would say, but guys, this is what he said. She only learned the hard way, Tiffany thought, always the hard way.

By mid-1999, Amanda was again learning the hard way. Becoming pregnant by one guy her freshman year and another before her senior year was not the norm at George Fox, whose stated values were "Students First. Christ in Everything. Innovation to Improve Outcomes." Amanda's family, whom Tiffany met a few times and thought very, very conservative, were members of a church where wives were expected to be obedient to their husbands. Tiffany had the impression that Amanda was seen, by her parents, as a rebellious sinner. Amanda said she wanted to please them, to change their minds. She started going to church all the time and told Tiffany she was trying to not smoke, drink, or swear. Amanda said she really tried to be who God wanted her to be. She wanted to make her parents happy.

And they had been happy when she planned to marry Shane Cook, the father of her second child. Maybe, Tiffany thought then, Amanda had been right; it was all going to work out. And then Shane killed himself. Tiffany sat with Amanda on the floor of her apartment and went through the profiles of Christian families looking to adopt. Tiffany kept looking at Amanda, who was already filling out her maternity top, and asking, "Are you sure? Are you sure?" Amanda was sure.

Around this time, something curious happened, something that could be filed under "Be careful what you wish for," or as recompense for Amanda bearing up under a bad situation: the deus ex machina that was Jason. Jason was the one by Amanda's side during her last month of pregnancy, who was in bed with her when her water broke, who drove her to the hospital when contractions began.

Tiffany never liked Jason. He was stiff in his demeanor, not light on his feet; she and April would crack jokes that he never joined in on. He told Amanda he didn't like her friends, that they we were a bad influence, and the whole time Tiffany was thinking, little do you know; Amanda is a strong girl, and she has a mind of her own.

After the baby left with the adoptive family, Amanda was swept up in Jason's largesse, eating seven-course meals, shopping at Saks, and just getting decked out. She was no longer the girl to whom guys lied about phat vacations. She was the one with the rich boyfriend, with the new jewels. She showed off her sparkles to Tiffany and April, until she'd lose a bracelet, maybe at a club downtown—honestly, she didn't know where.

Tiffany did not know that Amanda was not losing her jewelry. Amanda did not know it either. She believed Jason when he told her she was careless, that he was keeping a wedding ring he bought her in a safe-deposit box and that's why she could not see it. She did not know the diamond Ebel watch he gave her for graduation, the Rolex he bought himself, and the leather jackets from Neiman-Marcus were later pawned or sold for cash. Amanda tended to trust what guys told her, and Jason could talk and talk until she believed what he was saying.

Amanda graduated from George Fox University in spring of 2000. By July, she and Gavin were occasionally staying with Jason in a small apartment on Belmont Street in southeast Portland. Dogwood trees and Japanese maples lined the surrounding residential streets, and three blocks away was Lone Fir Cemetery, a thirty-acre memorial garden that looked like an enchanted forest. The location had the makings of a peaceful beginning for the young couple, and they had the added cushion of more than $200,000 in stocks, established years before by Jason's maternal grandmother, that Jason had been given control of some months earlier. The funds might have provided a secure boost for two young adults launching their lives. Instead the money proved an accelerant. Jason and Amanda bought no property and made no investments; they spent it on $6,000 bike frames and $1,000 cameras;

they burned through cash so fast they might as well have piled it on the living room floor and set it on fire.

Christine Duncan's petition to the court in October 2000, seeking to wrest control of the funds from her son, included a letter from Anthony Cubito, who had "worked as a counselor with Ms. Christine Duncan and her family periodically since April, 1992."

Cubito wrote, in a two-page document faxed from a Mail Boxes Etc., that Christine Duncan reported her son was "drinking up to a fifth of liquor and half a case of beer on a daily basis, is resisting checking into a residential rehabilitation program, is in an apparently dysfunctional relationship with a woman named Amanda, is rapidly spending thousands of dollars each month on his girlfriend, alcohol, expensive restaurants, etc., has gained approximately 40lbs. in two months and has a history of addiction. . . . If some intervention is not effected quickly, the end result, as in most cases with this high degree of alcohol intake, will end in disaster."

The disasters of the summer of 2000 included the slashed tires, the thrown keys, the bites and scrapes, and Tiffany seeing Amanda after she said Jason had choked her. Tiffany believed her. She saw the bruising across Amanda's throat and was so disturbed that she told Amanda, "Here's the deal: you've got to leave this guy."

Tiffany's concern, Christine Duncan's alarm: neither moved Amanda. She dug in. She hoped to marry Jason. It was true he could talk and talk and make her believe anything. It was true a former girlfriend of his named Keli Townsend told Amanda on the phone that she needed to know one thing about Jason: that he will never stop lying. Amanda at the time thought she could figure things out a little better than her predecessor, and in April 2001, she and Jason, with Gavin in tow, made a quick trip to Hawaii and got married.

Amanda—the bubbly girl, the la-di-la—started to be seen less. She left her job as a receptionist at a marketing agency in downtown Portland around the time of Trinity's birth in March 2002. Eldon was born in August 2004. The family moved to several condos and apartments, rarely staying longer than a year. Jason was promoted at Ricoh, while Amanda, in her way, was demoted. She rarely saw Tiffany and April, and she did not look for work. She stayed home and cared for the house and the kids, which she did to varying degrees of people's satisfaction. At the time of her arrest in May 2009, she had no Facebook profile or Twitter account; friends knew her to have no social media presence. Amanda lived in a tighter and tighter loop of communication, the criticism of a few people carrying the sort of weight that could change the way the outside world saw her and how she saw herself.

Tiffany stepped inside this loop in March 2005, when she and her then-boyfriend were invited to dinner at Amanda and Jason's before the family moved to Hawaii. Though Tiffany seriously could not stand Jason and the way he spoke to Amanda, saying things to her like, "Are you retarded?" in a tone so sharp that Amanda would freeze and not even blink her eyelash for what seemed like weeks, Tiffany thought, okay, one last hurrah.

Trinity was running around in a princess outfit when Tiffany got to the house. Gavin was playing on his own, and Eldon, less than a year old, was asleep upstairs. Amanda was making homemade enchiladas and told Tiffany to come into the kitchen. She mixed Tiffany a cocktail, some horrible thing with coffee, Grand Marnier, and Kahlua. Tiffany abandoned the drink to entertain Trinity by painting the girl's nails, until Amanda put the enchiladas on the dining table and started to eat.

Amanda? Jason said. How many times have you made these enchiladas?

I don't know, honey, she said. Maybe ten times?

Well, you know what? They taste like absolute dog shit. Our guests don't want to eat these.

Tiffany's date practically choked. I love it, he said, I really love it. It's totally fine. It's delicious. I'm not really a very spicy guy.

Do not try to smooth it over with her, Jason said. She needs to know this is not okay. She knows how to make enchiladas the way they're supposed to be. You know what, Amanda? You were in there chatting, and you were not paying attention to what you were doing. You need to go back and remake them.

Tiffany and her boyfriend spoke at the same time, saying there was no need to remake them, it was eight o'clock, they were already sitting down, and the kids were starving . . .

The kids can eat, Jason told Amanda. But you need to remake them for us.

Amanda went back to the kitchen to remake them.

Tiffany thought, this is insane, but Jason was not done yet. Trinity had taken three bites and refused to eat any more. Jason took her upstairs. Tiffany could hear her being spanked, which of course woke Eldon up. Now he was screaming. Tiffany went upstairs to get Eldon. She brought him downstairs and was trying to soothe him when she noticed Gavin had gone into the corner and was playing with his little cars; he had finished his food in like ten seconds because he *knew*. Tiffany and her boyfriend finally went into the kitchen.

You don't have to do this, he told Amanda, a woman he had known for all of an hour.

No, I need to, she said. It was wrong of me. I was visiting. I wasn't paying attention, and I really should have made more of an effort.

No, Tiffany said. Look what you are doing to yourself.

But Amanda was almost in a trance. She said, God said that you need to be a submissive wife, and you need to listen to your husband and do what he asks you to do.

Tiffany was still holding Eldon when Trinity came downstairs bawling. Jason sat her back down at the table.

This is your choice, Jason told Trinity. You can eat, or you can sit there all night. So you decide for yourself what you want to do, because you're a bad girl.

Amanda recooked dinner and re-served it. Trinity would not eat; it became a battle of wills between a three-year-old and her father, who took her back upstairs for another spanking and then sat her back down at the table. She was still sitting there at midnight when Tiffany and her boyfriend left. Three days later, the Smith family moved to Oahu.

Their troubles went with them. Unpaid bills and overspending had destroyed Jason's and Amanda's credit histories, which made renting a house difficult. Not until Jason's mother interceded were they able to get a split-level home with a tiny side yard on a cul-de-sac in the Mililani neighborhood. I visited the street in 2011. It looks like Any Suburb, USA. The closest beach is a thirty-minute drive, mostly on freeway. Friends who visited found conditions in the home unnerving. Ryan Barron stayed with the family several times.

"It was the worst," he said. "[Jason] would be gone all day and leave me at the house with Amanda and the kids. I'm, like, in paradise, and I can't go anywhere. He wouldn't give her a car."

Ryan said the reason Jason gave for leaving his wife without a car was that she might drive drunk with the kids. Amanda had started drinking heavily in Hawaii, "about a bottle of port wine or vodka a day," Ryan guessed. But he did not think leaving her with no way to get around was as much about safety as it was confinement.

"She lived a classic abused life, more mental than physical," he said. "Jason controlled her like a communist; he controlled her like Nazi Germany. He didn't want her to go anywhere and do anything. She was a prisoner. Where it really, really went sideways, it's all about Hawaii."

The family moved back to Portland in 2007, first to the condo in downtown Portland, then to the house on Southwest Cayuse Court in Tualatin, the last home they would live in as a family, until Jason left in June 2008. Amanda was alone with the three children. As she had when Gavin was a baby, she applied for state assistance. She asked her husband to come home. He delivered the ultimatum about her needing to lose weight, stop smoking, stop drinking, and get a job.

September 2008 was a lousy time to be looking for a job. Amanda did not find work. Jason did not return home. Reports show that the Department of Human Services and Child Protective Services received numerous calls between August and October of 2008 from people concerned about the children's welfare. On September 12, Gavin returned from school to find he was locked out of the house. He went to a neighbor's, who reported the situation to DHS. On September 17, a CPS worker interviewed Gavin and Trinity, who "denied drug or alcohol use by their parents, denied fighting by the adults in the home and denied physical discipline." When asked about Jason's substance abuse issues, Amanda "refused to provide the worker with any information." On October 17, DHS received a report that Gavin "had been physically abused by his mother." Gavin again "made no disclosures about abuse." Trinity admitted nothing.

Tiffany had not seen much of Amanda after she returned from Hawaii. She was married to Shanon at this point, and in fall 2008 was preparing to have her second child. Amanda called in September, sounding like her old self, sounding happy; Tiffany was glad to hear her voice and said, come to my baby shower; it's in two days.

April gave Amanda a lift to the party. April was agitated when she arrived and took Tiffany aside. She told her, there is something really wrong with Amanda; on the drive here, I could not make sense of one thing she said. There was no direct line from what I was saying to her mind. And she's too skinny, way too skinny.

Tiffany was eight months pregnant, and it was her shower; she did not have a lot of time to take the situation in hand, if there was a situation. As the party coalesced, Tiffany and April tried to talk to Amanda, who was both amped up and spaced out, more than spaced out. Tiffany said, Amanda, wait, wait, wait, we are not following what you are saying. The people at the baby shower were noticing, and they later asked Tiffany, was that friend of yours high? Was she wasted? Tiffany did not know and could not devote the time she might have given the question in the past. In October, she delivered her second baby in 363 days.

Tiffany did not see Amanda again until Christmastime. Tiffany and her daughters met Amanda, Eldon, and Trinity in Pioneer Courthouse Square. Eldon was in his stroller, and Tiffany had her three-month-old in a baby carrier on her chest. Trinity was the only child big enough to be awed by the square's seventy-five-foot holiday tree. It should have been a festive occasion, but the weather was raw and the friends did not stay long. They promised to catch up soon.

When Tiffany had her birthday dinner at a local restaurant in May, she did not invite Amanda. April was there and asked Tiffany if she had seen Amanda. Tiffany had not, not for a few months. April said she'd had a couple of messages from Amanda, and she sounded super out of it. Tiffany had her hands full but said she would try to call her. This had been on May 18. The next day, she and Shanon and another couple had driven to the Oregon Coast.

By 2016, Tiffany would have three more babies, and sixty thousand followers on Instagram, where she posted about "mothering five miracles, saying yes & telling my story the only way I know how. Now is now." She did not see her public devotion to her children in any way as a reaction to Amanda's destruction of hers; Tiffany had, for the most part, put what Amanda had done behind her. She had decided the murder was not about revenge and that Amanda never said anything like that to Shanon. No, instead it was, "I had nothing left. I had nothing. I was completely broken. I'd rather have the kids be gone than be with Jason." It was as simple as that.

But Tiffany vividly remembered who Amanda had once been: a young woman who, at least for a time, had not been easily torn down; a woman who had a baby by a guy who committed suicide and still walked with joy in her step, and who found a good family for that baby. Tiffany at the time had asked her, was it so painful? And Amanda had said, my tragedy is someone else's treasure.

21

I was in San Francisco at a friend's party drinking wine when my cell phone rang.

"You don't know me, but I am going to do everything I can to make sure Trinity is not hurt any more than she has been," the caller said.

I took the call to an upstairs bathroom. Contrary to what the caller said, I did know who it was, and I told the caller so.

"Okay," he said, and that he was calling because he'd had "a couple of beers." He was calling because he was mad—mad at me, mad at Amanda. She was "no angel" and stayed in her marriage only because "she was greedy, staying as long as there was money." The caller was also mad at Jason.

"I know a million bad things about Jason, but I am only going to tell you a few," he said. "He currently has a lawsuit against him from a paraplegic he was taking care of. You should check that out." Also, that some years back Jason had smuggled "thousands of opiates back from Mexico, on Gavin."

I asked if he was implying that drugs were packed into Gavin's diaper bag or on his body. The caller did not know, or chose not to elaborate, or was making things up as he went along.

"He told Amanda they would make so much money," he continued, but instead Jason "became an addict" and stopped going to work, telling his bosses Amanda was having a rough pregnancy and that he needed to be home with her, but she wasn't pregnant. I noticed my cell phone did not have as much juice as the call might warrant. It was after midnight and the caller still had a lot to say: Gavin and Trinity had been very close, Jason was a neglectful father, Eldon was small for his age. The caller said that no one close to the families would speak to me and that he did not want his name mentioned. He twice apologized for having driven past my house. Had I, he wanted to know, driven past his? I told him I had.

It was twelve thirty. I listened to the caller breathing.

"I'm a Christian," he said, "and unfortunately, I think Eldon is in hell."

That the caller, that anyone, would add the concept of eternal suffering to the fate of a four-year-old boy murdered by his mother—what relief could this bring? Or was the point to extend the suffering of the living?

We were not going to debate Scripture, me standing in a bathroom, him cracking another beer and saying again that no one would speak to me.

"Listen, Jason is a heroin addict," he said. "He used to score down the street from your husband's business."

The caller knew my husband's business?

"I've been there before," he said. I asked whether we could meet for coffee to talk further. The caller said we could "sometime," but before we set that time, at 1:03 in the morning, my phone went dead in my hand.

In the wake of Amanda's sentencing, those who reached out to me had information they felt was substantive. Some of it was not. The offer of information was more about the need to tell the tragedy again and again. If a stranger on the other end of a phone line was all they were going to get, then okay. They would convey the doubts and distress they had carried about Amanda, about Jason, but they wanted it understood that they had their own troubles. It wasn't the caller's job, he let me know, to fix these mendacious people, and even when he'd tried—and he had tried—he'd been foiled. There was too much subterfuge, too many ways for what was happening, with the kids and the marriage and the drug use, to be hidden or explained away. How you lived with the outcome, or how the caller lived, was to protect his family, stick to his faith, and make one late-night, beer-fueled, not-for-attribution phone call. Then maybe he could sleep.

"Where are you?" asked Molly. I was in Salem, Oregon, standing under the sky bridge of what I thought must be the ugliest shopping mall in America.

"Oh, I see you," Molly said. "Stay there."

Where was I going to go? I had driven from Portland to see Molly, whose emails had arrived intermittently for a year. She initially said our meeting was out of the question but had recently decided we needed to meet, which was why I was standing in the full sun of a mid-August day waiting for someone who did not want to be identified by her real name.

Molly's emails indicated she knew more than most people about Amanda and Jason. She had met both Trinity and Eldon, knew the Smiths, and knew the family of Jason's new wife. She knew about members of the Stott family I had never heard of. And her anger with Amanda had not cooled, not in fifteen months. In one email, she imagined Amanda in her cell, where "she probably dwells more on the fact that the final—ultimate—revenge was poorly executed and only half successful. By her standards and to her dismay Jason won the battle that was to be hers."

The person who met me under the sky bridge wore a sundress and looked like a college kid, though she had told me she was closer to forty.

"Let's go inside," Molly said. We took the escalator to the top floor. The food court smelled of Chinese fast food. A woman two tables over changed a baby's diaper. I had barely gotten out my tape recorder when Molly started talking. Her primary concern, she said, was for Trinity. Did I have any idea what was going on in her life? Did I know the Department of Human Services was not monitoring her? I told Molly I did not know much more about DHS's involvement beyond what had been released in the CIRT report earlier in the month. Molly had read the report.

While she had told me she worked with kids, Molly's familiarity with the case struck me as unusual. Also unusual was what she wanted from me, which was "everything, please"—everything having to do with Amanda's mental state at the time of the incident and everything I had learned from her attorneys. I had come to trust Molly, to believe she had legitimate reasons to be invested in Trinity's safety. Still, I told her I could not give her documents but that, just as she had accessed the CIRT report, she could procure public records. I would be doing so myself later in the week in Eugene.

"I'll meet you there," she said as a mall worker pushed a six-foot-high container of trash past our table.

"Did you speak with Amanda yet?" she asked. When I said no, she looked let down, as though there were things at stake I might not fully appreciate.

The number of people working their way toward me a year and more after the murder and the attempted murder told me that certain barriers—of propriety, of distance, of "not my problem"—had been breached. There was Samantha Hammerly, Amanda's friend from junior high school, who felt the Lord had made sure she had been watching television the night Amanda's mug shot was shown so that she might become reacquainted with her friend after seventeen years. There was Amanda's college classmate who, having children the same ages as Trinity and Eldon, experienced such a transference after learning what

Amanda had done that she questioned her own mothering, her own sanity, until her husband told her, "Get over it. It's awful, but you don't have anything else in common with her." There was the late-night caller and his stories of Gavin as a drug mule and the fleeced paraplegic.

There were many ways to ethically address the provocative arcana people offered. One was to be comfortable with a certain amount of uncertainty, to accept that the story of a murdered child had expanded to the point where more and more people would seek access points, and that some of these people might be conspiracy theorists, or stayed near the story because it gave their lives meaning, or because they could not let it go.

Another way was to verify what they said.

The paraplegic was named Brian Burr. He was born in 1973. He attended Milwaukie High School, where his senior year he was student body president and captain of the wrestling team. When Burr was seventeen, he fell off a ladder and broke his neck. Burr retained some use of his arms. He was able to drive his own van and live independently. Sometime around 2003, he met Jason Smith. Four years later, Jason began to do some work for Burr as a caregiver, helping him with light tasks, such as cooking and cleaning. Jason sometimes brought Amanda and the kids to Burr's home.

On November 7, 2008, Burr sent Amanda, via certified mail, a summons stating that she needed to "appear and defend the complaint filed against [her]." Both she and Jason were defendants in Case No. SC082908. Burr, the plaintiff, alleged the following:

"On or around January 2008, Plaintiff loaned Defendant Jason Smith $3000.00. On or around April 29, 2008, Defendants issued Plaintiff a check (check number 1010) in the amount of $3000.000 as repayment for the original amount loaned to them." The check did not clear. A photocopy of the returned check, issued from the Bank of Hawaii in Mililani and signed by Jason Smith, was included in the complaint.

"On multiple occasions," the complaint continued, "Defendants acknowledged owing the Plaintiff the original amount of $3000.00. On at least three occasions between April and July of 2008, defendant Jason Smith showed up unannounced at Plaintiff's home and offered Plaintiff cocaine in lieu of payment. On at least one occasion, Defendant Amanda Jo Smith phoned Plaintiff and asked Plaintiff what she could do to settle the claim besides making payment."

Lee Burr, Brian Burr's father, told me, "I was there when that guy called a couple of times trying to get Brian to leave him alone about the money. He wanted him to take drugs instead."

Burr told his father about Amanda asking what she could do besides repay the money. "But he said, 'What else can I have her do? I have someone to clean my house.'" Lee laughed. "And Brian had a girlfriend!"

The complaint continued:

> Since May 2008, Defendant Jason Smith consistently harassed Plaintiff by calling him up to four times a day. Defendant Jason Smith verbally abused Plaintiff by badgering Plaintiff and making Plaintiff feel guilty for suing Defendant. . . . Defendant Jason Smith threatened violence to Plaintiff if Plaintiff mentioned the money owed to any of Defendant's family members. . . . Defendants' acts consisted of some extraordinary transgression of the bounds of socially tolerable conduct and exceeded any reasonable limit of social toleration.

The complaint asked for repayment of the original loan plus bank fees incurred, as well as relief and damages, plus court and attorney costs, for a total of $10,000.

By May 23, 2009, Burr had yet to receive any money.

"I was there when he first heard about the kids," Lee said. "Brian saw it on TV and said, 'They worked for me!' He was really upset."

Lee remembered Jason contacting Burr afterward. "Jason called for relief, but I think Brian was going to go ahead with the case," he said.

Brian Burr's mother, Patty Bacon, did not think Jason asked for relief from the debt after Eldon's murder. He would not have needed to.

"After the baby died, Brian didn't have the heart to go through with it," said Bacon. "Brian was brokenhearted. He knew those kids and Amanda; they came over and had hot dogs in the backyard."

Bacon did not know in what capacity Jason worked for her son.

"He didn't work for Brian very much . . ." She hesitated. "Look, Brian was on medical marijuana, and he [Jason] came over to smoke it."

She did not know how the two men met, and we could not ask Burr, who developed a blood clot and died in December 2010.

I waited for Molly outside of Lane County Circuit Court in Eugene. Across the street, a gourmet farmers market was underway, with people wearing bike helmets and nibbling pesto-and-lamb empanadas.

"I'm sorry about the mess," Molly said, moving a soda cup from the passenger seat of her minivan. She wanted to take me on a tour; it would be easier for her to drive. She first asked if I had found what I was looking for at the courthouse: criminal records for Jason and Amanda. I told Molly I had. She asked if I would make her a copy. I told her no, but she could get the same papers I did; it was public information.

"But let me ask you one thing," she said. "Does he have any felonies?"

I confirmed that this had been reported, and wasn't I the one who was supposed to be asking questions? Molly smiled and took us out of town. I had found the address of where I thought Trinity was living with Jason and Keli. Molly thought she knew where it was and said it could be our first stop. We drove past broad fields, farmhouses, and barns until we came to the property. All we could see from the road was a long driveway leading uphill.

"I think that's Jason," Molly said as a black SUV passed going the other way. I turned to look. The SUV's brake lights blinked once. Molly made a sharp left up a rural road. She did not want on record how she knew Jason, and as she drove farther up unfamiliar roads until we hit a dead end, it seemed she did not want to run into him now.

After Eldon was murdered, everyone had been angry with Amanda, for reasons that were obvious. Now, people seemed angry with Jason, for reasons that were sometimes opaque. The anonymous caller, and now Molly, made accusations they might have confronted Jason with but had not. Who was trustworthy here, whether there were sour grapes or guilt or fear, was not immediately discernable. I did not doubt, however, that these people were trying to get under the nub, to expose the root of how the crime happened.

The tour's next stop was a strip-mall pawnshop. Molly said Jason used to sell stuff here, that he habitually stole jewelry from the women in his life. I said I'd heard that. Molly asked if I knew that Jason and the woman to whom he was now married had dated in high school. I did not know that. As she put the minivan in reverse, she asked if I knew how Eldon got his name.

Molly's earlier claim that the Department of Human Services was not monitoring Trinity had me look over the DHS reports again. On July 6, 2009, DHS had opened a temporary "Child Welfare Case Plan" for Trinity, wherein the "Child (is) in the home, DHS has custody." By

October, with Trinity "still a current ongoing assessment," a schedule of planned visits was enacted. Though the reports were heavily redacted, the schedule appeared to have broken down immediately. On October 9, 2009, a DHS caseworker received a call from Jason saying he needed "to reschedule the face-to-face today due to some things coming up." The meeting was rescheduled for October 13. The caseworker canceled this meeting. She left phone messages for Jason on November 2, and again on November 5, to "set up a face-to-face." Jason called back to say "that him [*sic*] and Trinity [redacted] are really not feeling well." The meeting eventually took place on November 24. "Trinity was quiet but friendly during my visit," the caseworker noted. The next meeting appears to have been on January 20, 2010. Despite the report's redactions, the number of in-person meetings with Trinity between October and January, as noted in the reports, appeared to be two.

Molly drove us into Coburg, a farming community whose downtown looked to be two blocks long.

"If we see anyone, we used to work together," Molly said. She mentioned that several of Amanda's relatives lived here and that this was where Trinity went to school.

Coburg was also, I would later confirm, where Amanda found out the provenance of Eldon's name. In early 2009, Amanda had driven to Coburg looking for Keli Townsend, whom she suspected of being romantically involved with Jason. Jason had denied this. Jason's mother also told Amanda she was wrong, that Jason and Keli had been friends since high school and that was all it was. Amanda did not think that was all it was. She knew Jason had been spending time with Keli. Eldon had come home with stories about going to the park with her; Trinity had talked about playing with Keli's dogs.

Believing that Keli lived in Coburg, Amanda had gone to Coburg City Hall, where she asked for Keli's address. Amanda was told that information was not available, but the person working had just seen Keli's father, Eldon, up the street; maybe Amanda could catch him. Amanda might have asked this worker to repeat the information she was learning for the first time: that her son had been named after the father of the woman she suspected her husband was having an affair with. Or maybe she didn't ask again.

Molly drove us back toward Eugene. There was a gold haze in the air.

"Grass seed," she said, and asked if it was true that Amanda had not been allowed in her mother-in-law's home after she was caught trying to impersonate Christine Duncan on the phone "to gain access," Molly said, "to the money." I wondered where she got this information, but, tit for tat, she would not say.

Molly dropped me at my car and pointed toward a scenic way out of town.

"Don't hit any cows," she said.

I drove past sheep shorn for summer and trucks coming in from the fields. It was seventy-two degrees and a good hour from sunset. It was the kind of evening where you roll down the car window and let the wind hit the cup of your hand. I turned on the radio. An oldies station was playing songs from when I was young: "Loves Me Like a Rock," and "Hello It's Me," and "Oh What a Night," and "How Long Has This Been Going On?" The songs made me feel nostalgic, and I thought about how Eldon would never feel nostalgia. He would never sing along to songs from when he was thirteen, or learn to drive, or fall in love, or creep into middle age. I continued north, passing the prison in Wilsonville, where the woman who extinguished his life would spend the next thirty-five years of hers.

22

Summer 2008 had gotten out of control. Ryan Barron had been okay initially with Jason staying with him and Sara. But his friend had become spooky and gross. Sara would look under the bed in Jason's room and find thousands of crumpled-up napkins or a bowl of vomit with a T-shirt stuck in it. She'd had it by September and asked Ryan, "What is going on with your friend?"

Ryan knew about Jason's drug history. Ryan should; he had been hanging out with the guy nearly every day for seven years. Jason had been using OxyContin back in 2001, though not in crazy amounts; he had been heavy, heavy into weed back then. Ryan had gone over to Jason's apartment the first day they met. Amanda was there, and she had just made some pot cookies. Ryan didn't know how to make these and was told that you sauté the pot in butter and use the butter in the cookie recipe. Ryan ate a cookie, went outside, lay on the grass, and stared at the clouds for two hours.

That seemed funny now, innocent. It seemed a long way from when Jason showed up at Ryan's this past June with welts on his back and shoulders, saying he'd been asleep on his couch and woke up to Amanda beating him with a coat hanger. Ryan took pictures and told Jason that there was no way he was going back to that house; it wasn't safe. "Plus," Sara said, "what if Amanda beat herself up and called the cops and said that Jason did it?"

This kind of violence, and his long history with Jason, made Ryan willing to put up with Jason's drug use in the house. Jason would chew Vicodin like candy every five minutes. They had no effect. He was taking up to twenty-five or thirty OxyContin pills a day, and he was doing Dilantin. He tried phenol patches and MS Contin. He would sit in front of the television in a daze and pass out. Sara saw all this. It became impossible for Ryan to explain away, to pretend his friend was not in their guest room snorting anything he could get his hands on.

Ryan tried to reason with Jason. He told him, "Dude, you've got to knock it off. You cannot mix cocaine and Xanax."

But Jason was too far gone. He looked like shit and like he didn't care. Ryan was sympathetic to the guy's problems, but still, Jason was taking serious advantage of the situation; he was staying with Ryan and Sara for free, not paying any bills, making probably eighty grand a year for a job he was phoning in, constantly broke, and stealing, including trying to make off with one of Ryan's guns. It was too much, and Ryan finally told Jason he couldn't stay with them anymore. Jason asked Ryan what he was supposed to do. Then he called his mom.

Ryan knew Jason had no easy place to land: his mother would have her own set of demands, Amanda would have hers, and the kids needed food, needed attention. Jason was in no condition to provide what any-one needed. Any environment he walked into these days, everyone else paid. Maybe it had always been this way. Ryan had lost his job during the time he was partying with Jason. Ryan didn't want to pay anymore.

And Jason would find a way to skate through; he always seemed to. He knew how to hustle.

When Ryan was still partying with Jason, they would sometimes score along Northeast Eighty-Second Avenue, a miles-long strip of cheap motels, tire stores, and Asian steam-tray restaurants. There was a lot of drug activity and hookers, especially on payday or when people got their relief checks. Ryan and Jason would head over in the afternoons, sit at different cheap-ass bars with about fifteen other people, everyone drinking lite beers and waiting for the dealer to show up and then going single file into the bathroom with the dealer to get their eight ball or whatever. Jason had been going there for years. He was tight with this woman named Shannon, whom Ryan met a bunch of times. She was a former prostitute and slept on the floor of someone else's trailer. She told Ryan she had a stage-four brain tumor. She did not need to tell him she was a raging alcoholic. Jason would give Shannon money, give her rides, buy her lunch. Maybe it got sexual; Ryan had no idea. Shannon had tons of pain pills, and sometimes Jason shared those. He was kind of her caretaker, the way he had been with Brian Burr. Ryan had gone over to Burr's a few times with Jason, had watched Jason help Burr in and out of bed with a sling, watched Jason cut up lines of coke for the guy. It was sad all around, but it gave Jason access to what he wanted. Shannon did, too, and she had something to offer in addition to her meds: an ex-boyfriend who was getting shipments of cocaine in quantity. Befriending people with access to drugs was a way to get closer to the source, and that, Ryan knew, was something Jason always tried to do.

At 1:30 a.m. on September 18, Ryan woke to the sound of his front door busting in. He pushed Sara out of bed and to the floor. He grabbed his .357 and yelled out. No answer. Moving through the bedroom with the hammer of the revolver pulled back, Ryan was ready to shoot whoever was out there, and then the hall light went on.

What's going on? Jason said, so out of it he didn't seem to register that Ryan was pointing a gun at his face. Jason practically knee-walked to his room, saying only, sorry, man; so sorry, before going inside and locking the door.

It was two in the morning when Ryan called Jason's boss at Ricoh. Part of him felt like a shit-heel for doing so, but he had to. He laid out Jason's problems for Fred Smith. It took forty-five minutes. Ryan also told Fred that Jason had been using a company credit card to buy things and then returning them at other stores for cash. Fred, who had fired Ryan the year before, told him he had done the right thing by calling, that this was what a real friend does.

Ryan was not sure he could call Jason a friend anymore. The guy had been testing their friendship for years, and though Ryan would not put it this way that day, he would come to think of Jason as the classic profile of the man that puts on a strong front but who needs everyone's admiration and can take zero criticism. Ryan had always known Jason as the guy who constantly handed out his business cards, the guy who tried to be impressive because he needed an identity to hang on to, and that inside, Jason was empty. Sara, who had a master's degree in psychology, would later tell Ryan that the entire time she knew Jason, she never saw him express any emotion but anger, and that nothing seemed to affect him.

It was three in the morning when Ryan got off the phone. He felt guilty about turning Jason in and knew Jason would be pissed if he found out. Ryan also thought he should have done it sooner.

Jason called Ryan two days later to say he was going to rehab. He made it sound as though it was his idea, when Ryan knew Fred Smith had told Jason, go to rehab or get fired. Ryan did not call Jason on this, said only it was a good idea, if not that he had been the one to call their boss.

Jason showed up at Ryan's house later that night. He was driving a pickup truck he had rented with a company credit card. Eldon was with him. Jason was visibly impaired, very high on something. Ryan asked Jason what the hell he was doing. Jason said, dude, I have no money. I don't know. I'm going to rehab tomorrow.

Ryan did not want him in the house, but he also did not want Jason driving. Ryan got in the truck and drove Jason and Eldon to a nearby Motel 6. He took off Eldon's shoes and got him in bed. Eldon, who had just turned four, went right to sleep. Ryan told Jason he had to chill, to get some rest. Jason instead pulled out a bag of coke and said, I can't take this with me. I'm just going to cook it down.

Jason went into the bathroom. He broke a light bulb in half. He put the coke and some baking soda and a little water in the top of the broken bulb. He heated it with a lighter and rolled a penny in the hot liquid. The liquid bonded to the penny and dried to a rock that could be smoked.

Ryan watched Jason make the crack cocaine. He could not stop him. He also could not leave. He called Sara and told her, "He's smoking crack in the bathroom right now." He said he didn't know what he was supposed to do. Call the cops? Grab Eldon and run? Sara told him he could not leave Eldon, which of course Ryan would not do. He stayed as Jason smoked the entire eight ball, until he was nodding out and asking Ryan to drive him to Eugene. Ryan told Jason to sleep it off and that he needed to call him first thing in the morning, that Ryan would need to know that he and Eldon were okay.

Jason did not call Ryan in the morning. Instead he got behind the wheel of the rented Ford F-150 and smashed into the back of a Dodge van parked four blocks from his and Amanda's house in Tualatin. He drove away from the accident. Several people witnessed the hit-and-run and called the police.

By the time Officer Chris Kish caught up with Jason, he was parked on the corner of the house he had not been living in all summer. There was significant damage to the front end of the F-150, primarily on the passenger's side. Officer Kish asked Jason what happened. Jason said that an early 1990s four-door blue Volkswagen had turned into his path and caused the accident. Jason said he chased the Volkswagen for several minutes before he lost sight of it. He further explained that a passenger had jumped out of the vehicle and took off running; he chased the passenger but lost him. Another officer had spoken with witnesses, who said there had been no Volkswagen and no runner, only the F-150 smashing into the van. Its owner had heard the crash from inside his house and, seeing his rear bumper smashed in, followed a trail of debris and leaking fluid to the parked F-150.

Learning this information, Officer Kish asked Jason if he wanted to amend his story. Jason said no and again told him about the blue Volkswagen sideswiping him. Kish inspected the white F-150 and saw no traces of blue paint. He also noted that, according to Jason's story, the damage should have been on the driver's side, whereas all the impact was on the passenger's side. He told Jason the damage to his vehicle did not match the story he was telling. He said there had been a witness to Jason smashing into the parked van. Kish again gave Jason the opportunity to change his story. Jason did not. He said, "I swear on my life and my family that I did not crash into a vehicle."

Officer Kish wrote down that Jason was acting "twitchy" and "became agitated several times" during the conversation. He asked Jason directly why he was not telling the truth. Jason said he was not lying and that another vehicle had crashed into his. At 3:16 p.m. on Sunday, September 21, Jason Smith was arrested for failure to perform the duties of a driver and issued a citation to appear in court.

After not receiving a call in the morning, Ryan started dialing Jason. He finally reached him around six at night. Jason said he was not in rehab yet because something had happened. He told Ryan, dude,

I fucking fell asleep at the wheel, and I fucking crashed into a telephone pole, and I wrecked the truck.

Ryan asked about Eldon.

Eldon was fine, Jason said.

Ryan asked whether Jason had been high at the time of the accident.

Jason said, no, I fell asleep.

Ryan told him, "I don't believe you."

23

In August 2010, I was falling asleep when a text message came through on my phone. Someone was saying he had seen abuse in the Smith household. I took my phone from the nightstand and typed that I'd heard things were pretty fraught.

"Amanda's parents taught her to obey her husband," came the reply. "They claimed it was the Christian thing to do."

My husband rolled over and looked at me with one eye. "Who are you texting with?"

I took my phone to the next room and let the texter know we could talk if he wanted to. He called immediately.

"The first thing I thought when this happened was 'Jason contributed,'" said Isaac LaGrone. "I want to say he's a psychopath."

Isaac's voice sounded thick in his throat, as if he was either coming off a cold, or from emotion. I asked Isaac if he meant Jason's behavior was like that of a sociopath.

"Sociopath, yeah," he said. "You have a best friend for ten years, you spend time with his kids, this happens, and you realize you don't know the guy at all."

That someone would call at nine thirty at night to say Jason was a psychopath or sociopath—each condition is on the antisocial personality disorder spectrum, and the terms are sometimes used interchangeably; I tend to use sociopath—surprised me less than it might have a year earlier, when I did not appreciate that everyone who spoke about the story brought their own considerations, whether personal, ethical, or theological. Some of these people had avoided reporters. In Isaac's case, it was because he expected there would be a trial, at which he assumed he would be legally compelled to testify to what he had seen.

"I was looking forward to a trial," he said. "I wanted all this stuff about him to come out. I'm thinking, 'Don't settle!' But they did."

Isaac told me he first met Jason in late 2001, when he hired him at Ricoh for a two-week temp position. Jason moved up quickly, from mail room to account manager.

"He was good!" Isaac said. "He could sell ice to an Eskimo. He could sell you the dream."

At the time, Amanda was working as a receptionist in downtown Portland, not far from where Jason and Isaac worked. The three sometimes met for lunch near the waterfront; they were all young people with entry-level jobs at big companies.

"He hadn't been working when I [hired him]. She was the breadwinner," Isaac said. "But he made her quit her job, because he was jealous. He was jealous of everyone! She smoked clove cigarettes, and if she'd go outside their house with Ryan [Barron] to smoke one, Jason would say, 'I'm not letting you out there with her!' and he'd go out and stand with them."

Isaac had known Trinity and Eldon since they were born. He loved both kids and, as a bachelor, was happy to eat dinner with the Smith family as often as several nights a week. When Trinity saw him at Eldon's funeral, she ran into his arms.

Isaac said, "She's shouting, 'It's my Uncle Isaac!' and these people are thinking, 'She's got a black uncle?'"

He laughed, the only time he did during this phone call. He had been trying to reach Jason since the funeral, to find out how he was doing, how Trinity was doing. Jason never called back. Isaac at first attributed the cold shoulder to stress. Later, he saw it as another sign that a near-decade-long friendship was a sham, a game Isaac had not known he was playing.

"I'm telling you, the guy is good. He will knock your socks off," he said. "He's like a pimp."

Like a pimp?

Isaac repeated, "He's like a pimp."

I thought Isaac was using the terms "pimp" and "psychopath" synonymously to indicate a person who could make you believe what he wanted you to believe, who could "sell you the dream," when really you were fulfilling his dreams, his needs.

Soon after Isaac called, I went to a Volkswagen dealership to buy a new car. After choosing a model, I walked into the office of the man who would arrange the financing. Mario was tall, with strong features in a large face. He sat behind his desk, tapping at his computer and speaking to me in an engaged and relaxed manner. He occasionally directed a comment to my husband, seated farther away by the office door. Soon after he asked what I did for a living, Mario admitted to being a newshound himself, to reading *The Economist* online every morning in German. I was impressed and turned to nod at my husband, whose expression was less enthusiastic. As Mario typed up my lease, we spoke in friendly ways about books and our shared lineage—he mentioned that he, too, was part Greek. After he offered tips about his favorite happy-hour spots and told me he was deeply interested in reading an interview I'd done with serial killer John Wayne Gacy, Mario said I could come back tomorrow to grab a copy of the paperwork, which I had signed.

"Wasn't he an interesting guy?" I commented to my husband as we walked to my new car. Din had no particular reply.

Before I went to the dealership the next day, I rummaged around the basement for a hard copy of the Gacy article. I could have brought

Mario the text-only, which I had on a file on my computer, but I wanted him to see the images. I only had two copies but decided to give him one; I could always get it back later.

I drove to the dealership to find Mario again at his desk. I told him I had brought him the article, and he looked at me as though he had never seen me before in his life. He told me I could get my paperwork at the front desk. I left him the article, certain that by the end of the day it would be in the trash. And when I read my lease, the rate was not what Mario had quoted, or maybe it was; I had not been paying close attention. I felt humiliated, though here also was proof: you can write about sociopaths, you can read all about them, and chances are you will not recognize one when he is taking you in. And while it is the case that my husband is harder to fool than most people, Mario did not that day target him. Also, there is no online edition of *The Economist* in German.

I wondered, after being taken in by Mario, if sociopaths played long games or only short ones, where they got a quick hit off your shame. I knew about the superficial charm of the sociopath, the stories that rarely checked out, the unwillingness to admit wrongdoing. Not every sociopath is a killer—most are not—but they are all to a degree out to con others, taking genuine pleasure in getting one over on the rest of us dupes, saddled as we are by emotions and a conscience.

"Psychopaths take great personal pride in their deceptions and extract tremendous joy from them," Dave Cullen wrote in *Columbine*, his exploration of the Columbine massacre and shooters Dylan Klebold and Eric Harris, the latter a textbook sociopath. "He's not just conning you with a scheme, he's conning you with his life. His entire personality is a fabrication, with the purpose of deceiving suckers like you."

We become grist for the sociopath's mill, in other words; we become his fuel. Dr. Hervey Cleckley, in his seminal work on the psychopathic personality, *The Mask of Sanity*, posited that what sociopaths lack is "soul quality." Another work I came across called sociopaths "soul eaters or Psychophagic." Reading this, I pictured Goya's painting *Saturn*

Devouring His Son and considered the idea that sociopaths must feed on others because they lack souls of their own.

"Psychopaths tend to see any social exchange as a 'feeding opportunity,' a contest or a test of wills in which there can be only one winner," wrote Robert D. Hare, PhD, in *Without Conscience: The Disturbing World of the Psychopaths Among Us.* "Their motives are to manipulate and take, ruthlessly and without remorse."

Contrary to a crop of recent books that claimed such qualities make for successful CEOs, consuming the faith, time, love, and money of others, however essential to the sociopath, proves thin gruel.

"Why are all sociopaths not in positions of great power?" Dr. Martha Stout asks in her bestselling book, *The Sociopath Next Door.* "Why do they not win all the time? For they do not. Instead, most of them are obscure people, and limited to dominating their young children, or a depressed spouse, or perhaps a few employees or coworkers. Not an insignificant number of them are in jail. . . . They can rob and torment us temporarily, yes, but they are, in effect, failed lives."

I had started out determined to learn about Amanda, but as more people contacted me wanting to talk, it was Jason they wished to talk about.

Isaac had denied interview requests from the press immediately after the kids were dropped from the bridge. He had been a solid friend of Jason's for eight years, and he was not going to go blabbing just because someone wanted to stick a microphone in his face. It had also been a confusing time. There was no playbook that tells a person how to act when your best friend's wife murders their child, and so Isaac figured he would take Jason's lead. Whatever Jason needed to get through this awful time, and whatever would be best for Trinity, Isaac would do. But he never heard from Jason after Eldon's murder, and now, fifteen months later, questions had rushed into the void.

Three days after our initial conversation, Isaac and I sat in my back-yard on what would prove to be the hottest day of the year in Portland. Isaac had a dome-shaped head he kept shaved, small ears, eyes with half-moon lids, and a wide gap between his front teeth. He was heavyset and borderline diabetic, and he'd brought his own Diet Pepsis to drink. He drank a lot of them as we sweated through the afternoon.

"He's the only person to this day that I've ever been with that can pull the wool over my eyes, you know?" he said of Jason. "I still don't see how he did it. I was so mad at myself. I was like, man, how can you be that stupid?"

Isaac should not have been an easy person to fool. Raised mostly by his grandmother in a rough section of northeast Portland, he had grown up around gang activity and drugs but had never been in any real trouble himself. He was thirty-five now and had spent his entire career at Ricoh, where he'd started not long before Jason in 2001.

"One of the first things he told me was, 'You gotta see my wife; she's beautiful. She's Filipino, blah, blah, blah,'" Isaac said.

Jason almost immediately invited Isaac to the couple's home for dinner. Isaac was impressed with Amanda's cooking. She made Thai food, tacos, and the best biscuits and gravy he had ever eaten. He appreciated the homemade meals. He appreciated, too, Jason's honesty about some troubles he'd had.

"He told me that he blew through the money," Isaac said of the stock Jason had inherited. "He told me, 'Man, I used to have [drug] problems, really potent,' but he never went into specifics."

Isaac noticed small elisions, like Jason claiming he'd be late for work because he had a meeting when Isaac had Jason's schedule on his com-puter and knew there was no meeting. But friends cover for each other. Isaac understood how Jason might need to cut corners after Trinity and then Eldon were born, considering Amanda's chronic overdrawing of their bank account.

"He would have to borrow money from me to get the account caught up—and then she would do it again," Isaac said. Her spending and her refusal to get a job, Jason said, were the reasons they could never catch up financially. Jason mentioned, too, how this was putting a strain on his relationship with his mother. She was always loaning them money and had also bought the family a minivan, a Honda Odyssey.

What did Isaac know about the cost of raising kids? Nothing, so he believed his friend, though he did not see how Jason's own spending habits were helping.

"You'd think people with financial problems would do things to make them better. He was doing the opposite," Isaac said, recalling Jason's obsession with expensive food, how he would only buy "the freshest cuts of beef."

Isaac was cool with things not quite adding up. He believed in having his buddy's back. Jason had a friendly wife and fun little kids who liked having Isaac around. Isaac was at the Smith home for dinner, he reminded me, "at least twice a week, with the whole family."

"I love Trinity; that was my buddy," he said. Isaac loved the way Eldon spoke, mispronouncing words the way three- and four-year-olds will, including the name of the Nerds candies Isaac used to bring him, asking as soon as Isaac came through the door, "Do you have any *nuuuwhds*?"

"Yup, that was my boy," Isaac said. "Every time I come over, he'd run to the door, 'Uncle Isaac's here!' Then we'd go to the store and run off from Jason. I'd push him in the cart through the store. Jason's like, 'Dude, what are you guys doing?' We'd kind of ignore him. It was really weird, but I never got the . . ."

Sweat was running down Isaac's head. "I just never got that father-son relationship, that 'I'm glad to have a son,'" he said. "He was always like, 'Eldon, don't do this' and 'Eldon, don't do that. You're not listening! Go to your room!' . . . Once Eldon was gone, he spoke passionately about him, but he never did when he was around. I mean, I'd be stoked to have a son, but he wasn't."

I mentioned that in court Jason had said of Eldon, "I would whisper in his ear, he was my favorite person in the world."

"That is not true. That's not true at all," Isaac said. "I think that's what he really feels guilty about, that he didn't use his time wisely with Eldon."

While Isaac liked being made to feel part of the Smith family, there were times when he felt uncomfortable, or as though he had misread situations. For instance, Jason would make Gavin eat hot peppers, telling Isaac it was "a running joke" he had with the boy, who to Isaac looked "afraid of [Jason], kind of jumpy." Jason told Isaac that Amanda was not disciplining the kids and this was why he needed to be hard on them.

"He even had me snowballed," Isaac said. "Like, if he didn't rule with an iron fist, there was chaos in his house."

Isaac attributed Amanda's attempts to be an obedient wife to what he saw of her parents.

"I don't want to say brainwashed, but then, I do want to; some religious people are brainwashed," he said. "Her dad didn't even know me and says, 'Isaac, you need the Lord in your life.' My dad's a pastor, and I go, 'Yeah, I'm a Bible child. I know all about religion and right now I'm not choosing to go that route.' So that's how he was. And the mom, ironically, the one time I met her, her and Jason was having a fight because Jason wouldn't let her see Gavin. He said that she was butting in their business all the time, so they got into a shouting match, 'I'm going to see my grandchild and you can't stop me!' What I thought was really weird was, if I am telling you that you can't see your grandchild, and you're not the parent, that's the first bullet that's coming out of my gun. She didn't! Which I thought was really weird. You're a stepparent? I go over your head. . . . But she didn't. She accepted that [the decision would be Jason's]."

Isaac knew of one time Amanda went over Jason's head. Isaac graduated from Portland State University in 2005, after taking classes on and off for twelve years. When Amanda congratulated him, he told her getting the degree had been a struggle.

"I'm not the smartest guy around. Like Jason, who did it in four years," he said. "She goes, 'Isaac, Jason didn't graduate from college—and if your job knew that, he'd be in a lot of trouble.' I said, 'Yeah, he would.' He told me he graduated in 1997."

This lie ate at Isaac. He sought out a University of Oregon 1997 graduation program. Jason was not on it. Isaac asked me in the backyard if I knew whether Jason graduated from the school in 1997, or any year. According to the National Student Clearinghouse, which provides degree verifications for most postsecondary institutions in the United States, Jason Frederick Smith did not graduate from the University of Oregon, nor is there record of his having attended classes there.

In March 2005, Ricoh transferred Jason to Hawaii in order to oversee the mail room needs of the Kamehameha School District. Isaac did not know much about what happened to the Smith family on Oahu, other than that Jason continued to occasionally borrow money from Isaac and, despite his sometimes-spotty work attendance, proved to be a prized employee.

"We lost a major account when he was no longer around," said Isaac. "They preferred to work with him."

When the family returned to Portland, Isaac was again a frequent dinner guest. The kids, he said, were "always well behaved." Jason and Amanda, not so much.

"He was cussing at her, like, 'You're being a bitch. You're being a dumb bitch,'" he said, and that by this time, Amanda had changed. "That's when the drinking really increased. I never knew it was that bad. It was more like she went from more being herself to trying to please, you know what I mean?"

The memory, the way it was now rearranging, looked to pain Isaac. "I just felt like she was going out of her way, like walking on eggshells," he said, and, later, "On *Law & Order*, they would say, this is abused woman syndrome. Because she was. I witnessed it with my own eyes. I never witnessed no physical violence, but it was mental abuse."

As people who live through the same tragedy need to keep telling the story in order to understand what happened, so sometimes do journalists who walk similar beats. This was the case when I interviewed Walter Kirn about his book *Blood Will Out*, the true story of how Kirn was taken in by a sociopath and double murderer who'd for years posed as a philanthropist named Clark Rockefeller, of the Rockefeller dynasty. Kirn had his reasons for communicating with Rockefeller, including believing he had lucked into a good story, before learning the person he was dealing with was a con man and killer whose real name was Christian Gerhartsreiter.

Kirn and I spoke in 2014, in the *Oregonian* newspaper's offices. The paper was about to sell its iconic building, and all of the furniture on the fourth floor was gone but for two chairs my editor helpfully placed there. Kirn and I sat knee to knee and discussed how sociopaths walk among us, how they have jobs and husbands and wives, but that most of the time their lives end badly.

"They tend to overplay their hands, finally," he said.

I agreed. John Wayne Gacy had been executed; other sociopaths I'd written about had torpedoed their careers by piling on lie after lie. Still, resentment can have a long life, and even after the sociopath's death or dishonor, people can remain angry and astonished at their having been taken in, as were some of the people who spoke to me about Amanda and, increasingly, about Jason.

There was not really any way, Kirn and I agreed, to avoid being the target of sociopaths, with their terrible talent to identify and play to whatever is important to a person, to shape-shift into what that person wants to see. We do not assume the motives of others are custom made to fool us, that they will dangle a morsel made of our best morality until we take the bait.

"We project our own humanity onto them," said Kirn. "We keep on in this fantasy that they have some resemblance to us."

Having no fixed identity, or none they think will get them what they want, sociopaths try on masks, emulating qualities others seem to find admirable. Clark Rockefeller rescued sick animals, which made him appear selfless. Gacy dressed as a clown and entertained children in the hospital. Nursing others provided cover for the less admirable things they were up to.

"They do like to take care of sick people and to ostensibly seem to be feeling," Kirn said. "They'll sit there and tell you how devastated they are, and they'll use all the right words, and maybe even emote, but it's overdone or just off in some way. Because emoting is something they are imitating."

This inability to love and to feel joy struck me as deeply sad. To constantly mirror the emotions of others in order to get by must be exhausting, and lonely. And yet it was difficult to muster sympathy when you were the person who's had your soul eaten.

The last time Isaac saw the Smith family was Easter 2009. He brought the kids Easter baskets. He never saw Eldon alive again. He found out about his murder on the news and became frantic. He called Jason, who did not answer. He called Ryan Barron, who was with Jason.

"Jason gets on the phone and says, 'She killed my son.' That's all he said: 'She killed my son,'" said Isaac. "I said, 'I'm so sorry, man.' He just hung up."

Isaac found out about Eldon's memorial in an email sent through Ricoh's corporate offices. He rode down to Eugene with a few people from work. Jason shook his hand at the memorial, but that was it. Trinity ran into his arms.

"She said, 'Don't cry, Uncle Isaac; it's okay,'" Isaac said. "She was a stronger person than I was. I was just bawling as soon as I saw her, I was so heartbroken."

Eldon was laid out in the front of the Eugene Faith Center. Isaac watched Ryan Barron go up and said his final good-byes; Ryan would later say he thought Eldon looked like "a waxed doll." Isaac could not bring himself to go up to the casket, but he could see Eldon there, in his little suit.

Isaac wanted to stand and say a few words at the memorial. He was not given the chance. Of the several hundred mourners, only Jason was permitted to speak.

"He got up and spoke, and it was like his words came out clearly, like he was giving a presentation," Isaac said. "'I'm going to dedicate the rest of my life to my son, blah, blah, blah,' but it wasn't heartfelt. It was kind of like, 'Hey, I'm a Fortune 500 CEO, and this is what we need to do to get our numbers up.' The people I rode to the funeral with, coworkers, were like, 'How the hell did he do that?'"

Isaac and I had been in my yard three hours and were soaked with sweat. He had been exerting himself all this time, trying to work something to the surface.

"I feel hurt by both parties in this, you know?" he said. "I'm hurt that Amanda did this, and I want to say, I'm more hurt by Jason. . . . If I had money to buy a commercial, I would send one out right now to Jason to tell him how unhappy and upset I am."

Isaac made a thick sound in his throat, twice. "But he won't talk to me."

After Amanda was sentenced, people offered information that both confirmed and countered any ideas of revenge. They'd seen horrible things happen to the children, to Jason, and to Amanda, yet had felt stymied to help or had once believed lies they no longer believed. Five people used the word "toxic" to describe Jason and Amanda's marriage. It was as though two elements that should never have been mixed were mixed, with predictably volatile results.

Thomas Parrish spent thirty minutes with the couple before needing to get out.

He and Jason had been friends since fifth grade. They lived a block and a half from each other and went through elementary school, middle school, and high school together. Jason's family was well off; their house was stocked with cookies and chips, which came in handy when the boys became high school stoners. Except, Jason's mom did not play that way; she did not like Jason's friends hanging out. When Thomas heard her coming home, he'd book out the back way and over the fence. That lady was intimidating.

Jason was not intimidating. He was a supergenerous guy, and loyal, too. He and Thomas and their friends called themselves the Trooper Posse, after the Isuzu Trooper they used to ride in. The posse was mostly African American at a time when Eugene was 90 percent white and 1 percent black, as Thomas was. Some students at Sheldon High School at the time were tagging lockers "SFP"—Students for Prejudice. There were fistfights, and people were getting suspended; it would have been easy for Jason to hang with his more usual clique, mostly rich white kids whose families had been in Eugene a few generations, but he stuck tight with his new crew. He lived kind of a charmed life, played on the football team, dated the most beautiful girls, including Keli Townsend, and treated his friends to fancy lunches at bistro Marché when most kids from Sheldon High were headed to McDonald's. Even as a young guy, Jason liked nice things; he dressed well and carried Visine and cologne so he would not look or smell like the weed he'd been smoking.

Thomas knew Jason was troubled underneath. Jason was a year younger than most of the other guys in the posse, and when the rest of them graduated in 1992, Thomas saw Jason get quiet, saw him get depressed. He did not want to do anything but get high, which was okay when they were fifteen or sixteen. But now it was time to move on, and Jason didn't. Thomas thought Jason was somewhat beaten down by his mom. She favored Jason's younger brother, who had something like a 4.5 GPA and could speak Japanese. Jason had to compete with that, and he couldn't.

Thomas did not think Jason had graduated high school by the time he was renting a room at the Campbell Club, a co-op on the University of Oregon campus, not as a student, just as a place to live during one of the times his mom kicked him out. He was overindulging at this point, smoking a lot of pot and probably doing other drugs. Thomas stopped by one time and found Jason in a state of extreme paranoia, saying he had not left the room in days. In the closet were mason jars filled with pee; Jason was apparently too freaked to use the communal bathrooms down the hall.

By 2000, Jason had moved up to Portland to be with his new girlfriend, Amanda. Thomas drove up to spend the night with them, and Jason answered the door with a black eye. He was hesitant to talk about it but eventually told Thomas that Amanda had clocked him. She and Jason argued the whole time Thomas was at their place. Thomas couldn't take it and left after about a half hour, telling Jason, "This is not a good situation for you."

He and Jason made a plan on their own to camp out at the three-day Sierra Nevada World Music Festival in June. The drive from Eugene to Marysville, California, took seven hours. Jason was on the phone the whole time, arguing with Amanda. After setting up camp, Thomas went off to check out some acts. When he got back to the campsite, Amanda was sitting in his lawn chair. She had flown from Portland to Sacramento and taken a forty-mile cab ride to Marysville. It was obviously she wanted to be the center of Jason's attention, that she did not want him hanging out with his friends. To fly all that way and spend a couple of hundred dollars on a cab—who did that? Thomas left the couple arguing. When he returned, Amanda was gone.

That relationship, as far as Thomas was concerned, never got better. He thought Amanda was a bad mother to Gavin. They all went out to sushi one time and she was goading him, telling him he wouldn't get some toy or something if he didn't eat his sushi. Thomas watched Gavin put piece after piece in his mouth, trying to do what his mom wanted, but Thomas knew this was not going to be good. And sure enough, Gavin spat it all out on their $200 sushi platter, whereupon Amanda grabbed him and left the restaurant. Thomas was embarrassed for Jason, though he was not doing a sterling job with Gavin, either. Jason was rough on the boy—nothing physical as far as Thomas saw—but Jason talked to him in a belittling way, really harsh, and the kid was like four.

After a few of these incidents, Thomas no longer wanted to hang out with Jason and Amanda. It was too uncomfortable. He had a lot of love for the guy, but that situation was ugly. He never knew what was going to happen, if someone was going to start throwing knives or plates, if someone was going to go crazy.

Thomas did not have any contact with Jason for almost a decade. Thomas had kids of his own, troubles of his own, including doing a stretch on a domestic violence IV charge. Thomas was in jail when Amanda dropped the kids off the bridge and did not speak with Jason afterward, not more than a few Facebook messages, Thomas asking Jason how he was doing and Jason just saying good. He and Keli were back together. Thomas was glad to hear it. Jason deserved some happiness after what Amanda had done. Thomas knew Jason was not a perfect guy, but he did not see anything his friend could have done that would have pushed Amanda into doing what she did. If she had been having troubles and thought about hurting the kids, she could have left them at a fire station, or a police station, or with neighbors. She could have been upset about her husband leaving and dealt with it.

24

I picked Isaac up from his office near Portland's waterfront. It was a crap day, raining and cold.

"Jason will need a fresh pair of underwear," Isaac said as we made the three-minute drive over the river to the east side.

"Look, there's the boat." Isaac pointed at the Portland Fire Bureau's new high-speed rescue boat, which at 2:00 p.m. would be christened the *Eldon Trinity*.

We parked near the news trucks. A public relations woman standing beneath an umbrella handed out pamphlets: The 35-foot boat cost $400,000. Its top speed was 45 mph. It had a night-vision camera and 120-foot floodlights for night rescues, and its design specifications were ideal for rough-water rescues.

The doors to Portland Fire Station 21 were rolled up to make room for the maybe eighty people inside, including officials talking to reporters, firefighters in full uniform, and a cameraman setting up mics in anticipation of hearing from people here today about what had happened downriver 563 days ago.

City Commissioner Randy Leonard, Portland's former fire chief, said he had pushed the city council to fund the boat.

"I authorized a review of all the incidents in the core area downtown, to find out how we are responding to less notorious incidents," he told me as I watched Jason's family arrive.

"Such as, there are people that consistently and on a fairly regular basis jump off the bridges intentionally," Leonard went on. "And what we discovered was a consistent pattern of overly long responses on the river. . . . We didn't want to react to one incident and do this. We didn't really understand the need existed until this happened."

Less notorious incidents on the Willamette—rowing accidents, kayakers flipping, the very occasional person jumping from a bridge—passed quickly from the news cycle, if they made mention at all. None, as far as I knew, had been influential in moving the city to fund a new rescue vehicle.

In his bid to get a yes vote on the boat, it had been Leonard who told his fellow commissioners, "As I listened to the 911 tapes, I could hear the little girl screaming, 'Don't, Mommy, don't.'" There was no tape of Trinity screaming this; the first 911 recordings have her calling for help when she is in the water. Still, it might have been an innocent enough mistake. The audio had been poor. As Leonard strained to hear what was on the tape, perhaps he was hearing a child fighting off her mother, a child fighting for her life. Leonard would later tell me he had leaned into the recording and listened to the screams over and over, that they had been very hard to hear.

When I asked him at the boat dedication whether he had met Trinity, he replied, "I have not. Fire bureau members have been dealing with her."

Jason's stepmother, Kim Smith, motioned me over. She held both my hands.

"Can I ask you something personal?" she said. "Have you spoken with Amanda yet?"

Jason and Trinity arrived. He was holding her hand. He wore the cantaloupe-colored tie, a white dress shirt, no jacket, and a baseball cap with the Ralph Lauren Polo insignia. Trinity had on a little girl's velvet party dress, white tights, black Mary Janes, and a white headband. She was tear stained, her cheeks flushed. Jason kept an arm around her and stroked her hair as officials stepped to the lectern and said, variously, that today they honored "the memory of Eldon, who perished in the waters of the Willamette," and Trinity, "who's shown, at such a young age, that she is a hero and that she will grow up to be a strong and courageous woman."

The speeches were part of the protocol and heartfelt, but they were not what most people had come for. They had come to see Trinity, who looked from her father to the crowd with deep apprehension. Jason remained solicitous; he looked to be comforting her. The cameraman had to make an adjustment, and Jason and Trinity needed to step away from the lectern. The only place for them to go was into the fray of Amanda's family. The crowd had no reason to think the families were not here today in unity. This is what the speeches were about. The crowd did not hear Jason say to Amanda's grandmother that Trinity was crying because she was scared of her. They saw Jason carry Trinity back to the lectern and stand her on a box.

"My daughter, Trinity, would like to say a few words," he said. "Here, honey."

Trinity leaned into the microphone. Her voice was so soft as to be inaudible. I had to watch that night's newscast, where the boat dedication was the lead story, to hear what she said.

"I'm here to feel my brother's, my little brother's love. And I'm here to honor him because I miss him so much," Trinity said. "My whole entire family is here to come onto the boat that the firemen have got for us. Friends and family are all here for me, and I think it's great that you guys all get to be here for me."

The room applauded. Jason took the mic.

"I've said from the first moment this all happened that I truly believe my daughter is a superhero. I think you can see why," he said. "She truly is a testament to the human spirit, and it is absolutely amazing to see her here today in front of all of you, dedicating this boat after the horrible ordeal that she and my son went through that dark night on the bridge."

Jason's voice was rich, reassuring. We could easily hear it over the click and whir of the cameras.

"I just want to thank the city of Portland, the fire department, the police department, everyone who has been a part of making this happen," he continued. "Out of tragedy has been born an opportunity to save many, many lives for years to come. In the name of my son [and] my daughter, we just only hope that just one life can be saved, let alone hopefully many more for years to come. This tragedy has affected us all in ways that we can't even begin to explain, but at the same time, it's brought us together as a family."

A baby started crying in the back of the crowd.

"It's brought out the resiliency, and how wonderful and beautiful and strong and amazing a little girl can be. My daughter beside me, she truly is the most wonderful person in the world, as you can all see."

Trinity, who had been fighting tears, looked past her father's shoulder. She mouthed, *mom-my, mom-my, mom-my.* She was looking at Keli Townsend.

"You come and you expect in a sense to see someone who . . . um, doesn't in any way reflect the state that she's truly doing better than we ever could have hoped," he said. "Every day is full of happiness and joy, and her life is full, with school and Girl Scouts and all that good stuff."

Jason leaned toward Trinity and chucked her under the chin, tried to get her to smile. She did not smile.

"I love you, sweetheart," he said. "I want to thank you for being here and being so strong."

As the room applauded, as the baby screamed full bore, Trinity walked quickly from the lectern and buried her face in Keli's waist.

When I was Trinity's age, my father told me something, a realization he had come to when he became a father. He said, "I could have taught you and your brother that 'yellow' was called 'red' and you would have believed me."

My father told me this story more than once, not because he wanted lauding for not having tricked little children, but as an example of how power might be misused.

Power was being misused today. Randy Leonard had, if unintentionally, dissembled about hearing a 911 tape when asking for votes for the boat. Jason spoke of how tragedy brought the family together when the families had never been further apart. And he spoke of how full of joy his daughter was as we watched Trinity look as miserable as I have seen a child look. There was disconnection here. There was whitewash.

Amanda's immediate family—her father; her sister, Chantel; her brother-in-law, Daryl Gardner; their three children; her grandmother, Jackie Dreiling; her son, Gavin Beck; and his stepmother, Chelsea—watched Trinity cry into Keli's waist. They stood close enough to touch her. Trinity had not seen most of them since the incident. When she told the crowd, "my whole entire family is here to come onto the boat," she might have expected this to be the case. Or maybe this part of the entire family had been scrubbed from her mind; we could not know. Those in attendance may not have noticed that when Trinity saw her mother's family she stopped crying. It was at this moment that Keli told Jackie Dreiling, a woman to whom she had never spoken or been acquainted, "Leave."

What stories had Keli been told that she felt it prudent to order a seventy-eight-year-old woman to leave? Was this a stupid question? What more beyond what Amanda had done did Keli need to know? Who had Trinity run to for comfort? Amanda's family was superfluous, if not guilty by association. If Jackie had considered saying something sharp to Keli in return, if Daryl had wanted to slug his former brother-in-law for saying Daryl's wife was the reason Trinity was crying, there was no way to do so. The cameras were rolling.

Gavin kept his eyes on Trinity. He had given some thought to what he would put in the gift bag for his sister. Inside was a small blanket made for her by a Christian organization, a poem he had written and framed, and a photo of himself. He would get the bag to Trinity if he had the chance. He had the chance. He reached past Keli to Trinity and said, "I love you." Trinity grabbed the bag.

As the cameras recorded the event, Amanda's mother, Kathy Stott, sat in the family's parked car, out of sight of the news trucks. She was afraid, she had told her mother, Jackie, of what Jason would do if he saw her, afraid the day would become more difficult for Trinity than it was bound to be. Maybe she was telling herself, as she sat alone in the car, that not seeing her grandchild was part of the penance to be paid for what her own daughter had done.

I did not think Amanda had any idea what she had set in motion or, perhaps more precisely, kept in motion and pushed through to a devastating end. Which was not an end. There was no end; the long-term stress the families endured would gain and lose strength as it jumped hosts. It would make and break alliances and transform into a rescue boat that saved the lives of others.

With the talking part of the dedication over, the crowd exited the firehouse, past a man standing just inside the roll-up door. He might have been thirty. His cheeks were drawn and his clothes looked as though he had been sleeping outside. He was leaning on the handles of a baby stroller. A baby too young to sit upright was curled in the seat. I thought this must have been the baby we heard screaming, and that the man might have wandered over from a nearby homeless encampment. Suzanne Townsend, Jason's mother-in-law, found the man's presence odd and asked Jason who the man was. Jason told her he had worked with the man at Ricoh.

People made for the dock ramp, which had been given a fresh coat of white paint. The press took more photos. Other vessels pulled behind the *Eldon Trinity*. A fireboat blared its horn and shot six arcs of water forty feet in the air, cascades in blue, pink, and clear. Cars on the nearby Morrison and Hawthorne Bridges blew their horns. People said "Ohhhh!" the way they do when watching fireworks, creating new reasons why we were here, trying to get ahead of the original reason. They wanted to impress upon a little girl who had almost died in the river that other things happen on the river. The loss could not be compensated for, but look: there was a red ribbon on a boat with her name on it.

Amanda's family did not walk to the boat, onto which they had not been invited. They watched from a nearby overlook. If they were moved by the chorus of ship horns, shutter-flies, and helicopter blades whipping the air, they did not show it.

Two boats were preparing to leave. The *Eldon Trinity*, which was not designed with river cruising in mind, had limited capacity for passengers and would carry a few members of the Smith family and several Portland officials. A press boat would follow. I was not planning on boarding either boat. Randy Leonard was on the dock with Keli Townsend. She was dressed glamorously, in a pencil skirt and high heels. Her champagne-blond hair looked no worse for the rain. The wind made it hard to hear what she was shouting to Leonard as she jabbed a finger toward me. The commissioner looked confused: Was Keli saying she did not want the reporter, who had just interviewed him, on the boat?

Isaac came up behind me. I told him I was not getting on the *Eldon Trinity*; that much had been made clear.

"To hell with them," he said, and walked up to the boat. Trinity saw him. She shouted something that turned out to be, "Uncle Isaac! Get on the boat!" Isaac stepped on, and the boat motored south.

The second part of today's ceremony would be held on the spot in the river where Trinity was rescued and Eldon was found drowned.

This part of the event had not been explained to the crowd, and it was unclear whether the people who remained onshore knew what was going on. Amanda's family stayed on the overlook and, when the boat was not back in an hour, drifted back to their cars. Chelsea and Gavin remained. He sat alone on a bench, staring in the direction of the rescue boat, which was long out of view. I sat next to him. The hood of his snowboarding jacket hid his face. I asked whether he'd had a chance to speak to his sister. He kept looking at the river. He gave the impression, not unusual for a thirteen-year-old boy, that he might prefer to never talk again. He turned and looked at me for maybe ten seconds, then said only, "Yes."

Everyone else who had stayed ashore was in the firehouse. The homeless man with the baby was still there. Suzanne Townsend and Christine Duncan were there. They were attractive women of around seventy. Their clothes marked them as women of some means. Suzanne, especially, was striking; she looked like a prettier version of the actress Colleen Dewhurst, with something steely about her. I could picture her shooting rattlesnakes. The women had known each other for decades and today formed a natural bulwark, gracious but unyielding as they avoided speaking with me beyond a few pleasantries. But they laughed together. Seeing that the boat was not yet returning, they staged a mock duel with their closed umbrellas.

"The latest dispatch we got is, they're at the Sellwood Bridge and waiting there," the PR woman said. "The press boat hasn't gotten there yet."

The *Eldon Trinity* returned almost ninety minutes after it left. Those onboard were knotted in the wheelhouse, out of the weather. I would later hear criticism regarding keeping Trinity in the cold so long, for making her wait in the spot where she'd almost died in order that the press might get their photos. But as she walked up the ramp, she was beaming.

Gavin was at the top of the ramp. Chelsea quickly posed the kids for a photo.

Trinity and Gavin. Photo courtesy of Chelsea Beck.

A reporter approached Gavin as Trinity was led away. She wanted to know what had been in the bag he gave his sister. Gavin said nothing.

Isaac watched Trinity disappear into the firehouse, and then he broke for the parking lot.

"That was rough," he said when I caught up with him. "I held it together on the boat, but not now."

Isaac was overcome. I put my hand on his arm. His fleece jacket was soaked.

We were back in the car by 3:43. I blasted the heater as I drove him back to work.

"Trinity invited me on the boat, so that was cool," he said. "We rode down to where the incident occurred at. They pointed out to

Trinity where they found her. She was really curious. I thought maybe it would be too emotional for her . . . They pointed right to where she was, and it was a good ways away, too. She didn't even know how to swim, which is the most miraculous part about it. So like they said, she held on to Eldon."

According to what Trinity had told a social worker during an interview three days after the crime, she had not known Eldon was in the water. She thought he was in the car with their mother. I did not tell Isaac this. It gave him comfort to believe she had tried to save her brother. Maybe she had.

"Yup, she held on to Eldon the whole time," he repeated.

Once on the water, Isaac did not say the things to Jason he'd imagined he would.

"We kept it cordial," he said. Jason told Isaac that he could see Trinity again and that they would stay in touch. Isaac let that tale blow away in the wind.

"We threw some flowers into the water," he said, and Trinity read something she had written for Eldon. "Just like, 'I love you; I miss you; I'll always remember you.' It was pretty sweet," he said. "And then his favorite toy went into the water; she threw that into the water. His favorite Transformer."

Isaac laughed at my suggestion that he'd thrown some Nerds candies in the river.

"No Nerds," he said. "That's all she wanted to talk about on the trip! Was the Nerd song, so we sung that several times."

Isaac sang the Nerds song as I drove him back over the river. He said Trinity had gotten to drive the boat and toot the horn and was told by someone in the fire department that any time she wanted to go on the boat, she was more than welcome to.

"We actually had a blast," Isaac said as I dropped him at his office. "Under the circumstances, we had a good time."

I came home feeling as though I had been in a washing machine with a bunch of rocks. I told Din the day had been sort of a wreck, seeing children split apart, families cast adrift, seeing what Trinity was required to navigate. She had lost her younger brother and was not allowed to see her older brother, her grandparents, or people like Isaac who had been part of her life. The harm that Amanda had done to this child, to all her children, harm that other people were working double time to fix—all of it made me so angry at her.

"It's about time," he said.

Later that night I received a phone call. The caller, whom I had spoken with before, wanted to know if I had noticed "the bummy guy" with the baby at the ceremony. I said I had. The caller said Suzanne Townsend had not been reassured by Jason's explanation of the man being a former coworker. She had approached the man and asked how he knew Jason.

"And he said, 'I met him here in Portland three weeks ago, with Lisa,'" said the caller.

"Who's Lisa?" I asked.

"Exactly."

The cover photo on the next day's paper was of Trinity standing at the back of the rescue boat and staring at the water. Her father had his hand on her head. Commissioner Leonard was at center, smiling for the camera that finally got its shot.

Trinity, Jason, and family aboard the rescue boat, 2010. Photo courtesy of Jamie Francis, The Oregonian.

Within hours of the story going live on the *Oregonian*'s website, Jack Bogdanski, a professor at Lewis & Clark Law School and a popular political blogger, posted the following comment:

"That was really, really creepy. That little girl should have been in school, and she should be allowed to forget her unspeakable nightmare. To wheel her out to support Randy Leonard's fireboat fantasies is nauseating. A fire bureau boat (and the seven harbor pilots that the bureau has on its payroll) wouldn't have made a darn bit of difference in her case."

Disdain at playing politics with one child's murder and another's trauma was inevitable. People would tell stories about what happened on the Sellwood Bridge for as long as they thought the stories useful. The story I was telling myself was that the boat bearing Trinity's and Eldon's names had made a difference. It had taken Trinity back to the death zone, and, as it turned out, she did not want to forget her "unspeakable nightmare."

"She's a strong kid. She's overcome a lot. Just to even show up there. She was *curious*," Isaac had told me. "When [the guy who rescued her said], 'This is where I found her,' she said, 'Where?! Where?!' She was curious and she wanted to know."

She was curious and she wanted to know.

The firehouse dedication, strangers calling her a hero, and what some saw as the deployment of a small child for personal gain caused Trinity visible distress. The spectacle was shallow; it could not mean anything to her because it was not for her. That she would go back on the water and be curious, this was her story. She looked into the abyss and was not afraid.

"I would like to think of this girl as emerging tough and extraordinary, even fearless; knowing that the worst thing that could ever happen to her or any human has already happened," my sister-in-law wrote me in an email. "This may sound corny and optimistic (because it is), but there will be enough people suggesting to this girl that she is broken and doomed to a lifetime of victimhood and therapy. I hope instead she rages!"

25

Fall 2008–Spring 2009, Tualatin and Eugene, Oregon

People working in the yard next door on Southwest Cayuse Court told Amanda that Eldon had sat on the curb crying as Jason was interrogated, handcuffed, and put in the back of the police car following the hit-and-run. Amanda was home now; she would take care of things. She immediately asked God to please not let Jason's work find out he had been under any sort of influence while driving a vehicle rented with the company credit card. Amanda believed in the power of a praying wife, that God had helped her out of previous tough spots and would again.

Amanda had seen her husband sporadically all summer and thought his hitting rock bottom, if this was rock bottom, provided her with opportunity. Maybe now Jason would see they needed each other. Maybe all of them banding together—she as his wife, and Jason's mother, and his employer—would make Jason realize they could have the life she wanted, where he paid the bills and she took care of the children. They had been each other's allies for almost ten years; she had guarded his secrets and moneymaking schemes: selling arrowheads on eBay, selling baseball cards, and buying time with a fake baby.

Amanda could not know how many people Jason told she was pregnant when she was not. He had certainly told some employees at Ricoh; several higher-ups even gave Jason a baby gift. Jason initially told Isaac the "pregnancy" was the result of Amanda having an affair, and that a cousin of hers was raising the baby. Jason later said they had given the baby up for adoption. The adoption story was perhaps recycled from Amanda's past. Regardless of who had been told what, Amanda's credibility among Jason's coworkers had been long eroded.

"We had all heard rumors that his wife was pretty much batshit crazy," wrote someone who worked for Jason, with the caveat that "if anybody would drive a human (clearly beyond mental stability already, and truly sick as she was) crazy enough to flip out so abhorrently, Jason would have been that guy." If Isaac thought Jason was beloved by clients, this coworker saw Jason as "making everybody crazy with being such a smug fuck—the clients hated him and so did both employees and colleagues."

The day after Jason committed the hit-and-run, Amanda got the children to school and arranged for them to be picked up. Then she drove her husband the hundred miles to Eugene. Had the couple been listening to the radio during the drive, they might have followed the deepening subprime mortgage crisis, or learned that *Mad Men* had won its first Emmy the night before, or that the fall equinox was tonight. It is doubtful Amanda and Jason listened to the radio. They had immediate concerns.

Amanda hoped to find a way to check into Serenity Lane, the inpatient rehab facility where Jason would stay for the next several weeks. She wanted to go to rehab because she'd heard the chances of a marriage holding together when only one partner goes through treatment were poor. She thought Jason would want her by his side. She thought, immediately after Jason entered rehab, that her mother-in-law would want the marriage to succeed. Learning how deeply the family was in debt, Christine Duncan paid the household expenses. She gave Amanda gas money so she and the children could make the occasional trip to see Jason. He left rehab in under a month but did not return home. He told Amanda he wanted to do an intensive outpatient program, and that this required he stay in Eugene. Amanda asked if she and the children could rent an apartment nearby. He asked where money for that was going to come from. The plan was for her to stay in the Tualatin house with the children and tell them that Dad was away working.

Amanda thought she did well the first few months. She got the children to school. She took them to church. She kept asking Jason when he was coming home; he kept putting her off. He started taking the children to Eugene for a few days at a time. Amanda did not know why they could not be together as a family. Eldon and Trinity would bring home stories about Daddy and his friend Keli. Amanda accused Jason of becoming involved with his former girlfriend. He told her she was being paranoid, that Keli was an old friend who'd just gone through a bad divorce, and anything Amanda was imagining probably meant she herself was guilty of something.

Amanda did not know that since leaving rehab, Jason had been spending more and more time with Keli. What may have started innocently was becoming something more. Keli suffered from several medical conditions that might have complicated her ability to have children. Jason had children. They could all spend time together, which, as the months went by, led to Eldon telling Amanda how Daddy and Keli had wrestled on the bed, and to Trinity telling her mother that Keli was skinny, way skinnier than Amanda was.

In November, Sara Barron received repeated calls from Amanda telling Sara that she really missed seeing her and Ryan, that the children missed seeing them, and asking if they could come to the Tualatin house for dinner, sort of an early Thanksgiving.

Sara and Ryan had reservations. They had not seen Jason since he'd gone through rehab. Ryan knew Jason was now involved with Keli Townsend and that this was the reason Ryan no longer heard from Jason, that he had found a new host. Ryan had concerns about this. He thought Keli's medical issues probably meant she had unlimited access to pills. He hoped this would not prove a temptation for Jason, who had called Ryan to say rehab had worked and he was now clean. Ryan saw no reason to broach the subject of relapse when he called Jason to ask whether he was cool with Ryan and Sara going to Amanda's for dinner. Jason said anything that allowed them to have contact with the kids was a good thing.

Sara and Ryan were a bit disoriented by the condition of the Tualatin home: everything was tidy and clean. Amanda was cheerful and sober. It was as though the household had been put through the normalizer. Sara and Ryan tried to go with it. They'd brought appetizers and sparkling juice and cheese. They sat with Amanda and made small talk, but something was off. Sara saw it especially. It was as though Amanda had been putting on a show. She had her script, which seemed to be, "This is us, and I haven't been drinking, and the kids are going to school. We are doing wonderfully, and it would be nice if you guys would tell Jason how great we are doing, because I think he is talking about staying in Eugene and that is really going to break our hearts."

Sara was sure the purpose of the dinner was for her and Ryan to give Jason the message that the home life he had left was worth going back to. Sara told Amanda it was great to see that things were working out, and that she was happy to know Amanda was not drinking. The evening went well for about forty-five minutes, and then Amanda cracked open the first bottle of wine. That was how long she was able to hold it together. The dinner she meant to cook never got cooked.

Sara and Ryan fed the kids Brie and crackers until he left to buy them all some real food.

Ryan drove two miles to Lee's Kitchen, thinking, this was it: Amanda had finally retreated to the alternate world inside her head. It had been bad enough in Hawaii, where Ryan had been stranded, watching TV as Amanda roved around the house, sometimes after a breakfast of vodka and chili peppers, saying things like, I think rainbows are a way to attract happy people to the same area so that they can meet each other and be happy together. Then she'd start rearranging the furniture or taking everything out of the kitchen cabinets and putting it all back in. It was all movement, no logic; it was Looney-freaking-Tunes as far as Ryan was concerned, and then Jason would get home from work and a whole different cycle of craziness would begin. Jason would start in on what Amanda was wearing. In Hawaii, she was so skinny none of her clothes fit. She'd have on a tank top and a pair of shorts, and Ryan could see everything because her clothes hung off her so much. It was made worse by Jason yelling that she looked like a homeless person and that she was embarrassing him in front of his friends. He'd call Amanda a fucking idiot and kick over the garbage can and say, that's fucking bullshit. I'm working all the time, and all you have to do is clean this bathroom, and it looks like shit. Ryan thought Jason yelled like this partly for his benefit, that Jason would pump up the anger when someone else was around to see it.

Just like Amanda was putting on a show tonight. What was it with these two? Ryan could not know what they were like when they were alone. Jason had told him there was no sex in the marriage, not for years. No surprise there. Ryan could see there was no love, no affection; he couldn't even tell that they liked each other. It was more as though they were roommates who had these kids that were just a terrible inconvenience in their lives.

Ryan got back to the house with two big bags of Chinese takeout. The kids dug into the food; they ate and ate and ate.

***

For the Thanksgiving holiday, Amanda and the children went to Southern California with Jason and his mother to spend time with Christine Duncan's family, as they had done in previous years. For the first time, Amanda was put in a hotel room alone with Gavin, while Jason shared a room with Eldon and Trinity. Amanda continued to think her husband was being unfaithful to her. Christine Duncan said Keli Townsend was an old family friend and that was all there was to it.

In December, Jason told Amanda that Eldon and Trinity would have Christmas with him and his mother in Eugene. Because Gavin would be spending the holiday with his father, Amanda would be without any of her children at Christmas for the first time since Gavin was born.

An arctic blast moved through the Pacific Northwest in late December 2008, dumping nineteen inches of snow by Christmas Eve. The city of Portland was not prepared. Buses became stuck and sat in the street for days. Wind blew traffic lights sideways, lights no one needed to heed because motorists were told to keep off the roads. Amanda decided to drive to Eugene anyway. The drive south on I-5 would have been difficult, and without knowing how, she cut her hand. Jason met her at the front door of his mother's home. He told her she was not welcome to come in. Amanda asked to use the bathroom to wash the blood off her hand. Jason's mother allowed her to do so. Christine Duncan called Amanda's mother and complained about her daughter showing up uninvited. Amanda spent the night in her car across from the house, watching her children celebrate Christmas.

When Amanda first met Jason, she believed that she was or would become a good mother, a good wife, that she was beautiful and desirable and smart enough to work with her husband-to-be's changeable sense of the truth, with his drug habits as well as her own drinking and pot smoking. As 2008 turned to 2009, most or all of these things had failed to be true. Amanda had lost one identity after another. Whether Jason was deliberately robbing her of these could not be established to everyone's satisfaction. It also did not matter. Amanda felt robbed of them and humiliated. She had mishandled or lost every identity she had once assumed was hers. She had thought herself shrewd for marrying Jason, and that was being proved to be very far from the truth. A slow diminution was near complete. Just as her children were almost wholly out of her grasp, so too was her sense of self.

Photos taken of Eldon and Trinity at Christmastime reflect none of the tumult of their recent lives. The children show off a house they built from Legos; Trinity is smiling a goofy smile, and Eldon is looking directly into the camera. The baby fat in his cheeks is gone, and his chin is defined. He has the face and countenance that make people say to boys his age, "What a young man you are turning into. How old are you now, son?" Eldon was four years old. He was four years old in a photo taken with his dad, the two of them together in an oversize chair, Jason's arm relaxed around his son's shoulders, Eldon resting his hand in his father's lap.

Trinity turned seven in March 2009. In the pictures, she and Eldon gaze at a tall cake with fluffy white frosting and her name in script on the top. It had been a busy fall for the children, a busy spring; there were new schools and new friends, a new place to live with their dad in Eugene, and a new place to play out at Keli's, where there were dogs and sheep. The children look even older than at Christmastime, Eldon especially, in his collared shirt.

They were acting older, too. Trinity decided in the spring she would cut her hair and donate it to Locks of Love. She wanted to grow it to the ground, but Keli convinced her that her waist would do. At the hairdresser's, Trinity wears a smock imprinted with dogs and houses and holds the cut lock of hair. It was long and shining, the bottom lighter than the top; like Eldon's, her hair turned blond in the sun, but most of her hair was darker now, almost as dark as her mother's.

In a last photo of them together, Trinity is sitting in her mother's lap. Amanda is holding her daughter tightly around the waist, resting her chin in the crook of Trinity's neck. Amanda is smiling. Trinity is smiling, too, but there was a little "eek!" in it, the anticipation of her first professional cut; until now, only her mother had cut Trinity's hair. After the haircut, there is a photo of Trinity looking pleased, looking thoughtful, as though she knows she has taken a step into grown-up land.

26

Chelsea Beck said Amanda's grandmother wanted to speak with me, and that I was to approach her at the boat dedication. I did, introducing myself as Nancy.

"Rommelmann?" Jackie Dreiling said. She had a deep nasal voice and a frown that turned her chin into a pad of crinkles. She was tall, broad-shouldered, and walked with the aid of a gnarled wood staff, which she used that day to get away from me.

"The timing was just bad," she later told Chelsea. "Give Nancy my information."

The week after the dedication, I drove to the home Jackie shared with Amanda's parents. The well-kept one-level ranch had a semicircular driveway set behind an evergreen with a crucifix at the top.

Jackie opened her front door immediately upon my knocking. Her hair had not grayed but yellowed. She had small eyes behind large glasses. She motioned me to the kitchen, where she had plated some muffins. She asked if I wanted coffee. We took the muffins and coffee to her carpeted living room and ignored them. Jackie sat in a recliner across from a TV showing Fox News on mute. I sat on a footstool with a velvety yellow seat that made me think of Miss Muffet's tuffet.

Jackie stared at the TV and told me about her late husband, who had died of a brain tumor thirty years earlier. She and her three children had cared for him at home until his death, leaving Jackie a widow at age forty-nine. During our visits, which would stretch over the next fifteen months, Jackie sometimes rocked her recliner and stared past the sliding glass patio doors and into the garden.

"How do you understand the not understandable and forgive the unforgiveable? I don't know," she said. Family members could not speak with one another about what Amanda had done. But the loss of Eldon, of Trinity, and the damage Amanda did were things Jackie needed to talk about.

She was also looking for information. She wanted to know, for instance, why Keli Townsend had been "nasty" to her at the boat launch. She wanted assurances that Trinity was safe. She wanted it on record that Amanda had deliberately been driven crazy.

"Mandy did it. She's guilty; she's in prison and deserves to be," she said. "But you have to think how she got to that point."

Jackie charted how she thought Amanda got to that point—from adored baby and piano recitals and good grades and love of Christ, to a woman standing on a bridge in the middle of the night throwing her children away.

"She didn't throw them over. She dropped them," she said. "Not that it makes any difference, it's the same result."

Jackie told me she thought Amanda was more shaken by Shane Cook's suicide than she let on. The family had been pleased when Amanda said she would marry the father of her second child; they all liked Shane Cook.

"And she really cared for Shane, but he didn't have any money," Jackie said. "She told me he just wasn't what she wanted. She wanted somebody with money."

Jackie believed Jason had been "waiting in the wings" when Amanda delivered Shane's child. I wondered about the timing and asked Jackie how Amanda and Jason met. She did not know. No one seemed to. Tiffany Gray thought they met at a gym. April Anson said they met when they bought pot from Jason. Isaac said Jason told him that when he first met Amanda, she wasn't interested in him, and that he had won her by "laying on the charm and the money."

Whatever Amanda and Jason's origin story, Amanda herself would later write, "I was close to a person who committed suicide . . . that's another story of my life, one that my husband was part of in a way. He had met the guy, Shane, once." This might provide a chilling image: a young man eager to win the affection of a young woman carrying another man's child, a woman ready to have her affections won. Amanda may well have been grief stricken by Shane's death, but if she met Jason before Shane's suicide, she would not have been in that state of mind yet.

Jackie said she "did not see a lot of Mandy from the time she took up with Jason," and that at her graduation from George Fox, Amanda said a quick hello to her family and left with Jason.

"That was pretty much the end of us," she said. "She hasn't admitted to this since she's been in the facility, but Jason hates all of us, and she was expected to hate us, too. Jason hates everybody. He doesn't come across as a person that hates people, but he does."

It was Jason, she said, who "stole [Amanda's] mind," Jason who ruined Amanda's credit, Jason who insisted he be Gavin's father.

"Mandy tried to give Gavin to Jason, that was her whole *purpose*," she said. "Jason wanted to be a father."

I did not understand why it had been important for Jason to be seen as Gavin's father. Was he giving Amanda what he thought she wanted? Was taking on her child a way to bind her to him? Jackie said it was the other way around: Amanda wanted to stake her position in the Smith family, and Gavin was part of the exchange. Jason did not tell either Ryan or Isaac for years that he was not the boy's biological father, and several times Amanda sought to change Gavin's legal last name from "Stott" to "Smith."

"Of course, it wasn't the issue," Jackie said. "*She* wanted to be a Smith; she wanted Gavin to be a Smith. She wanted to be a part of that family so bad, and she thought she was, and she thought . . ."

Thought they would accept and love her?

"Yes, yes, because they had all that money," she said, money Amanda continued to believe would be coming to her.

"She sat here in my living room after Jason was gone, and she's telling Daryl and I, [she's] describing the motor home she and Jason were going to get someday—it was a million dollars," Jackie said. "She was so convinced she was one of them and she was going to get all this, because Jason was going to inherit it all, and Kathy would say to her, 'How many people have to die, Mandy, before it gets down to Jason?'"

Sheriff's Office Classification Summary Report [selected]:

> 5/23/09: Ms. Stott Smith will be a high profile individual for some time. . . . She came into our custody already on SU [suicide] watch. . . . She appeared to be in the "shock" stage and stated several times, she didn't know the answer to the question. She did, however, say she was having Suicidal Thoughts. . . . She did go from one extreme emotion, crying and holding a conversation with self, to calm, cool, and collect. So Ms. Stott Smith definitely has some MH [mental health] issues.

If Amanda and Jason's arrangement contained the seeds of its own destruction, it was easy to see how the couple thought they might prop each other up, might capitalize on the other's attributes, might play to the other's vanities and exploit the other's weak spots. The illusion had not provided much protection. Ryan Barron had seen the welts on Jason's back after Amanda beat him with a hanger. Tiffany Gray noted the strangle line on Amanda's throat. Someone suggested Jason gave himself the black eyes. Who punctured whose tires can never be known.

What is known is that police complaints repeatedly show Amanda and Jason pointing the finger at each other. Having people believe you are a victim is a form of control; it elicits sympathy and concern. Amanda's friends felt sympathy for her when the man whose child she was carrying killed himself. It is doubtful she told them that Shane "just wasn't what she wanted. She wanted somebody with money."

And Jason had money, or at least the illusion of it. While Amanda had evidence that their finances were nearly always in the toilet, there was also the promise of the motor home and the wedding ring of her dreams, which she had never seen but Jason said was locked in a safe place. Amanda had taken these things on faith.

"She was totally devoted to him. She wouldn't say anything bad about him," Jackie said. "She sat there with a cell phone in her hand and said, 'I don't know what to do unless Jason tells me what to do.'"

Jackie was alluding to something I had considered, that Amanda had been gaslighted. The term is from a 1938 play called *Gaslight*, later made into an Alfred Hitchcock movie, wherein Charles Boyer's character isolates his wife, played by Ingrid Bergman, slowly breaks her will, and convinces her that his transgressions are her fault.

"I tried to tell her. I said, 'Mandy, don't you see that Jason is a controlling person?'" Jackie said. "And her response was, 'Oh no, Grandma. I am the one who's a controlling person, not Jason. Jason is a wonderful person.'"

In the months after Jason left, Kathy Stott checked Amanda into the hospital twice for depression, once to an eating disorder clinic. Amanda was either released early from the programs or walked out. Jackie said Amanda did not want to give up her eating disorder, and that Jason would buy her size-two clothes and say, "Fit into that."

"She could throw up the most expensive meal in town," Jackie said, and the only food she saw Amanda consume in the months leading to the bridge was ketchup; that Amanda's car was littered with hundreds of fast-food ketchup packets, which she would suck on as she drove. Amanda was also drinking heavily. Perhaps with the kind eyes of a grandmother, Jackie saw an objective here, as well.

"She was trying to become an alcoholic, because Jason went to that place," she said.

Did she mean Serenity Lane? Yes, Jackie said. Amanda had asked Christine Duncan, whom Jackie called "Chris," to pay for her to enter treatment.

"Chris wasn't going to do *that*," she said. "She probably would tell Jason, 'I'll send you to rehab, but you're going to have to get rid of Mandy.'"

Later, Jackie would further demote Amanda's status in the eyes of the Smiths. "She was the babysitter," she said. "That's what her function was."

By fall 2008, Amanda was no longer performing this function. She was a woman who drank herself into oblivion in front of her children. She was a woman stalking someone she believed to be her husband's lover. She was a woman who, once her house had been emptied of furniture, sat on the floor picking little craft beads out of the carpet.

"Mandy told me one day, she was sitting right where you are talking. I said, 'Mandy, if you would just get yourself together and straighten out, you will get your kids,'" Jackie said. "'It doesn't matter how much money they've got, no court is going to take children away from their mother unless you give them cause to do so.' She said, 'Grandma, no one wins against Jason and Chris.' She truly believed it was going to be however they wanted it to be, and there was nothing she could do about it."

5/27/09: [Stott-Smith] has been very quiet and doing a lot of sleeping. She seems really out of it and still doesn't seem to know what's going on.

5/28/09: Amanda is on Psych Medication and should be considered to be moved off suicide watch.

5/29/09: Inmate Stott-Smith tried to cheek meds, so the meds are being crushed.

6/3/09: Stott-Smith will be on Suicide precautions for the indefinite future. They found comb under her mattress and added cell searches to the plan. Ok to have sanitary napkins but NOT underwear.

Jackie and I were finishing our first visit when Daryl Gardner, who drove a forklift in the warehouse of the paper products company where Mike Stott worked, walked in. He stood in Jackie's kitchen holding his one-year-old son and said he thought the boat dedication had been "a debacle," that Randy Leonard was "an asshole," and apropos of nothing, "Jason stole Vicodin from me when I was living in Mike and Kathy's garage."

I mentioned to Daryl I'd heard about opiates being smuggled from Mexico. He confirmed this. He said Jason came from a "family of enablers."

"Chris has a real track record of buying Jason out of every problem he's ever had," Jackie said, but that there was no reason he should have needed her protection.

"He is perfectly capable of being successful on his own right. He's perfectly smart," she said. "You'd be amazed how charming this guy can be."

Jackie was not charmed. She had seen Jason throw the family Chihuahua over her back fence. She said that Amanda had been "sent off to doctors to get pain pills, which she turned over to him."

April Anson had said that when she bought pot from Jason in 2008, "there was probably a kilo, in jars." Daryl Gardner knew about the pills; Thomas Parrish knew about the pee. Ryan Barron said he watched Jason smoke an eight ball of crack, and two days later, Jason Frederick Smith was admitted to rehab for at least the fourth time. Maybe the gaslighting theory was too ambitious by half. Maybe what we were seeing was a garden-variety drug addict. Maybe Christine Duncan was a mother trying to protect her child from himself. She had helped support Jason, Amanda, and the children for years, bought the family a car, rented them houses, made sure they lived well in the teeth of her son's instability and, in Duncan's view, her daughter-in-law's inability to do anything right.

Jackie wondered, "Why didn't Chris spend more time looking out for Mandy?" and suggested that "if she had, her grandson would be alive now," but I could see Christine Duncan thinking she had done nothing but look out for Amanda. Who was the perpetrator here anyway?

7/15/2009: Violation: Inmate Stott-Smith asked Deputy —— where the [television] remote was. Stott-Smith said deputy did not know. Stott-Smith said she had seen the remote in the officer's station and "just barely leaned in to get it."

8/7/09: Staff has noticed Stott-Smith and Inmate Joseph Wild [a former Portland police officer arrested for sexually harassing women by phone, including a fourteen-year-old relative] have been talking together more frequently.

8/10/09: Amanda requesting general housing and wants to go to church. She can be very manipulative. Does not currently pose a suicide risk.

8/18/2009: Move to 8B on Wednesday. Need to monitor closely.

8/20/2009: Moved back because another inmate was yelling baby killer out there [*sic*] door.

I was back at Jackie's the third week of January 2011. We drank diet root beer and talked about Eldon, whom Jackie said the family had not gotten to know well.

"Jason kept Eldon very close to him," she said. "He carried that kid around."

The last time Jackie saw Eldon was spring 2009. Amanda's children and Chantel's boys had been playing in Jackie's garden. Jackie had yelled, "Who wants ice cream?" Eldon, she said, was the first to run up.

"He stood there looking up with this scowl—Eldon scowled a lot," she said. "I said, 'If you want an ice cream, you're going to have to give me a smile.' And he flashed me the biggest, most beautiful smile you ever saw in your life."

Jackie cried now. "I can't tell you why she did it, because I don't think she herself knows," she said. "I've been told she told the officers it was revenge."

That was the widespread story, I said.

"You have to be mad at somebody to feel revenge, don't you?" she asked. "She's never shown any sign of being mad at him. Never. Not once."

She was trying to fit what she had seen to the popular narrative. I empathized with the difficulties of doing this. Both of Jackie's daughters had accused her of seeking vengeance.

"I don't want vengeance. The Lord says vengeance is His. But I want justice!" she said. "I am waiting on the Lord; Lord, I am getting tired of waiting! Kathy says Jason lost Eldon—who most people believe is the only person he ever loved beside himself. 'Eldon was taken from him, so if you want vengeance, there it is.'

"But I don't believe like the rest of them do that he loved Eldon," she continued. "Eldon was *useful* to him."

Jackie believed Jason had used Gavin, and Eldon in turn, "to move his drugs on I-5." She said the entire family thought so. I asked if anyone had confronted Jason with these suspicions.

"No!" she said. "We had no proof. To this day we have no proof."

They did have proof of the marks on Gavin. At age six, while in the bathroom at church, someone had seen the boy with bruises from hip to knee. Jackie's daughter, Hildy, as an officer of the law, was a mandatory reporter. Though I was told the story by different people in different ways, it seemed someone photographed the bruising and told Amanda that if she did not file a report with Child Protective Services, they would. Jackie implied it had not been easy for the family to call CPS, a call that would perhaps get Amanda in trouble.

It became easier. In August 2008, during a custody hearing with Nathan Beck, Amanda's family testified against her. Daryl described how Amanda had driven drunk and into a ditch with the kids in the car. Jackie relayed that her granddaughter had dumped a milkshake on her head after Jackie tried to convince her Jason was seeing another woman. Amanda did herself no favors that day by acting as her own attorney.

"She came to court in a very expensive suit, her long hair braided down the back. She looked real classy," Jackie said. "She has this brief-case, and she pulls out a jar of peanuts. Nuts! And the court clerk says, 'You can't eat in here!'"

10/22/2009: Cell searched, [found] sugar, pepper, elastic from clothing, two sets of linen, newspapers, too many books & mag—verbal warning. Needs to make her bed every day.

10/29/2009: Stott-Smith's room still a mess. She had extra clothing, a bedroll and two cups of ice tea from dinner. I gave her a Rubbermaid bin and told her everything needed to be on table, rail or in box.

10/30/2009: Stott-Smith not listening. Stuff all over her room; trash on floor, books on floor, pencils all over the floor. Seized everything not in the box/shelves.

"Did I make it clear why I wanted Nathan to have custody?" Jackie asked.

The subject of Amanda giving custody of Gavin to his biological father had come up several times during our visits.

"The big thing with me was fear . . . that she would get back with Jason," Jackie said. "Even if they didn't get back together, Jason could still—anything that he told her, she would do. So it was just very important to me, from the standpoint of getting Jason so totally out of [Gavin's] life, that he could have no little crack to seep in. The only way that could happen is if Nathan had custody."

Jackie wanted Nathan to have custody, she said, "because he is a good guy; he's stable, he's intelligent, he's his *father*." She knew that Amanda—ketchup-eating, over-drinking, milkshake-dumping Amanda—was in no shape to be a mother. Amanda seemed to recognize this, too, and asked Jackie in early 2009 to help her draw up a custody agreement giving Gavin to Nathan. Amanda made Jackie promise she would tell Jason and Christine Duncan that it had been Jackie's idea.

"I did *not* talk Mandy into it," Jackie said. "Maybe if I had needed to, I would have; I sure wanted him away from Jason. But Mandy came to *me*."

Amanda, Jackie said, "would leave little notes at my doorstep" about child support and visitation, notes Jackie fashioned into an agreement. After several drafts, she and Amanda were satisfied. They drove to Jackie's bank to have the agreement notarized, after which Amanda went to her parents' side of the home and started to make dinner.

"She had no qualms, no misgivings; she knew exactly what she was doing," said Jackie. "And then she told Jason what she had done."

Jason told Amanda she had made a horrible mistake. Christine Duncan thought she'd made a horrible mistake. Kathy Stott told Amanda she should not have done it. She told Jackie that she would seek to have the agreement nullified on the grounds that Amanda was not mentally competent to sign it. Jackie countered that if Amanda weren't competent to sign it, how was she competent to be a mother? I pictured Amanda standing in her parents' kitchen, being berated by everyone except Jackie, who had held on to the signed agreement and had already called Chelsea Beck to tell her, "Come and get it, come and get it *now*."

Whether Jason did or did not care about Gavin was not the point; the point was that Amanda had done something without asking permission. She had made a play, for which she could expect to be penalized.

"When everyone she looked up to—Kathy, Jason, and Chris—all told her she'd made a mistake, this was a turning point," Jackie said. "She thought she did something wrong and bad when actually she took the first step I thought was right since this all started. Had they not done that to her, I think she was ready to go ahead [with her life]. They did her in right there."

Circuit Court of the State of Oregon for the County of Multnomah, Judgment of Conviction and Sentence:

> 04/13/2010: Defendant agrees to a life sentence. There is a possibility of parole only after the defendant has served a minimum of 35 years in prison.

> No contact with surviving victim or victims' immediate family without prior written consent. This includes contact in person, in writing, by phone, by email, and through third parties, and includes coming to the homes, workplaces, and schools of surviving victim and victims' family as well as coming into visual or physical presence of the victims.

"What do you have against railings?" Jackie asked. It was a warm August afternoon, and she was climbing the front steps to my house with the help of the walking stick. She had called the night before and said it was "urgent" that she see me.

The urgency had to do with a two-year-old photo she had given me, of Kathy Stott surrounded by her grandchildren. Kathy knew her mother and I had been meeting and had asked that Jackie never speak for her. Jackie thought giving me the photo might imply she was doing so.

"I have just been sick about this," she said. She needed the photo back. I went to my office to get it. In the photo, Kathy is seated on the floor. Trinity sits on her left knee, Gavin holds her right, and Eldon is in her lap; the other grandchildren lean in, and behind them all is Amanda. With the exception of Eldon, the children are all smiling, as is Kathy at center. Half of these people had been lost to each other in an instant.

When I got back to the living room, my cat was in Jackie's lap. She petted it for a long time. Her favorite place, she said, was the Oregon Zoo. She had mentioned the zoo before, with regard to Jason's ultimatum about how he would come home if Amanda got a job.

"He knew she couldn't. He had her to where she couldn't have gotten a job to save her soul," she said. "I told her, 'Well, Mandy, what you probably ought to think about doing is volunteering. Why don't you volunteer at the zoo?' And she says, 'I can't do that; it's too close to Suicide Bridge.'"

Vista Bridge sits 120 feet above a roadway in southwest Portland and has proven compelling to jumpers, hence the name Suicide Bridge. The jumps often prove fatal, including to the five people who went over in 2013, after which a suicide barrier was installed. Within months, a fourteen-year-old boy scaled the barrier, shot himself, and fell to his death.

That Amanda had not jumped, from anywhere, was "a real puzzle" to Jackie. Or maybe not: Jackie said Amanda had several times told her, "Grandma, I don't think I'm saved." She was concerned, Jackie said, "that if she committed suicide and she was not saved, she could go to hell."

Amanda had nevertheless been talking suicide for months. The family, Jackie said, had been "scared to death" she'd hurt herself, never the children.

"I consider her to be a coward to tell you the truth," she said.

I told her my husband felt the same way.

"Very, very cowardly, yes," she said, and later, "I'm sure people wonder why she didn't just jump with her kids."

The question had come up.

Jackie said the answer was that Amanda had worked summers as a lifeguard.

"She's too skilled," she said. "She would know she wouldn't drown."

Oregon Corrections Intake Center—Intake Assessment Report

STOTT-SMITH, Amanda
Report date: 29 Apr 2010
Reported Drug [and Alcohol] use in 12 Months Before
Lockup: [Answer]: "Never"
How serious do you think your alcohol or other drug
problems are? [Answer]: "Not At All."
Marital Status: Married
Children: 1
Living with: 1

For a visit in October 2011, I brought Jackie a bag of coffee beans.

"That's funny," she said. "I have a present for you, from Mandy."

I considered how this could be as Jackie handed me a box from Hilo Hattie, a chain of stores on the Hawaiian Islands.

"The last time Mandy went to Hawaii, she brought this back for me," she said of the ceramic mug imprinted with hibiscus and Bird of Paradise. I told her our swap was like "The Gift of the Magi," and we took our usual places, she in her rocking recliner, me on the tuffet, the TV news on mute. I caught a glimpse of a corpse on-screen, its face and hair caked in what looked like plaster dust.

"Did you hear about this already? Gaddafi's dead," she said. I asked who had taken responsibility.

"The rebels," she said. "Though I would not give you two pennies on a bet that they will set up a democracy over there."

We watched the news until Jackie said, "Well, we have some things to get to."

She slid open her glass patio door. We walked through it and into another on its right, into Kathy and Mike Stott's side of the home. The living room was immaculate and had the powdery scent of Love's Baby Soft, a cologne I wore as a teenager. I followed Jackie to a home office. Mike Stott had given permission for me to see photos on the family computer. Jackie narrated the slideshow: Chantel and Daryl Gardner's son Noah playing an electric organ; Kathy taking a nap on the beach; Chantel on her father's riding lawn mower; Mike and Kathy with their faces close together.

"These two have been madly in love since they were sixteen," Jackie said.

One slide showed goldfish swimming in a little pool in Jackie's yard, as well as a big turtle Jason brought back from Hawaii. Was it still alive?

"Oh, yes," Jackie said.

Gavin and his cousin Luke on skimboards, Gavin looking tall . . .

"He's a freshman at Benson [High School]," she said.

Kathy holding a giant Hershey's chocolate bar . . .

"Kathy is a devotee of 'smores," Jackie said. "Show her a flame."

The boys by a fire on the beach two years and four months after their cousins were dropped off a bridge. The people in the photos were smiling—smiling at a child's birthday, smiling at a rock-climbing gym. There was one quick shot of Trinity from years earlier and the slideshow started again.

"I asked Kathy, I said, 'You know, [Nancy] has asked me a couple of times how you got through this,'" Jackie said. "I'm going to give you an exact quote—she doesn't know I'm doing this but it will be all right with her. She said, 'Without the Lord, I'd be in a psych ward.' And I am sure she would!"

"And I'll give a you a quote from Trinity," she said when we were back in her living room. "They were sitting in the back seat of the car, and Trinity was trying to comfort Mandy, and she was patting Mandy, and see Trinity knew all about Keli, and Trinity said, with her exact words, 'Don't worry, Mama, he loves you better.' It was so heartbreaking. If any wife ever had her husband's girlfriend shoved in her face . . . Chris told Mandy that Jason and Keli were good together because they were both coming off bad marriages."

Jackie was under the impression Keli Townsend's family had money, and if this were the case, then what did Keli see in Jason? I had been told certain things: that starting in fall 2008, Jason asked Keli to watch Eldon and Trinity, saying he had no one to look after them. That Keli became close with the children, a closeness perhaps kindled by the possibility that she could not conceive children of her own. [This would prove not to be the case: in January 2013, Keli gave birth to Jason's fraternal twin daughters.] That Jason wooed Keli the way he wooed Amanda, buying her jewelry and designer jeans and fifty-dollar pieces of cheese. And then the jewelry started to go missing.

Jackie circled back to Amanda finding out for whom Eldon had been named. It galled her that the Smith family knew the name's genesis but never told Amanda. She thought her granddaughter had been set up from the beginning.

"I told Kathy, 'Just you wait. When they don't need Mandy anymore for those kids, they'll get rid of her one way or the other,'" she said. "And that's exactly what did happen."

I did not know whether Jackie was suggesting Jason wanted the mother of his children dead or that he did not, once he had primary custody of the kids, concern himself with the histrionics of his estranged wife. He had just gone through rehab. He had nearly lost his job. The lawsuit with Brian Burr was pending. Maybe Jason was exasperated with Amanda's repeated run-ins with DHS, her driving to Coburg to track down Keli, and her calling him dozens of times in the middle of the night. Maybe the suicide threats had a numbing effect on whatever feelings he had for her. Amanda had not been able to punch her way out for a long time, and there was no reason to think she could now. What was she going to fight with?

"None of us ever thought that Mandy would hurt one of the kids," Jackie said. "It never even crossed our minds."

I suggested that people who act in good faith assume others will, too.

She nodded. "Naïve."

Jackie walked me through her garage. On the wall was a message Amanda had written years earlier, in lipstick: I ♡ GRAMS. I asked if I could take a picture of it.

"Of course," she said.

We stood in the driveway.

"If you speak with Keli, tell her to come see us. We are not the terrible people she thinks we are," Jackie said, and that if things with Jason went the way Jackie thought they might, Keli would need support. Jackie's thinking about Keli had turned around since the boat dedication, a turn that had Trinity at its center.

"She's lost so much, have you considered that? Her mother, both her brothers, her cousins, the rest of the family that is us," she said. "And who knows what she's being told about us?"

I knew that for the past two years Trinity had referred to Amanda as "that girl," though she sometimes slipped and called her "Mommy." I told Jackie as much. I thought this might upset her. On the contrary, standing today in the sun she looked as strong as I had ever seen her.

"She loved her mother," she said, nodding. "Very much."

Coffee Creek Corrections Information Systems—Offender Chrono History, with comments [selected]

6/15/2010: Placed items in back pocket after breakfast.

7/3/2010: [Warned] not to change clothes while her door was open.

11/5/10: No show for legal library.

11/9/10: Sleeping during count.

11/18/10: Sleeping during count.

12/18/10: Had 10 hard-boiled eggs in cell from breakfast.

Jackie called in early November. She had been "going through some papers that needed to be shredded" and came across writing Amanda had done on her mother's computer and given to Jackie to hold on to. Jackie suggested we meet at a restaurant near her home.

We were the first customers of the day. No sooner did Jackie sit down than she handed me the pages. I did not look at them at the table. We ate pad Thai and talked about Occupy Wall Street. After lunch we walked a block to a French bistro whose owner I knew. He was solicitous in the way of the French, oh-la-la-ing and doing everything but kiss Jackie's hand. She gave him the frown she had given me at the boat dedication, which today I found so funny I laughed out loud.

I did not wait to get home to look at the pages. I read them in my station wagon, parked near the light-rail tracks. Amanda, sometimes typing late at night, wrote of her isolation in the months leading up to the bridge. In every document, on every page, sometimes in the same sentence, Amanda wrote what she knew of Jason and what she hoped of him. These often contradicted each other.

"He is the smoothest talker around . . . and his memory allows him to form lies in a way that seems to be foolproof as well unfortunately," she wrote. "He has taught me everything I know and I will never not love him." She wrote she trusted him when others accused him of theft, followed by an itemization of jewelry and household goods he pawned or sold.

"I will agree to anything that man says," she wrote. "If he told me we were going to sail the ocean blue in 10 years, I'd wait."

What were her objectives in writing these pages? Was it a chronicle, a confession, an indictment, and if so, against whom? Was she leaving a trail, and if so, for whom? Whom did she want to know of her "joy and peace" at having given up her and Shane's baby for adoption? That Jason "did hurt Gavin leaving several bruises on his upper thigh" but that she and Jason had "fervently prayed" that Nathan and Chelsea would not see them? That she was "told one thing by my mother-in-law and another thing by my husband and trying to follow the authorities God had placed above me, I became more codependent than I'd ever like to admit"? That knowing of Jason's affair with Keli, Amanda "was dying in side [*sic*] trying not to be depressed"? That "alcohol became my friend"? Was Amanda a reliable narrator when she said she had gone to a doctor for depression, took one Zoloft, and "thought about suicide for a couple of days and didn't take any more"?

One of the documents was typed into the body of an email. It was in draft mode. There was no addressee. Amanda began the unsent email, typed on Valentine's Day 2009, "To whomever this may concern." I had no idea who she envisioned this concerned person might be, but today it was me.

"I am self-centered. A narcissist. A dramatic interpreter. For some reason, worthy of love, and for another reason going mental. Not really. That's what everyone else thinks. I am kind of smart. But I am in la la land part of the time because I choose to be. Anyways. This is not my plan," she wrote, and later, what her plan might be.

"I thought maybe the right thing was to make sure that everyone knew how perfect and wonderful Daddy was and I would take all the heat."

A plan she had followed through on.

3/18/11: Sleeping during count.

4/2/11: Had discussion with inmate tonight regarding her lack of hygiene. Explained that she is expected to shower on a regular basis and that she is also expected to wash her clothes and bedding on a regular basis.

4/6/11: O was experiencing stress over her high-profile case and stated inmates on H unit were harassing her, not letting her sit at tables etc.

4/9/11: Disobedience for standing on top of her toilet and talking through the cell vent.

5/9/11: Covering cell vents with pads.

6/20/11: Disobedience, horseplay—Inmate was sprinting in dayroom trying to make line movement, which she missed.

12/31/11 (misconduct report): "We found in your bag the following items: 1 large bag of sugar that was wrapped in plastic and placed inside a serving glove, 1 large bag of butter placed in a serving glove, 22 individual packets of sugar. . . . It has been my experience that inmates in possession of sugar in that quantity are attempting to create what is called pruno (or prison wine)."

3/15/12: Inmate plugged toilet by flushing food (oatmeal).

3/28/12: Sleeping during count.

6/11/2012: Told to get along with her cellmate and be aware of how long she is running around in the cell nude.

6/24/12: Verbal warning given for foul language—using the word "fuck" several times.

7/17/12: Failed to dispose of contraband (picked flowers from yard)

9/10/12: Daily failure [in] ability to follow direction and hiding food and horseplay.

9/13/12: Sleeping during count.

6/21/13: Inmate sent me a kyte [inter-prison memo] wanting to move to J-Unit as her crime is "so high profile" that she finds it difficult in G-Unit. . . . I advised her if other inmates are threatening or harassing her, she needs to bring that to the attention of the unit officer.

9/13/13: Sleeping during count.

3/28/14: Inmate Stott-Smith wrote me a kyte stating she is "sorry to be a burden" . . . and she normally would not persist but her cellmate is very "sick" of her. According to Stott-Smith, her cellmate calls her names and she would like again to request a move.

9/7/14: Contraband butter.

11/21/14 (misconduct report): "During the [cell] search the following items were found: 7 extra pair of underwear,

2 pair red shorts, 2 pair extra socks, 6 envelopes and 1 pair
hospital socks. On 11/10/14 there was an amnesty day for
all inmates to turn in extra clothing. They had a 24-hour
period to comply. Inmate Stott-Smith failed to comply."

In February 2012, Jackie and I again met at the French bistro. There
was no comic interchange with the owner this time. Jackie sat at a table
against a wall drinking water in silence. She looked tired, closed in on
herself.

"You don't have to write this book, that would be okay," she said.
Maybe she was reading my mind. The troubles that might have led
Amanda to murder—finding out the origin of her son's name, her
drinking, feeling both persecuted by and obligated to her husband,
losing custody of her children, and being unable or unwilling to fix any
of it—sometimes weighed on me, as did the late-night phone calls from
sources I could not name asking about grandparents' rights, and hiring
detectives, and whether I thought it possible that Jason had poisoned
Keli's dogs. People remember things differently; they lie to be kind,
and they lie by omission. I knew that. Still, the layers of obfuscation
here, told by those who wanted to retell events, to sound the alarm
or to spread culpability, were sometimes a lot to sort through and see
clearly. Maybe, I told Jackie, I would not write about Amanda and the
children after all.

Jackie's face perceptively brightened, and I had a flash, oddly, of
white doves flying up from her shoulders. She had told me more than
once she was ready to be done with this part of her life. When I called
her a year later to say hello, she seemed nearer to that readiness, asking me to repeat my name three times before saying, "Oh . . . I *think* I
remember you."

When we left the bistro this day, the sun had come out. Jackie and
I knew without saying as much that we would not see each other again.

"I want to thank you," she said. When I asked her for what, she said that no one in her family would talk about what happened but that she had needed to.

"It helped so much," she said. I told her for me, too.

Coffee Creek Correctional offers more than 130 rehabilitation programs. These include life skills, education, behavioral and mental health, and other opportunities, from a beekeeping apprenticeship to barista training to volunteering in the prison hospice.

From April 23, 2010, to March 5, 2015, Amanda participated in dozens of activities. She had jobs with a floor-cleaning crew and as a food handler. She attended Toastmasters, where inmates learn "better communication strategies." She did yoga. She went to lectures on frogs and on birds. She had six mental health sessions in her first month, and none after. She attended grief and loss classes in fall 2011. From June 2010 to March 2015, she engaged in numerous religious activities, some of which were ongoing and included Baptist services, choir, prison fellowship, OWP (Oregon Women's Prison) Ministry, and Insight: Victim/Offender Education, a program that, according to its website, "supports incarcerated individuals in the process of understanding and developing insight into the underlying circumstances of their lives and the choices that led them to prison."

27

Justin Montgomery was in the middle of his shift at Foxy's Den on the south end of Main Street in Milwaukie's business district. Foxy's was no bigger than an average suburban rec room, and from the doorway, customers could see the whole of it, including video poker machines and a counter at which to buy cigarettes, beer, and snacks. Every vice, Justin thought, except strippers and drugs. Foxy's was open from 7:00 a.m. to 2:00 a.m. and was slow in the early afternoons, leaving Justin time to get his homework from community college done or to just stare out the scratched front window.

Justin watched a woman on a bicycle ride slowly past. He adjusted his thick-framed black glasses. The woman was wearing white shorts and a white top; she was attractive, with long hair and a tan. It was a sunny day, and watching her ride past provided a nice reverie. Justin had spent almost thirteen years in prison not being able to casually glance at a pretty woman, and at thirty-three, he was glad to do so now.

The woman rode past again, coming from the other direction. Justin watched her stop before Foxy's front door. She straddled her bike and looked up at the business's sign for so long it did not seem normal—all the sign said was "Foxy's Den." The woman looked down the street, back at the sign, and started to roll her bike inside.

She stayed in the entryway and looked at the video poker machines and at a side table covered with last week's newsweeklies. She looked at the man behind the counter. He wore a navy fisherman's cap pulled low over his coarse black hair.

Justin said, "Hi. How are you doing? Welcome to Foxy's."

The woman did not respond. Justin worked with the public; it was his job to read people, to make them feel relaxed. This woman's smile looked painted on; it did not touch her eyes. She told Justin she had just moved to the area and was looking for a job. He told her Foxy's was always accepting applications, that he would give her one, but she would need to turn it in to a different Foxy's, about two miles away.

The woman said, *Okay* . . . in this slowed-down way that made Justin think she might be on drugs. Not smoking pot or hard drugs, more as though she had taken Valium, as though she had overmedicated.

Justin gave her a Pepsi. He gave her a job application and, seeing as there were no other customers, asked her name. She said her name was Amanda and she was riding around today looking at the area. Justin asked where she lived; she said with somebody in a house, and that she recently had been having some problems.

Amanda sat on an old kitchen chair near the side table and started to fill out the application, though Justin noticed she really didn't; she was more just looking at it.

"You're having some problems, you okay?" he asked when he saw her further dislocate, her eyes sliding over the walls, past the TV.

She said, I had some problems with my husband . . .

She stopped. Justin prompted, "Your husband."

Oh, he's my ex, she said, and seemed to get agitated, but again, to Justin her emotions did not touch her. She had a spacey, robotic quality as she continued. It's our kids, she said. He won't let me see them. I really miss them, and his family is involved, and they won't let me see them because they think I'm . . .

Justin watched her work hard to not say the word "crazy." As she repeated that she no longer had her kids, she did not get to see the kids, the smile on her face stayed fixed. It was a dead smile, really a dead smile. Justin told her a job at Foxy's could help her, that it was a good company to work for, and that they were very understanding. He gave her everything she needed to turn in the application and told her that, if she wanted, to go ahead and put his name on there, that it might help her get hired.

They spoke maybe forty-five minutes before Amanda rolled her bike outside. Again she looked up at the sign, almost as though she had been trying to memorize the place, and rode away.

Justin and his girlfriend were watching the news a few days later when Amanda's mug shot came on TV. With the tension on her face and her hair a mess, she was practically a different woman. Justin stood and shouted, "That's Amanda! I know her! I know her!"

The news detailed what Amanda had done. Justin's girlfriend said it was monstrous, and he found himself trying to explain what Amanda's mental state had been a few days earlier, how he did not think she did what she was accused of doing out of animosity toward her children. His girlfriend kept repeating, there's no excuse. Justin agreed, while pressing the point that Amanda did not deserve to die for what she did.

The next morning, Justin bought a newspaper in order to find the attorney of record in Amanda's case. He called the attorney, who said, I'm doing this as a favor; I will take your name and pass it on to the next attorney. Whether the attorney did, Justin did not know. He never received a call back from anyone.

Justin had wanted to speak with the attorney because he had faced the death penalty. He spent twelve and a half years in prison for killing a man during a meth deal. Justin had been eighteen at the time, and his involvement with drugs back then had been a bad, bad, bad experience. He began serving time at age nineteen.

Justin was released from prison in 2008. He had been thirty-two, a year older than Amanda was when she began serving time. His life was going one way, hers the other; they had intersected for less than an hour, but it was long enough for him to want to reach out to her attorney, to tell him he had seen Amanda's state of mind in the days before the murder, and that if Justin could provide any insight, he wanted to.

It was not that he thought the crime should go unpunished. What Amanda had done was horrible, horrendous, disgusting, but at the same time killing her would not solve anything. It would not bring her son back. It would not take back the memories that her daughter was going to have to deal with. Justin knew, from his own family's experience, that Amanda's daughter was going to be punished right along with her. Trinity was going to have that stigma for the rest of her life: her mother was "crazy Amanda," who tried to kill her.

Justin knew Amanda was in for a hard time, that prisoners who harm or kill children become targets of other prisoners' special hatred. He thought, for her own protection, Amanda would often be sequestered, kept in a tiny room, with no window and a light on twenty-four hours a day. If she were suicidal, she would not be allowed to wear clothes, or not more than the turtle-shell vest strapped on prisoners at risk of taking their own lives. In Justin's experience, people who hear of such conditions do not have a problem with them.

He interacted with hundreds of customers who bought a newspaper at Foxy's or listened to the radio tuned to the news. As the week went on, Amanda was the news. Justin listened as customers talked about what a vile, disgusting human being she was, saying that she deserved everything she got.

Justin knew Amanda would be dealing with the ramifications of what she had done for a long time. He was still dealing with his. And if he wondered why Amanda would murder her child, he also wondered what she had gained. Something, he thought, must have been satisfied.

The most common assumption of what Amanda had satisfied was a desire for revenge against her husband. This was where most people stopped. They neither needed nor wanted to think further. The idea that Amanda would sit in a cell for thirty-five years relishing what she had done struck me as provincial, a fairy tale. Her life would go on. Even if she were kept naked in a tiny room, there would be evolution; there would be losses and gains.

I had considered the possibility that Amanda's life in prison would be easier than her life had been outside of it. Her eating disorder would not be countenanced, or not as easily. She would not be able to drink alcohol, or not as much. She would not have to ask anyone if she could take a yoga class or go to a lecture on frogs. She would not have to listen to Jason call her a dumb bitch. Her movements would be prescribed in prison; while there were many things she would likely never again do, things I thought about when I walked on a beach, or flew in a plane, or curled up with my husband, or bought a dress at Nordstrom's, she had, if looked at one way, been released from one kind of hell. And if I thought she had put herself in another, because my idea of hell would be if tragedy were to befall my child, I could also see she had, at the terrible cost to her children, bought herself some freedom.

"It's almost as if prison has given Amanda her life back," Samantha Hammerly said.

Samantha and I were having lunch in a burger bar in Portland's Pearl District in 2014. Our exchanges had not always been friendly. In 2010, Samantha contacted me to say she was a long-time friend of

Amanda's, and "the last thing she needs right now is a book written about 'the crazy mom who threw her kids off the bridge.'"

Samantha had proved open to changing her mind. She found our subsequent communications "therapeutic" and shared with me details of her visits with Amanda in prison, visits that had taken place every few weeks for the past three years.

"When I first started seeing her and talking to her, she was incredibly depressed," she said today. "I was scared for her for a little while."

Samantha had learned what her friend had done from the news on TV. She had not seen Amanda since tenth grade. Maybe it was residual affection. Maybe it was because Samantha had studied for a PhD in psychology, a pursuit kindled by a fascination with serial killers. But in May 2009, she stepped back into Amanda's life. Samantha was the cried-out woman I had seen at Amanda's second arraignment. She visited and prayed with Amanda's parents in the days after Eldon's murder. She went to Eldon's funeral. She wrote to Jason, urging him to allow Trinity to see Amanda's family. He had not written her back.

Amanda dropping her children from the bridge had a magnetic effect on Samantha. She would stand by Amanda because "she really does need support." Visiting her friend, the child killer, in prison fulfilled what Samantha saw as her duty as a Christian and as a friend. The visits also provided a light that Samantha sensed she ignored at her own peril.

"I agree that Mandy suffers from depression, something I know a lot about, and her symptoms are a lot like mine," she once told me, and that if I were to write about Amanda, "then do it justice, please. Help that mom out there in the same situation."

Samantha today spoke of the changes she had seen in Amanda, who had been moved to "a special part of the prison that's for people that have been on good behavior." Her weight had stabilized. She had visitors, including Chantel and her sons, who played in the prison's playground and had a blast each time they came.

Samantha said Amanda talked and wrote about her life in the years leading up to the bridge, how she had not been able to see her friends or go out or do what she wanted.

"She said she felt really bad about herself for a long time," Samantha said. "But she's not like that. She's never been like that. She's not a depressed person. She's always been happy, and so, what made her that way?"

Whatever had made her that way seemed to Samantha to be reversing, a "transformation" she attributed to Amanda getting involved with the church inside prison and "back in contact with God."

"She's happy and go lucky the way she was when we were in high school," she said. "She doesn't seem oppressed, and she's not depressed. She's very much like she was."

I was shutting off my tape recorder when Samantha stopped me.

"I did want to say one other thing," she said. "I did one time feel comfortable enough to ask her about what happened, and she just hung her head and started crying and said, 'I can't talk about that right now.'"

Samantha also started to cry. "And that was after we were just joking around and being happy."

28

"We go through life mishearing and mis-seeing and misunderstanding so that the stories we tell ourselves will add up. Trial lawyers push this human tendency to a higher level. They are playing for higher stakes than we are playing for when we tinker with actuality in order to transform the tale told by an idiot into an orderly, self-serving narrative."

—Janet Malcolm, *Iphigenia in Forest Hills*

Defense attorney Shanon Gray was sitting in a coffee shop across from the main branch of the Portland Public Library in July 2014. It had been more than five years since his wife, Tiffany, had urged him to get down to the jail where Amanda was being held to see if he could help. He had walked in just as detectives were trying to get her confession.

"I said, 'I'm representing her. You're not doing any interviews,'" he said. "They were pissed."

As it turned out, Gray would not represent Amanda. He had reached out to Amanda's family to say his wife had been her college friend and that he knew Amanda personally and was offering his services as an attorney. He never heard back. It had been one of Gray's law partners who stood by Amanda during her first arraignment "as a courtesy to the family," after which he was replaced by Ken Hadley. Gray had reached out to Hadley. As a former Multnomah County district attorney, Gray had been through enough aggravated murder trials to feel he would be an asset to Amanda's defense team. He received no response from Hadley.

I had previously met Gray and as before was struck by his intense physicality. He had a granite jaw, sharp blue eyes, and the readiness of a wrestler, or maybe a lion, as if at any moment he might propel forward and bite his opponent in the neck. I had once asked him what he and Amanda spoke about in the hours immediately following her arrest. He had declined to tell me then, and today invoked attorney-client privilege, despite never having been her attorney. But he was willing to say a few things: that Amanda recognized him when he came to see her and that, contrary to what Tiffany had said, he did not sit with Amanda for hours, more like twenty or thirty minutes.

"I can say she was in a glaze," he said. "She was just checked out."

Gray had not known Amanda well and had never met Jason. He said he did not need to know them to understand the dynamics that had been at work. The factors here—someone threatening to take the kids, one side with money and power, the other side feeling cowed—were to Gray prosaic. If I thought the situation unusual, that Amanda was somehow an exceptional victim and Jason an exceptional abuser, I was fooling myself.

"You think some abusers are different? No! I've been a defense attorney for twelve years, and if you don't think he's a dime a dozen—he's a dime a dozen!" he said. "These guys have a certain thing: they knock 'em down, they cut them off from all their family and friends, they control the money, they control the resources. It's piece by piece by piece by piece to where they control everything, and in the process they're beating them down emotionally: 'You're not smart enough. You're not pretty enough.' I don't need to know who the abuser is. I *know* who he is: he's an abuser. It's not like it's a new way to do it."

Gray believed the end came about prosaically, too. "He was the kind of guy who was probably going to say, 'Hey, when I take [the kids]? You are never going to see them again,'" he said. "This has been years of him beating her down and him following through with his promises, and she thought to herself, 'How can I hurt him the most? How can I hurt Jason and his family the most?' I don't think she thought about the kids. I think she just thought, how can I hurt them the most? And that's what happened."

Gray was talking about Jason and Amanda as if they were classical characters. He was not the only one. As I wrote about Amanda and the children, people repeatedly brought up *Medea*. I reread the Greek tragedy, about the hero Jason and the sorceress Medea. I noted that Jason, who has left Medea to marry a king's daughter, does not seem so much cruel as an opportunist when he tells her, "What more need hast thou of children? And for me, it serves my star to link in strength the children that now are with those that shall be." I noted Medea's conviction as she makes her choice:

> LEADER: O lady, wilt though steel thyself to slay thy children?

> MEDEA: I will, for that will stab my husband in the heart.

> LEADER: It may, but you will be the saddest wife alive.

> MEDEA: No matter; wasted is every word that comes 'twixt now and then. Ho!

An old story. But was Amanda the saddest wife alive? She might have panicked when Jason committed the hit-and-run with Eldon in the car, might have seen this as evidence the children were not safe with their father. But she had driven drunk with them. And dropped them from a bridge.

When I asked Gray whether Amanda might have been afraid of Jason raising the children without her, he said, "I would imagine that. She knew he would probably raise a son that would be an abuser, and a daughter that would be bore down on; he was going to command that family. That may have been a secondary purpose. But the thing is, nobody ever gets to that second part. I don't even think her attorneys got to that part."

He snapped his fingers. "They got her in and got her pled so fast . . . I wouldn't have agreed probably with the way it was resolved."

Gray thought the case should have gone to trial. What needed to happen, in his view, was for Amanda's family and friends to have come forward; they needed to stand up and press with what mitigating evidence they had.

"Did they ever present any [mitigating evidence] in court?" he asked. I told him, not in open court.

"It disappoints me that her family completely abandoned her once they found out about the kids, the grandkids," he said, and asked rhetorically if I had seen them at any of the early arraignments. "No," he said, "because they had not been there."

"They were playing the game from the start," he said. "They could not come out on Amanda's side if they ever wanted to see their grandchildren again."

I knew Amanda's parents had not abandoned her. They visited her in jail. The family had been afraid she would receive the death penalty and so encouraged her to plead guilty. Still, Gray's idea that the Stotts felt they had to make a choice—publicly support their daughter, or try to keep access to their granddaughter—was one I had not considered. I told Gray the latter had not happened. The Stott family had not seen Trinity in five years.

"It didn't play out the way they wanted it to," he said. "They thought if they sucked up enough—bad Amanda, bad Amanda—that they would eventually be able to see their grandchildren and be part of [her] life. 'You were right, Jason; Amanda, our daughter, was a mess; she did this horrible thing!'"

Gray felt Jason never had any intention of letting the Stotts see Trinity. The only option the Stotts had was to fight in court, and they had not taken it. Gray understood their fear that Amanda might have received the death penalty. "And yeah," he said, "the DA might have pursued that," but the mitigating evidence, in his opinion, would have probably more than canceled that out. As I cited the drug use and the hit-and-run, Gray shook his head.

"The thing is, they're going to say that type of stuff isn't relevant in a trial for her thing," he said. "The mitigating damage is the abuse. The why she did it, the reason behind it, would have all been relevant."

Relevancy was the key to how the case would be classified, he said.

"I don't think it was premeditated in any way—and that, in essence, takes away the [aggravated] murder aspect of it," he said. He believed "the stressor at the time, whatever that stressor might have been, there was something that pushed her button that night. Maybe it was the lack of [Jason] returning the phone calls."

What had been said when Jason and his mother dropped off the children for the last time? Earlier in the evening, Chantel overheard Amanda telling Jason on the phone that she was trying to get a job but that it was hard. In February, Jason had come to pick up the children with, as Amanda would write, "a most beautiful and skinny and blond and smiling Kelly [sic] with a yellow shirt and a cute ponytail and Daddy all handsome with a new tie." Later in the month, Amanda gave up custody of Gavin and was made to regret doing so. Piece by piece.

I told Gray that Jason had a new wife, two new children, and a new job with a different office equipment company.

"Other than obviously losing a child, it worked out perfectly," he said. "He's got the kids all to himself, he's got a new woman to abuse, and he got rid of Amanda. It's perfect, and he's the hero. He's the father of the children. He got all the media attention. He's the knight in shining armor."

That phrase, I said, had come up again and again.

"I don't know the guy. All I can say is, he fits the profile of the guy who has the wife who does this type of thing," he said. "It's almost a kind of psychotic episode, of postpartum depression; women do these kinds of things, right? They do these drastic things, and then they drown their kids . . . This wasn't anything like that. This was a guy who'd been bearing down on her for years and was eventually moving her out of his life completely and moving her out of the kids' lives."

Amanda had been moved off the stage. And then she did something that put her front and center. I asked Gray whether he had been at the jail when Amanda wrote on her intake paper that she wanted no media attention.

"I don't know who would have filled that out," he said. "She wasn't in any position to respond to anything, especially 'Do you want media attention?' 'Hmm, hold on; let me think about it for a second . . .'"

I told him I understood the resistance, but after five years I also wondered why she would not want to set the record straight. Again, Gray was shaking his head.

"When you want to 'set the record straight,' that means you're opening up wounds," he said. "It's your worst day, and someone wants to write a book about your worst day—fuck me. I don't know if I would be as cooperative, either.

"Now as a journalist, I see you want to explain: 'It wasn't really your fault; it was your worst day because someone helped *make* it your worst day. There were factors that [contributed] and people want to know why.' I get that. But when you're in that spot, it's like, '*It was my worst day*. I want to leave it alone.'"

Gray planted his hands on his thighs. "It's surprising she didn't reach out to more people; she had a really good group of friends," he said. "But that's part of [being] the victim. You don't realize how many friends you have until something bad goes bad."

In the 2004 book *Are You There Alone? The Unspeakable Crimes of Andrea Yates*, author Suzanne O'Malley wrote, "At the end of the day, Rusty Yates hired a handyman to smash to pieces the white porcelain bathtub in which his children had died." I did not know whether the story was apocryphal.

In 2011, Multnomah County announced that the Sellwood Bridge would be replaced. The new Sellwood Bridge would be better able to sustain an earthquake and to accommodate cyclists and pedestrians, with LED lighting and benches where people might contemplate the river. The city had offered pieces of the historic bridge for sale. There had been no takers. A spokesman for the county said the distinctive orotund concrete railing, over which Amanda Stott-Smith dropped her two children, would be taken away and recycled.

PART THREE

Eldon and Trinity. Photo courtesy of Ryan Barron.

29

"It's one of those things you look for: the repeating thing, the thing that after thirty years probably contains some nugget of truth, though it comes in different iterations, because at its heart it's the same story."

—Leah Carroll, *Down City*

May 23–28, 2009, Portland, Oregon

A call was logged into Portland's Bureau of Emergency Communication just before 1:20 a.m. on May 23, 2009: an incident near the Sellwood Bridge. Police were on-site within minutes. Officer R. Storm entered the waterfront condo of Pati Gallagher in response to her 911 call saying she heard someone screaming for help from the river.

Storm could hear the screams, too; they sounded like those of a child.

A fireboat was requested. Dispatch said a boat would be available in thirty minutes. Another officer pointed his flashlight at the water but saw only blackness. He shone the spotlight from the patrol car at the river. Still nothing.

Sergeants Matthew Stimmel and Pete Simpson arrived. Simpson walked north in an attempt to triangulate the screams with the other officers. At 2:09, he saw a civilian boat heading toward him. A woman in the boat cried, "We need help!" David Haag and Cheryl Robb brought the boat in fast. Simpson called for Emergency Medical Services.

Haag told Simpson they had found two children in the middle of the river. The girl and boy were in the boat. Haag carried the girl to the dock and wrapped her in a blanket. Simpson carried the boy and laid him on the dock. He checked the boy for a pulse and found none. He began CPR but could not resuscitate him.

Simpson carried the girl to the top of the Oregon Yacht Club dock to meet Emergency Medical Services in the parking lot. He saw no visible injuries on the girl. He noted that her missing front teeth seemed age-appropriate. He asked if she had any "owies." The girl nodded. He asked where. She pointed to the right side of her jaw. Simpson wrote that she was "able to keep her eyes open and was crying." Stimmel noted that the girl "had a distant stare and a chatter about her mouth." She was taken by EMS to the hospital.

Portland and Multnomah County boats arrived and began the search for more bodies or evidence. The Sellwood Bridge was closed to traffic. At about 3:15, Stimmel drove the neighborhoods south of the bridge. He returned to the dock at 3:52. The medical examiner was photographing bruises on the boy's face and knees and a scrape on his back. Stimmel assisted the medical examiner in getting the boy's body on a gurney and into a vehicle.

At 3:22 a.m., the Tualatin Police Department took a missing person report on an adult female, a four-year-old male, and a seven-year-old female. The caller was Christine Duncan, who said she was the children's grandmother. The names of the missing children were Eldon Smith and Trinity Smith. The adult female was their mother, Amanda

Stott-Smith. Duncan explained that she and her son, Jason Smith, the children's father, had brought the children to the family's former house on Southwest Cayuse Court in Tualatin at approximately 7:30 p.m. Duncan said that Amanda "did not appear to be unstable or distraught at this time." Family members had become concerned when Amanda did not return as expected to her parents' home with the children. Duncan reported that after several attempts at calling Amanda failed, Jason reached her sometime between 2:00 and 2:40 a.m. He told his mother that Amanda sounded upset and "would not mention the children at any time . . . and told him she had nothing to live for."

Officer Bryan Belcher also spoke with Jason. "Mr. Smith told me that Mrs. Smith has a history of alcohol abuse and depression," he wrote. "She has been very depressed since their separation and missed her children."

Officers with the Tualatin Police Department called Amanda. She did not answer. They drove by the Tualatin residence and found it empty. They spoke with Kathy Stott, who had been trying to reach Amanda for hours.

Based on this information, the Tualatin Police Department submitted an Emergency Request for Transactional Records with Cell Site/Location with AT&T in order to track Amanda's cell phone. At 6:30 a.m., Amanda's phone sent off two pings, but officers were unable to identify an exact location.

Around 7:00 a.m., Channel 12 Fox News in Portland reported that the Portland Police Bureau (PPB) was investigating two children found in the Willamette River. Christine Duncan heard this report and called 911. An officer on call wrote that Duncan "was sure based on the description that it was her grandchildren and was hysterical."

At 7:45, the Tualatin Police Department received confirmation from PPB that the male child was found deceased. The female had been transported to Oregon Health & Science University and was expected to survive.

At 8:41, officers received an additional ping on Amanda's phone.

At 8:45, Jason and Christine Duncan met Detective Michele Michaels in the downstairs lobby of Justice Center in downtown Portland. They were brought to the thirteenth floor and joined by Detective Bryan Steed. Jason and Christine Duncan were very concerned the children found in the river might be Jason's son, Eldon, and daughter, Trinity. Jason recalled the last conversation he had with Amanda, sometime after 1:30 a.m. She sounded "odd" and "said something like, 'Help me. Help me.'" She told him, "You've taken all my joy away. I don't have my kids anymore." She accused him of having an affair with Keli Townsend. Jason told detectives Amanda had gotten angry over this issue before, to the point where she had driven to the town in which she believed Keli lived in an effort to find her.

During this interview, the children were positively identified. A Crisis Response Team officer helped to tell Jason of the death of his son, and that his daughter was in the hospital and expected to make a full recovery. Immediately after telling Jason of Eldon's death, detectives received word that Amanda had been located.

Amanda had stopped her car on the ninth floor of a parking garage two blocks from Pioneer Courthouse Square. She was parked nose to the wall. On street level, there was an Apple Store, a Tiffany & Company—places she might have gone to replace the computer she no longer had, a ring that in better days she had never seen. Dreams, all gone.

Around 9:00 a.m., Officer Wade Greaves and his partner received information regarding another cell phone ping on the phone belonging to the mother of the children in the river. The ping was traced to Southwest Fifth Avenue and Yamhill Street in downtown Portland. The officers drove the area and located the vehicle in the top level of a parking garage a block away. Greaves radioed that he had spotted the car, a 1991 Audi. He and other officers could see there was one female in the car. He further radioed that the car door was opening and the female was exiting; she was heading for the open wall of the parking structure. Greaves and other officers ran toward her. She climbed the wall and was over when Greaves grabbed for her.

"[She] dropped off the ledge while I held her from falling by her right wrist," Greaves wrote.

"He kept her from falling nine levels to the sidewalk," added Lieutenant H. Miller, who assisted in getting the female over the wall to safety and taking her into custody. She was handcuffed and placed in a patrol vehicle. She made no statement other than to complain that the handcuffs were too tight. Miller checked.

"They were not too tight," he wrote.

Chantel and Daryl Gardner had been up all night, first driving around looking for Amanda, including in Washington Park, where they'd previously found her drunk and passed out in her car. They had not found Amanda, and by 10:30 a.m. they were in downtown Portland. When they were a half block from the Police Bureau, officers drove up with Amanda in custody. Chantel was newly pregnant. When she saw her sister being walked into the station, she collapsed on the sidewalk.

At 10:40 a.m., Amanda was in a Detective Division Holding Room. At 10:50, the handcuffs were removed. She was searched by Detective Michele Michaels. The log said Amanda was wearing a red floral top, size-thirteen white shorts, a black belt with white stitching, and sandals. She had two one-dollar bills in her front pocket. Photographs showed "scrapes on her arms, legs and right hand," wrote Detective Steed. Steed's report offered no opinion as to whether the fingernails of her children might have caused the scrapes. Between 11:00 and 11:39,

Amanda squatted in the corner. At 12:30, she was taken out of her cell to be interviewed.

"Her words were not slurred nor were her pupils dilated or pinpoint," Steed wrote. "She was able to track and answer questions in an appropriate manner." After Michaels advised Amanda of her Miranda rights, Amanda was asked about the scratches on her arms and whether she needed medical attention. Amanda said she was okay. She asked twice how the children were. Detectives told her they did not have an answer to that question.

Detectives asked what happened the night before; Amanda told them they must know.

"You can just kill me," she said, and began to sob.

Amanda said she had "told everyone to just lock her up." She had lost too much. She said she had told Jason to take the kids, which was "the stupidest, craziest thing she had ever done to save the marriage." Details of what she meant by this are unknown. She said in response to Michaels asking about what happened the previous night, "I went a little crazy."

Amanda stressed she wanted no media attention, that she did not want to be on the news. This was at odds with Shanon Gray's opinion as to how lucid she might have been to make such a choice at this time. Also, with the opinion that, by dropping her children off a bridge in a major American city, Amanda had pretty much forfeited her right to privacy.

"I hurt the children. I mean, I didn't hurt them, I just let them [go]," Amanda told detectives. Asked where she let them go from, Amanda said, "You guys probably know."

Amanda said she let the children fall from the bridge and did not try to stop them. She said Jason had told her on the phone that one of the children had drowned and the other was hurt. If this were so, it meant Jason spoke with Amanda between his being told of Eldon's death at around 8:45 a.m. and Amanda being taken into custody at

10:20 a.m. There is no known record of this call, nor would Jason mention it to police.

Amanda described being in and out of hospitals all spring, of "going nuts and thinking she could just die." She said Jason had "taken her joy," which detectives surmised meant "she was going to take his so he would know what it felt like." They asked whether she thought she and Jason might get back together, without the kids.

"No," she said. "He'd kill me."

Told by detectives that the children had been found, Amanda again began to cry. "I am so dumb," she said. She went on to say she had heard two splashes. When detectives asked her to further pinpoint events, she said she had planned to jump. She asked about the children again and asked for a cigarette. Her statements further fragmented, "I told this one guy kill I told them guys" and "I was thinking bad thoughts. Not kill." She remarked that the chairs in the interview room were hard.

Detectives nudged her back on topic. They wanted to talk about the bridge.

"STOTT-SMITH admitted to dropping the children over the concrete part of the bridge," Steed wrote. "She stated she dropped TRINITY first and then ELDON and that ELDON had asked, 'Did you just put her in the water or something?'"

Here is the image: a four-year-old boy, woken from sleep, outside at night in a windy place, seeing the black line of the river run into the distance, seeing his sister drop from view. I see Eldon, as unfamiliar as he was with his surroundings, showing remarkable focus and logic. He asked a grown-up, what is going on here? He was using what coordinates he had to make sense of where he was.

Amanda added to the sequence of events, saying that Trinity was asleep when she dropped her, and that Eldon was awake. I am not sure his mother's recollection can be trusted, but it is the only one we have (but for those scratches). She repeated what Eldon said upon seeing his sister drop from their mother's arms: "Did you just put her in the water?" Eldon's question had not stopped Amanda from dropping him in turn.

At 11:15 a.m., Detective Rico Beniga interviewed Chantel and Daryl Gardner. Both were very upset. Chantel reported that she had eaten dinner with Amanda the night before. Amanda had been excited to see her children, and she appeared to be in better spirits than she had been for much of the spring, when, Chantel said, she had been hospitalized twice for suicidal ideation. Like her mother, Chantel was a registered nurse. She said Amanda had been noncompliant about taking her antidepressant medications, including Trazodone and Abilify.

During dinner the night before, Amanda mentioned to Chantel she would be taking Eldon and Trinity to see the fireworks. Amanda had asked Chantel to come, but Chantel had been too tired. She said her sister had not had any alcohol at dinner.

Daryl interjected that when Amanda did drink, she drank "an obscene amount of vodka."

Detectives received a phone message from a woman I will identify as KL, who said she had stopped at a Plaid Pantry market in Sellwood at around 12:15 a.m. on May 23. She had seen Amanda in the parking lot. Amanda had approached and asked if KL would watch the children while she went into the market. Amanda said she would give KL five dollars to do so. KL said she thought it was "really odd and was concerned the woman was drunk or high. She agreed to watch the children but refused to take any money."

KL saw the children inside the car. "One was in a car seat and the other was slumped over the lap of the one in the seat," Steed wrote. Both appeared to be asleep.

KL said Amanda was in the store for maybe three minutes and came out holding a small paper bag. She again offered KL money, which KL again refused. She said Amanda did not display "any noticeable drug or alcohol" impairment, yet KL was still concerned about her driving. But Amanda did not drive. She only sat in the driver's seat and was still sitting there when KL drove away.

KL said "the whole encounter was strange" and that she would have called 911 had Amanda driven away. Seeing news reports the following morning, KL said she regretted not having called. Video footage and a printout of Amanda's transaction showed she purchased a 500-milliliter (16-ounce) box of Bandit Chardonnay for $3.67.

After telling detectives how she had killed her son and tried to kill her daughter, Amanda said, "I think I need a lawyer or something?" Detectives noted they had asked several times if she understood she had the right to an attorney and whether she wanted to continue the interview without one, to which she had responded, "What's wrong with telling the truth?"

The truth, during this first interview, was as follows: Amanda's "life began falling apart" after Jason took the children and Amanda was told she had to move out of the house. She had not been able to handle being without Eldon and Trinity. She "went crazy" because she could not get her husband back.

"I'm in, really in big, big, big trouble," she said.

She continued talking about Jason, how he was nice to her in private but not "in front of his mother or anyone else." The detectives steered Amanda back to the kids, back to the bridge. She repeated that she wanted to take from Jason what he took from her, that she hated herself, and that she sometimes wanted to die.

Asked directly if her intention had been to kill herself, Amanda said, "Well, that wasn't really my plan." She said she had hoped "if I fell" it wouldn't hurt. She said she did not want the children to be hurt either, and she thought that by putting them in the water, their "pain of separation would end because hers hasn't."

She said after the kids were in the water, she was "going to go in and get them but changed her mind." When detectives asked what changed her mind, Amanda said only that she was "so ashamed, that she had no idea why she changed her mind and then because her car was in the way."

Detectives drew two lines representing the river's banks and bisecting lines representing the Sellwood Bridge. Where, they asked, had Amanda parked? She indicated that she had stopped the car midspan and dropped the kids from the bridge's south side. Steed asked whether Amanda had seen the children fall into the water. She said it had been too dark. He asked if she heard them yell. Trinity she had not heard; Eldon "a little." They asked how she had been holding the children when she dropped them. She indicated she had been cradling Trinity. She said no more about Eldon.

Amanda again asked if she could have a clove cigarette, and again she was told she could not smoke in the building. She would not tell detectives where she had gone after she dropped the children, only that she "needed to be executed and couldn't we just do that?"

Detectives said that sometimes people make bad decisions, but that trying to understand the roots of the decisions was important. Amanda did not seem in the mood to be placated.

"It's all calculated. Cold-blood murder," she said. When asked how so, she said, "Thought, thought, thought. How do I hurt Jason?" When asked how she would hurt him, she said, "I killed his kids."

Detectives paused the interview so Amanda could get something to eat. At 2:50, she was back in the holding cell. At 3:00, she was observed eating a granola bar. At 3:55, the interview recommenced. Amanda answered that she did not know whether she had consumed any alcohol before picking up the children the previous night. During a later interview, she told them she was taking the antidepressants Abilify and Seroquel. By my count, this made three antidepressants she was taking or had been noncompliant in taking. When detectives asked what the medications were for, she said she did not know, only that she was supposed to take them because her "life was in shambles." At the conclusion of the interview on May 23, 2009, Amanda was booked into the Multnomah County Detention Center on charges of aggravated murder and attempted aggravated murder.

Detective Steed spoke with Ray Pratt, the harbormaster for Portland. Pratt explained that the bottom of the Sellwood Bridge was "75 feet above the zero waterline," but because the river was running consistently ten feet higher, the distance shrank to sixty-five feet. Steed determined that from the bottom of the girders to the roadway was an additional twenty-five feet, and the cement railing another three or four feet, meaning the children had fallen a total of ninety-three to ninety-four feet. They would have been in the air for approximately 2.41 seconds before they hit the water.

Around 6:45 p.m., Amanda was offered something to eat. She had earlier seen investigators eating pizza and told Detective C. Traynor she wanted some. He explained the pizza was gone but offered to get her a sandwich from Subway. Amanda repeated that she wanted pizza. After being told this was not an option, she asked for a pen and paper in order to write down instructions for what she wanted. She wrote, "veggie sandwich, honey oatnut bread, no cheese, extra lettuce onions tomatoes pickles and olives, banana peppers, xtra vinegar, pepper, lots of dijon, honey mustard, no mayo." She told Traynor she wanted a six-inch, then changed it to a foot-long and added that she wanted some Sun Chips. Traynor purchased the sandwich. He later realized he had left the instructions at Subway. An employee retrieved the note from the dumpster, and it was logged into evidence.

Around the time Amanda was eating her sandwich, Detectives Lori Smith and Beniga were visiting with Trinity in Doernbecher Children's Hospital at OHSU. Beniga noted that an ICU nurse characterized Trinity as a "bright, polite child . . . cognizant of her surroundings." Trinity told detectives that she had broken a bone in her chest. When asked how this happened, she said she had been asleep in her mother's car and "fell into the water and was picked up by a boat."

She did not know how she wound up in the water.

Trinity said she and Eldon had been dropped off with their mother for the weekend. They were supposed to see the fireworks, but her mother could not find parking. Trinity said that while she and Eldon drove with their mom, they had seen some fireworks from the car. They stopped and ate cotton candy from a mini-mart and "drove all around town around midnight." She said again that she had been asleep when she fell in the water. When asked where Eldon was when she fell, Trinity said he was with their mom.

"I almost drowned," she told detectives. "I was crying for my mommy. . . . The river was fast." She repeated that she was "calling for her mommy" when she was picked up by the boat. She said she did not see or hear Eldon when she was picked up by the boat and said again that she missed her mother.

Trinity was asked about her parents. She said her dad did not like her mom "because she smokes and does not have a job." Trinity also said her dad doesn't like her mom because he pays all the bills and her mom does not help.

When questioned about whether she felt "safe" with her father, Trinity replied, "Yeah." She said her favorite family members were her grandmother and her aunt "because they were both nurses and help her." She said that "Gavin is friendly and nice to her because he tickles her." She said there was no one in her family she was afraid of.

Trinity healed with remarkable speed.

Concurrent with Trinity's interview, Detectives McCausland and Ober were at the home of Jackie Dreiling. This was when she told detectives that Amanda was "the number one most self-centered, selfish person" she knew, adding that she thought her granddaughter had been "diagnosed with a 'Defective Character Disorder.'" Kathy Stott at this time described Jason as "a psychopath."

Shortly after 7:00 p.m., Amanda asked Detective Traynor whether a lawyer would come see her in her cell. Traynor explained that was not how things typically worked, that she would be assigned an attorney if she could not afford one, and that once she had legal representation, investigators would no longer question her. Amanda wanted to know "how long this process was going to take."

The holding room log indicates that at 7:00 p.m. Amanda was eating, at 7:20 she was reading the ingredients on the Sun Chips bag, and that she slept between 7:42 and 8:30.

At 8:35 p.m., her photo was taken. At 8:45, her clothing was seized. Amanda was "upset" by both actions and told Traynor "several times that she did not want to be on television."

At 9:00 p.m., Amanda was moved to a cell. At 9:15, she was observed to be crying. At 9:30, she was asleep.

Evidence found in Amanda's car included business cards for a clinical psychologist at Wildwood Psychiatric Resource Center and a primary therapist at St. Vincent Medical Center, and a black spiral notebook in which she wrote short notes. Her handwriting is spidery and hard to read, the notes dated but out of sequence:

2/12 Grandma Chris said she has to practically force Jason to come in & hug me.

2/12 Grandma Chris told me that Jason never said he wouldn't divorce me.

[Undated] We stopped @ the park on the way back & as Eldon ate his Flintstone push-up pop he told me all about how Kelly & Daddy had taken him to the park & how they sat on a bench together. . . .

2/19/09 He still won't let me talk to the kids on the phone when I call & ask.

1/12/09 It's a plan to make me jealous & do something stupid like get frustrated or bitter & I can't and won't because I love the children too much but Eldon tells me about Kelly [*sic*] Townsend & says she has no kids even though Jason says she does & is happily married even though a couple of years ago & just two days ago Grandma Chris told me & Jason that she had an asshole husband & that she and Jason were just friends.

3/11 Jason said that I could see the kids this weekend & that he just wanted to see them first so I waited though I haven't see them for a while so I called 3/12 3/13 to 3/14 & had arrangements . . . & then Jason called when I was on my way & he said no changed the plans.

On May 26, Detectives Michaels and Steed went to OHSU, where Trinity was still hospitalized, to meet again with Jason. The detectives had a few more questions. When, for instance, had he moved out of the house in Tualatin? Jason had stayed with Ryan Barron in summer 2008 but told detectives he had left the family home in September or October. He said he had continued to support Amanda after he left but told her she needed to be out of the house by May 31. Asked to describe how he thought Amanda was handling the move, Jason said she seemed "indifferent."

Jason said the last night he left the children with Amanda, she had a "big grin" on her face and "hugged the kids." When he asked Amanda what she and the kids were going to do, she said she didn't know, but "maybe the beach." She told him she wanted to see the kids more. He told her "what I always tell her. It's about her actions and what [she] has done [and that she needed to] get her life back on track."

The first 911 call from someone who heard screaming in the river was received at 01:19:23. Jason's phone rang at what detectives confirmed was 01:22:50. Jason heard it but did not answer. His phone rang again at 01:33:04. It was Kathy Stott, telling him the children were not home.

Jason began calling Amanda. He said they spoke several times, and during the "first few seconds of the first time, she said, 'Help me. Help me. Help me.' She said something like, 'I don't get to see my children. You've taken my joy away.'"

Asked to describe her emotional state, Jason chose the words "subdued" and "calm."

After Amanda refused to answer Jason's questions about the children, Jason said he hung up and called Kathy Stott, who told him that Amanda was not answering her calls and to call Amanda back. Jason did. Amanda told him he did not know what it was like to have everything taken away—your husband, your children. She accused Jason of having an affair with Keli Townsend, and at one point, police noted, "said something like he [Jason] had 'stuck his penis in Keli.'" She went on about how messed up he was and that he had ruined her." Jason said he told Amanda that if she did not immediately tell him where the children were, he was going to call the police, at which time Christine Duncan did call the police. Upon learning this, Jason said Amanda "freaked out. She said, 'Why did you do that?'" After asking Jason where he was, she hung up.

Jason said "there was no further phone conversations with her after that and she would not answer the phone," a statement that contradicted Amanda telling detectives she learned from Jason that one child had drowned and one had been hurt.

At 7:20 a.m., Jason received another call from Kathy Stott, who was in "a panic" because Chantel had seen a news report about two children found in the river. Jason said he thought, "There's just no way." He told detectives you'd expect someone who did this to sound "whacked out," and Amanda, according to Jason, had not.

Jason described his wife to detectives as "not a nurturer. Amanda focused on Amanda's needs." He said she was "extremely jealous" of his spending time with anyone other than her and for months had focused her jealousy on Keli Townsend, whom Jason described as someone he grew up with; their families were friends.

Jason told detectives that when he met Amanda she was nine months pregnant by a man who committed suicide, and that at the time Jason thought she "had a very hard life and [he] felt sympathy for her." He said he "tried to help her and used a lot of money to try to buy her the happiness she wanted" but had come to realize that she had "character flaws. She could be jealous and mean. She could be very vengeful. She would break things I care about to be vengeful."

The interview needed to be cut short because, detectives wrote, Jason "had an appointment to view Eldon."

Eldon Smith was four years, eight months, and twenty-seven days old at the time of death. He was forty-three-and-one-half inches long and weighed forty-five pounds. His clothing included a yellow T-shirt with gray sleeves and a bulldog logo on the front. He wore long black pants, white socks, and Marvel Comics underwear. He was wearing no shoes. Kayakers later retrieved a child-sized sneaker from the waters beneath the Sellwood Bridge.

"This unfortunate case involves the death of a young, currently unidentified Caucasian boy approximately 3–5 years of age who was found unconscious and not breathing in the Willamette River," the medical examiner wrote on May 23, the day the autopsy was performed and before Eldon had been identified. "Details await survival and a return to consciousness from the little girl who will, hopefully, shed some light on the mystery surrounding how these two children ended up in Portland's Willamette River near Oaks Park and the Sellwood Bridge in total darkness screaming for help."

With the exception of contusions to his face, neck, and upper chest, injuries later attributed to the blunt force with which he hit the water, Eldon was "well-developed, well-nourished, well-hydrated." His limbs, trunk, hands, and feet were, in autopsy parlance, "unremarkable." After Eldon's body was opened "with the usual Y-shaped incision," his organs were examined. These were likewise unremarkable. His heart weighed 107 grams. His spleen weighed 55 grams and was "smooth and glistening." His brain weighed 1,558 grams; it had suffered no trauma. Eldon was perfect in nearly every way, except that he was dead, and because of the manner of his death, the perfect boy had been taken apart.

Jason visited with Eldon when his son was put back together. He visited every day. Someone who asked not to be identified said that once Eldon was brought to the mortuary in Eugene, Jason sat with him there for more than a week, and even after the memorial, he did not leave his son's side.

***

On May 28, Detectives Steed and Michaels visited Amanda's brother-in-law, Daryl Gardner, where he worked at West Coast Paper. They wanted to speak with him again because the principal at his sons' elementary school had contacted the police. The principal told police that Chantel mentioned how Amanda had once asked Daryl something like, "How would you feel if you found your wife and kids floating dead in the river?"

The detectives and Daryl went to a break room. Daryl began by telling them he did not like Jason and was not "overly fond" of Amanda. He called Jason "a habitual liar" and said Amanda was "no saint."

Daryl characterized Jason and Amanda's marriage as "the most unstable" he had ever seen; they abused each other "physically and emotionally. . . . She has hit him and beat him up like crazy. He's had a knife. They have thrown each other's clothes out the window."

Daryl confirmed that Amanda had been pregnant when she and Jason met. She gave the baby up for adoption and hadn't "mentioned that in years." He told detectives, "Neither set of parents approved of the marriage. . . . He [Smith] married for control. She [Stott-Smith] married for money."

Daryl said Amanda was "a good mother, except for the cleaning up after, the feeding, and the caretaking part." He said she "used to be a very good mom, except for Gavin. He [Gavin] had a hard time with both of them [Amanda and Jason]." Jason had been "not good" with Gavin and caused the boy to be "withdrawn." Daryl described Gavin as being close with the Stott family, but "closed off. Distant. The physical abuse by Jason and Mandy and the mental abuse hurt him."

Daryl said Jason had been a "zombie" and used OxyContin prior to entering rehab. Daryl told detectives the story of Jason taking family leave from work by claiming Amanda was pregnant when she was not. "She felt she couldn't appear at his work after that because it was a lie," detectives wrote. Daryl said he believed Jason had wanted the time off so he could use some of the drugs he had brought back from Mexico.

Daryl said Amanda told him Jason had brought "50,000 pills of prescription medication" over the border.

Four sources had said that Jason had brought back drugs, and likely OxyContin, from Mexico. It was true, or it wasn't. There was no way to know unless Jason admitted to doing so, and even then, his reported reflexive lying, as well as his and Amanda's predilection to play the victim, would likely result in the story shooting off in another direction.

Daryl said Amanda lied to the family a lot. She had not, for instance, told them she had lost custody of Trinity and Eldon. Jackie Dreiling had said that Amanda "would not say anything bad" about her husband. Daryl confirmed this.

"Jason was her god," he told detectives. "When it came to Jason, she was an easy person to mess with."

Detective Michaels wanted to know more about the statements Amanda made to Daryl about putting the children in the river.

"It's not the kind of thing someone says and means," he said. "I'm not making excuses for her, but I believe in my heart she didn't know what she was doing when she did it."

Asked again about any statements Amanda might have made to him about doing something to the children, Daryl said, "She once said the perfect revenge against Jason would be to do something like this, but then it wasn't something she could do."

Here, finally, the word "revenge" appeared on record.

"[Daryl] said he didn't think she ever meant it and didn't take it as a serious threat but more of just being upset about the situation with Jason," the report continued. Detectives pressed: Had Amanda been more specific about what she would do?

"Roughly," Daryl answered, "it was that getting rid of the kid would be a good way to get back at Jason."

Michaels asked Daryl whether Amanda had asked him how he'd feel if he found his wife and kids floating in the river.

"She asked me," Daryl said, "'Can I throw your wife in the river?' She was just kidding because Chantel was giving her a hard time."

This was not germane to what detectives were trying to get at.

"I asked him," Michaels wrote, "if he could remember more specifically."

Daryl said, "She said, 'the perfect revenge against Jason would be to kill the kids. But I wouldn't do that.'"

And there it was. And just to make sure:

"I asked," Michaels wrote, "if she mentioned killing herself, and he said she did not."

Picturing Daryl in the break room, I wondered whether he realized what he had revealed, whether he understood that now the case could be built for premeditation. Daryl probably did not know, or did not know right away, that he had led detectives to a place where Amanda's idea was made tangible, because he did not see things the way detectives did. If he did not take seriously what Amanda said about exacting revenge on Jason by killing their children, if to him it was one more lunacy in the least stable marriage he had ever seen, the detectives did take it seriously.

Discussing Amanda's role in Eldon's death and Trinity's injuries, detectives noted the last thing Daryl said to them: "In my eyes, she is guilty."

The police apprehended Amanda nine hours after she dropped her children from the bridge. Within forty-eight hours, detectives had interviewed her and Jason's families as well as people who had direct and indirect involvement with her and the children on the night of the crime. More than three dozen officers, detectives, and criminalists from the forensic evidence department, at least two people from the medical examiner's office, and an uncounted number of medical staff were among those involved.

This was fast, solid, effective work. The officers and others operated in life-or-death zones, where resolutions were needed and outcomes expected. The public needed resolution in order to feel safe, needed consensus that what Amanda had done was monstrous and that she must be locked away. As subject to interpretation as the justice system can be, there is satisfaction in conclusion. Without it, we might have chaos; we might fall off the earth, or be dropped from a bridge. As a young teenager, my daughter drew me a Christmas card of the solar system, on which she wrote, "Thank you for being my gravity all my life."

Everything I had learned about this case showed that Amanda, for a short or long period of time, had been the center of her own universe. She defied or deflected the pleas of those around her and drifted further and further from putting her children's needs first. The alarm this caused others was palpable. Nathan and Chelsea Beck had repeatedly tried to convince various agencies that Gavin was in danger. Kathy Stott checked and rechecked her daughter into mental health clinics. During an August 2008 interview, she and Chantel told a Department of Human Services caseworker that "Amanda knows how to 'play the system' and that she is skilled at presenting well."

It would be easy to blame the system for breaking down, to say, "If DHS had done its job right, Eldon would be alive today." This would be asking caseworkers to see through the walls of lies Amanda and Jason had been building, together and separately, all their adult lives.

After years of looking, I could no longer differentiate between Jason's and Amanda's pathologies. Who was abusing whom? Who slashed whose tires? Did Amanda really sleep in her car on Christmas Eve and watch her children celebrate the holiday without her? What did she mean when she wrote that Jason "has taught me everything I know"? Did she mean it at all?

The exertions the couple employed to take each other down were sustained and, in their way, viscous. Amanda and Jason may have wound up in the same nexus by different routes, but by the end of

2008, and likely much earlier, they were both stuck there, together with their children. Maybe it felt, for a time, like them against the world. Then Jason decided he wanted out. He had the means to get out, and he took it. This for Amanda was heartbreak but also betrayal, not least because she could not find a way out herself, until she did. She would get them all out in 2.41 seconds.

30

Two dogs announced visitors at the front door of the Beck home in Vancouver, Washington. Chelsea Beck waved them down.

"Forgive the mess," she said of the boxes and craft projects on the dining table. Chelsea and Nathan had purchased the long, low ranch house in 2014. It was closer to the church they attended, and Nathan's brother planned to build a house on the footprint of a former cow barn on the three-acre property, a barn that Emily, Chelsea and Nathan's eight-year-old daughter, wanted to show me. In her shorts and cowboy boots, Emily hop-skipped toward the barn. The dogs stayed at her heels. Crickets, rarely heard ten miles southwest in Portland, chirruped in the green-gold landscape, hazy with dust on a hot Saturday afternoon in September 2015.

"Watch for holes," said Gavin, who seemed to make a point of staying beside me. He had turned eighteen in March. He said he was five foot seven but looked taller. He had straight glossy black hair, strong eyebrows, and the beginnings of a mustache that, asked to guess, I might have said had yet to be shaved. He wore dark Levi's, a black T-shirt, and rubber Crocs sandals, which he said worked well for the terrain. Were the pocks and dried mud holes the work of gophers?

"Rabbits!" Emily called over her shoulder.

"Maybe snakes," said Chelsea.

"Rats, Mom," said Gavin, who would be in a position to know. The previous summer, he had lived here alone for two weeks, except for drop-ins by his dad, to do scraping, painting, and cleanup. Had he ever been scared, staying on the property by himself?

"No," he said in a way that implied, what would there logically be to be scared of? When I asked if there were still rats on the property, Gavin broke into an open smile.

"The dogs," he said, "took it upon themselves to eliminate trespassers."

The Becks had also moved away from Portland to get some physical and psychological distance from the Stotts and Smiths, whose ongoing struggles Nathan had been sucked into essentially since meeting Amanda. Fighting to see Gavin had cost Nathan and Chelsea thousands of dollars and untold aggravation, for no good reason they could see.

Gavin graduated from Benson Polytechnic High School in June 2015. Within two weeks, he had a job at a Goodwill sorting center, five miles from their Vancouver home. Because he did not yet have a driver's license, he biked both ways. This and being eighteen kept him gangly.

"I am the least health-conscious person I know," he told me, again with the open smile. "You think I look this way from playing video games and eating junk food? You're right!"

We were seated at the end of an L-shaped couch in the Becks' living room. After showing me a new pair of pink cowboy boots ("With *gold*," she said, running her finger along a toe tip), Emily strummed a toy electric guitar. Chelsea maintained the illusion of not hovering over Gavin's conversation by sitting in a recliner across the room.

Gavin said he liked the work at Goodwill—trying to be the first to stock newly emptied tables—because it gave him the opportunity to observe acutely, to identify problems and come up with solutions.

Coming up with solutions was what Gavin liked to do. He decided his senior year that he would join the navy, because the navy would pay for college. He had been on his high school's robotics team for four years, captain or cocaptain for the last two, and worked on programmable logic controllers and industrial robot arms. He had taken apart his Kindle and added a program that allowed him to play Game Boy games on it.

"I want to see how this works with this and that," he said, "and why things are the way they are."

Gavin had the habits of an engineer. He had an example in his father, who had run electronic systems on nuclear submarines as an active member of the service. Nathan currently served in the reserves, including this weekend aboard a rescue vessel stationed off San Diego.

"When a submarine sinks unintentionally, it's up to teams like his to get the crewmen off, starting within seventy-two hours," Gavin said of his father's work, work that required precision and reliability, required doing what you said you were going to do lest other people die.

I noted that Gavin calling Chelsea "Mom" meant there were no longer any children who referred to Amanda as mother.

Gavin had been the one to wake his grandparents when Amanda did not return home with his siblings. That detectives had not interviewed Gavin until seven months after the crime, that the press had rarely mentioned him, struck Chelsea as yet more people showing Gavin he did not matter. Whether he wanted public acknowledgment was not the point. Chelsea wanted him acknowledged. To that end, she read a statement at Amanda's sentencing in April 2010, which read in part:

Since May 23, 2009, our family has forever changed. For my husband, Gavin's father and myself, we worry about our children in a different way now. We worry if they walk around the corner to the grocery store and we can't see them; if Gavin doesn't get home from school right on time; and the list goes on. You name something that a parent worries about and compound that times one hundred. Our family could be just as devastated as Eldon's because Gavin was with his mother for visitation that weekend and chose not to go with her that night to pick up the kids. When we think about that, it causes us as parents to not want to let our kids take any risks or do things on their own. That is unfair to us all. Amanda has taken that freedom and innocence away from us.

As the mother of Gavin I see every day how this has changed him. He loves stability and wavers when things don't stay the same. He has had to learn to talk deeply about his broken heart, his pain, his anger, all before he turned thirteen. He has to relearn how he and Trinity will relate to one another as they share this tragedy of having their brother taken from them, each child unknowing of the things that might bring up pain when they just discuss day-to-day life. No children should have to monitor themselves when sharing with their siblings, in hopes that they don't say something that will hurt the other more. Gavin faces life knowing he did not go with Amanda that night. He will continue to ask himself, if he had been there, could he have stopped her. The truth is that even though he thankfully was safe that night, with her choice, Amanda did throw Gavin away that day too.

Chelsea cried her way through this speech in court. Amanda did not cry or, as far as I saw, look Chelsea's way. She also did not let Chelsea adopt Gavin. Chelsea had written Amanda in jail, asking her to release her parental rights to her son. Amanda wrote back saying she wanted to hear from Gavin that this was what he wanted. Gavin had written Amanda, saying that it was.

"She wrote back to say that's not his 'voice,'" Chelsea told me in 2010. Gavin wrote Amanda again, as did Chelsea. Amanda did not respond. Chelsea wrote once more.

"I said, 'Show him you have some grace for him, the way the judge had for you and your life,'" she said. "It would show Gavin she was human and had some love for him."

Amanda responded to this letter.

"She said I was 'asinine,' and how dare I say she was not a good mother to Gavin?" Chelsea said.

Amanda instead suggested a rapprochement in jail with her surviving son. "Tell Gavin to forgive," Chelsea recalled Amanda writing. "The visiting area has so much warmth."

Gavin received another letter from Amanda after the boat dedication, a letter Chelsea paraphrased as, "It's me. How are you? Did you see your sister on TV? She looked good, but it made me sad. I mourned. I cried over it. But I'm fine now. You?"

I had seen Gavin a month after the boat dedication, in January 2011. Chelsea and I had been in the front room of their previous home in northeast Portland when Gavin walked in from school. He stopped just inside the threshold and seemed to assess the situation. After a moment, he said it was nice to see me again, went to his room, and closed the door. A thirteen-year-old boy wanting to hang out with some lady with a pen and a pad would be notable under any circumstance. Still, Gavin gave the impression of being someone who, at this time in his life, avoided interaction that was not essential. It did not surprise me to later learn he sought environments where he had control over the moving parts, that he preferred the reliability of robots and electronics, systems whose responsiveness were under his command.

Six months after the visit in January 2011, soon after his name was legally changed to Gavin Beck, I saw Gavin again. He was in his front yard, using a metal clamping contraption to dig up dandelions. He let me try it. I jammed it in the earth while he told me he liked math and science, liked Benson Polytechnic High School. I told him my daughter had flunked both algebra and geometry and had to take make-up classes at night school at Benson. Gavin found this very funny and laughed. Chelsea watched from the front door.

"I've had to let Gavin lead me," she said that day. He had recently told her he had forgiven Amanda, saying, "I had to forgive her to forget her."

By November 2011, Chelsea had not forgiven Amanda.

"I still *despise* her," she said. Chelsea was also angry with Jason, who had only once followed the court order that Trinity be allowed to see Gavin before cutting it off. That everything about Amanda and Jason enraged Chelsea was something she was starting to see as her problem.

"Nathan is very much 'action equals result,'" she said. "If getting upset causes more problems, he says, it's not worth it."

It was hard not to get upset when Gavin wrote letters to Trinity via Christine Duncan, who replied she could not go against Jason and thus could not show the letters to Trinity.

Amanda had sent Gavin a birthday card that March, albeit late. There had been no contact since. No contact, late contact, any contact: all of it ate at Chelsea, as did the families refusing, even after the murder, to confront what in her view they all well knew.

"It's ludicrous for people to say they didn't see this coming," she said. "Everybody knew it was coming, in terms of Amanda and Jason's behavior."

When I learned in 2009 that Gavin had not gotten in the car with his mother, I made certain suppositions. I supposed having not done so would be a heavy burden, that it would keep Gavin wondering if he could have done anything to stop her. I supposed he would be angry with Amanda and conflicted as to whether he wanted to see her again. I imagined that the loss of his brother and, in the aftermath, his sister, would cause him to feel upset or angry and that he would not want to talk about any of it.

When Gavin said he would speak with me in 2015, I took the suppositions and fashioned them into a soft landing: I would ask him only for memories of Eldon and Trinity. This would be the kind thing to do. It might provide relief in a story that sorely needed it. Wouldn't it be nice to see Emily showing off her gold-tipped boots? The silver Weimaraner and bluetick coonhound sleeping in a patch of sun on the living room floor? To see Gavin show Emily, on the acoustic guitar he had taught himself to play, the chords to "Wonderwall"?

"You can ask me anything you want," said Gavin when I told him I just wanted to hear happy memories of his half siblings.

In an effort to tread lightly, I had forgotten how math works, that the factors that put Gavin where he was would not be built from happy memories. Presupposition further discounted that Gavin would be a young man who had no interest, as most young men do not, in being handled gently.

"You can ask me anything you want," he repeated, but if I wanted to speak about Trinity and Eldon, "It depends on what time frame."

He laid out the time frame. There had been times he was left in the house alone with the children, in Hawaii, put in charge of feeding them, making sure they were okay. Gavin did not sound troubled recalling this. More recently, in Tualatin, he said, "was kind of when it all came tumbling down."

"When we moved back to Tualatin," he said, "you have less and less consistency with things like [eating]. By the time Jason was in rehab, we just ate what was available when we were hungry. When those two things were aligned, that's when we ate."

Trinity, Gavin, and Eldon. Photo courtesy of Ryan Barron.

How does a ten-year-old who finds himself in charge of a five- and two-year-old foster alignment? Gavin taught the children the words to the songs in the movie *Shrek*. He made up games for them to play. He fed them what he could reach and knew how to make: peanut butter and jelly, cereal when there was milk.

"They would just forget to keep buying milk," Gavin said. "Sometimes we'd have cereal with water."

He took pleasure in the memory of a small slyness.

"One time, *one time*, it was really great," he said. "We had no milk, but we had half-and-half. I had Frosted Flakes with half-and-half."

He learned to navigate two lives.

"There was the show that we put on, where we behave ourselves when people are around," Gavin said. "If we were with grandparents, we were not going to get in trouble. They [Amanda and Jason] are not going to really do as much because they're trying to display themselves as these great people."

Great people as in happy?

"Yes."

Caring?

"Yes," he said. "Things were also put under the category of 'family secret.' If something was a family secret, we weren't allowed to talk about it with anyone else."

The family secret Gavin cited—Amanda locking Jason out of the house until he bought her cigarettes—seemed innocuous. Gavin mentioned, but did not cite as a secret, Jason and Amanda using him as a go-between when they argued. He did not cite as a secret his mother slapping him when he did not turn in a homework assignment. He did not cite as a secret that Jason "was the main person who punished me, but at the same time, when he was angry it wasn't directed at me." It was directed at Amanda, he said, which meant Gavin could go be by himself.

"I always used to hide in my room. I would make stories and hid myself in these stories that I made," he said. "I chose to make up what was going on, fictional things, because they were better than thinking about what was actual."

"I don't think there was any authenticity in how people spoke to him," Chelsea said from the recliner. "There was never any, 'How was your day?'"

"No," Gavin said. "That never happened."

I thought it must have been especially taxing to a child with an analytical mind to live in a home where people did not mean what they said, or said something that meant its opposite. (There's an easy way to test how confusing this is to children: try sarcasm on a six-year-old. They will try to figure out why what you said does not match the way you said it, and when you tell them it's sarcasm, they may reply, as my six-year-old did, "Don't sarcast me.")

"I've decided I don't want to be someone who puts on a fake face when I'm doing something," Gavin said. "I try to talk to people the same way regardless of who they are . . . [and] I expect people to tell me when I do something that bothers them so I can then stop doing that to them. So [what I'm doing] changes a little bit, but not to the point where I am acting differently."

I asked Gavin what Eldon and Trinity had been like.

"Eldon was young enough that there wasn't really . . ." He paused. "I would say that, compared to other younger kids, he did not have the urge to kind of bug you about stuff. My best guess was that he was an introvert like I was, and that was one of the reasons he didn't do a lot. But it's also the environment. Growing up in that environment, I was very polite, I kept to myself; I didn't really do anything. I think that also had an effect [on him]."

Perhaps Eldon had been following in Gavin's footsteps.

"That very well could be," he said. "Trinity was more outgoing than Eldon and me. She liked doing karaoke. . . . Another [thing] would be, which I thought was really funny, was in the Tualatin house. Trinity was sick, and so she got up and went into Amanda and Jason's bedroom and was like, 'Mommy, I don't feel so good,' and then immediately threw up on Amanda, and it was just the funniest thing."

That was it for the happy memories.

On May 23, 2014, Jason Smith posted the following on his public Facebook page, a post Chelsea and I read together:

> Five years ago today my smart, handsome, funny, loving, confident, happy boy was taken from us. He lives on with the people that love him, and no more than I. As the years go on I hear his voice and continue to see his beautiful smiling face in the faces and voices of my other children, and in the special places I like to go alone to honor his memory. I love you so, so very much son. My life will never be the same without you, and I will continue to honor your memory by thinking of you often, and in the beautiful quiet places in the forest that mean the most to me. Eldon Jay Rebhan Smith in loving memory of you son. Your father adores you and carries on your wonderful memory.

I thought the message was moving.

"Yes," Chelsea said, turning off her computer. "After you talk to him, you always ask yourself, why don't I like that guy again?"

Gavin started his scheduled weekend visit with his mother on May 22, 2009. Maybe it was because he was playing with his cousins, or maybe it was because Nathan and Chelsea had told him, "If you don't feel safe with Amanda, you do not need to go with her," but when she asked Gavin to get in the car so they could pick up his brother and sister, he refused.

"I didn't want to be around her, so I said no," he said.

Gavin's life had changed dramatically by May 2009. He was living full-time with Nathan and Chelsea. He rarely saw Trinity and Eldon and never saw Jason. He had become mistrustful of his mother. These factors may have contributed to Gavin not being able to fall asleep the night of May 22, but none were the reason he woke his grandparents to say Amanda and the children had not come home.

"They were supposed to be there at ten o'clock, and it was ten thirty, and eleven," he said. "So it was reaching that point that something could be happening."

He tried to make sense of this until around three in the morning, when he fell asleep. He did not sleep long. By seven, the house was filling with people, with phones ringing. Someone—Gavin did not remember whom, or exactly what was said—told him what had happened to Trinity and Eldon.

"There's a cupboard behind the couch—that curved couch," he said of a couch in his grandparents' living room. "That's where I would go when Amanda came to pick me up, because I didn't want to leave. That was my hiding spot. And so, when it was explained to me what happened, I went to that cupboard and I stayed there for I don't know how long."

It was long enough for Kathy Stott to call Nathan and Chelsea and tell them what had happened to the children, long enough for Nathan to tell Kathy Stott that she was not to give Gavin any details, that he and Chelsea would do it, and that they were coming now. Gavin was still hiding when they arrived. Nathan and Chelsea brought Gavin out of the cupboard. Nathan told his son what happened, and then he and Chelsea did what Jason would later do with Trinity: they took him away from anything that would remind him of Amanda.

"It was hard. It was . . . it was the first time someone in my life had died, right?" Gavin said of his learning that Eldon and Trinity had been found in the river, that Eldon was dead. "It was kind of the idea, I'm never going to see them again; they're not here anymore. They're not here anymore. That was the sad thing all around. . . . I think what helped a lot was they were in heaven and eventually I'll see them, but I can't *see them right now*."

Gavin used the plural "them." Trinity was alive, but he had not seen her since the boat launch.

"I know that at a certain point I will be able to find her and go see her," he said. "But I don't necessarily want to see her with Jason around, that kind of thing."

"We invited Trinity to your graduation," Chelsea reminded Gavin.

"Yes," he said.

"We thought it sounded like a possibility because we met Jason's requirements," Chelsea added. Christine Duncan had called to say Jason would consider allowing Trinity to attend Gavin's graduation if Gavin promised that the Stotts would not be there. This had not been hard for Gavin to do. He said he saw Mike and Kathy Stott "twice a year, if at all." Through Christine Duncan, Gavin gave Jason his word. Jason had nonetheless not permitted Trinity to come. I asked Gavin whether he thought it possible Jason had no intention of letting Trinity attend no matter which of his demands were met.

"That's easily a possibility," he said. "There's no way to know."

I asked whether, at the boat dedication, Jason had spoken to Gavin at all.

"Nope," he said.

He didn't say, "Hello, son" or anything?

"Nope, nope."

Christine Duncan and her husband went to Gavin's graduation in June 2015. The families had not seen each other in five years. During the ceremony, Chelsea ran into Christine Duncan in the ladies' room.

"She said to me, 'I just don't understand why Gavin did not go with Amanda that night,'" Chelsea told me several days after the graduation. "She said she would not have let the children go with Amanda had she known Gavin would not be there."

This confused Chelsea. Hadn't it been Amanda's court-ordered weekend with the children? Duncan said it had been, but repeated she would not have let Amanda have the children if she had known they would not be going back immediately to Amanda's parents' home.

If this was revisionist thinking—Christine Duncan had not mentioned these reservations to detectives, while Jason had told them Amanda said she would be taking the children "maybe [to] the beach," which, as point of reference, is eighty miles from Portland—I did not doubt Christine Duncan's anguish. How many times in six years had she played over how she might have stopped Amanda? I imagined the loop to be endless.

Chelsea told Duncan that Emily wanted to meet Trinity, Gavin's other sister, and that Emily prayed for Trinity every night.

Chelsea said Duncan broke down upon hearing this, that she said, "Thank you. Thank you for saying that."

It's a near-immutable fact that parents will put their children's welfare ahead of or at least on par with their own. We assume this to be built into who we are. Or I had assumed this. Because I could not under any circumstance see myself dropping my child from a bridge with the intent to harm her, I did not see how Amanda could have done this to her children. We see through our own lenses. Sabrina Trembley saw Amanda as the mom next to her. Tiffany Gray saw Amanda as a mother-goddess-earth-mama. To others (the courts, the cops), this sort of rationalizing did not conform to the known coordinates, and further, it was decadent thinking. Lenses, their actions argued, must be made out of glass, not mirrors. I found this position increasingly hard to disagree with. Amanda had phoned Jason within three minutes of dropping the children and said, "Help me." She did not say, help your children; she said, "Help me." She was asking for attention. She was on the offensive. She had been locked in combat with Jason for years. They had all but cannibalized each other. People saw her as broken, and in many ways she was broken. And she had, after the fact and if we read the reports right, jumped from the ninth floor of a building. But before she did, she had the wherewithal to hurt Jason one more time. If he had been in earnest when he told detectives that, upon learning what Amanda might have done, his first thought was, "There's just no way," then he had not been paying attention.

"I'm basically done with Amanda. I have no interest," Gavin told me.

Part of his being "done" with Amanda, with whom he had not exchanged a word since telling her he would not get in her car, was about her having done "a bad thing, and she's bad for doing it." The other part was that Gavin sensed he was missing an emotional component.

"It was explained to me, when you're growing up, when you're really young, there are certain things you develop at certain times," he said. "Some of those things I didn't do. A good example would be I don't, or didn't—I haven't really checked recently—I don't miss people. . . . I have no interest in pursuing Amanda, and I don't miss her."

Did he miss Jason?

"No," he said, and also that he had "an active dislike for Jason because he is an active obstacle for me seeing Trinity."

Did he miss Trinity?

"I would like to see Trinity," he said.

When asked about his love for Trinity, for Eldon, Gavin paused.

"In my mind, Eldon didn't do anything wrong," he said. "In my mind he's a great person, because he got the shortest end of the stick. I wish things didn't happen the way they did, but they did; there's not a lot I can do to change that."

Emily crawled onto the couch. Gavin put his arm around her shoulders.

"I'm comfortable talking about what happened, but I don't . . ." He paused. "I've made a point not to rationalize it as much. I tend to overthink things. [With this] I did not," he said of his life with Jason and Amanda. "This was something that I did not want to do."

He chose not to run the program over and over.

"Right," he said.

He had evidence it might have been futile.

"Yes," he said. "But at the same time, it was probably a lot easier for them to lie about than it was to tell the truth."

The relationship, I suggested, had elements of deception from the start.

"They were both narcissistic people. They were both in it for themselves. . . . They are both not necessarily *good* people, but it was both of them combined that created the problem," Gavin said. "I think what it came down to, with both of them, was they tried to keep up this illusion that everything was fine for so long, and then to a point they just couldn't do it anymore."

It sounded like a lot of work.

"I imagine," he said, "it takes its toll."

EPILOGUE

On January 19, 2014, I sent a card to Amanda for what I sensed would be the last of our one-way correspondence:

> Dear Amanda—
>
> Please accept my apologies if my contacting you has brought you and your family unhappiness. I might have shown grace and patience regarding your wishes not to speak with me (rather than asking you to see things my way), and understanding as to why. I do understand. I send you as always my best regards.

Understanding is a fluid proposition, and a year later I would see things differently. That I did would not matter to Amanda, who stood firm, sending me two messages in six years, both times via Samantha Hammerly. The first came by email on New Year's Day, 2012:

> I did ask her [Amanda] about corresponding with you, either in person or by mail. She is not interested in any at all. She said to tell you that she sees it as rehashing her sins, for which she needed to answer to God about only, and He has forgiven her.

Amanda did not mention needing to answer to her surviving children. I wondered about that. Chelsea Beck did not wonder. She also did not give Gavin the letter Amanda sent each year on his birthday, with a check for thirty dollars.

The other message came soon after I sent the last postcard. Samantha and I were at the burger bar. She'd had a tough year. She had questioned her faith and left the church she attended with her husband and children. She had been a Christian since Amanda took her, in eighth grade, to services at the Stott family's church. I told Samantha I had heard less than favorable things about this church. Jackie Dreiling, who had worked in administration there, told me she had left because of the pastor's attitude, especially toward women, which included telling Chantel that if she left his ministry she would go to hell. April Anson recalled Amanda telling her that, during a marriage counseling session there, the pastor had said of Amanda, "'She's a whore; she's a bitch; she's a slut. You need to figure it out because you're living in sin, and the devil has a hold of your soul.'"

I could not know whether the pastor (who had been instructed by Amanda not to speak with me, and who has since died) said these things, only that Amanda said he had, or that this was how April remembered it.

A week after our lunch at the burger bar, Samantha again asked Amanda if she would speak with me. Why Samantha did this I did not know, but she had and received a variation on the first answer, which Samantha emailed to me.

> She is convinced you are only out to drudge [*sic*] up horrible memories and events and make a buck off her.

Depending on which end of the tube you looked through, Amanda's summation of what I was doing here was exactly true and exactly false.

More than a year after this lunch, after I learned things that would harden my sympathies toward Amanda, after official reports had shown that people rewrite their stories by the hour, that we read through subjective lenses, I came to a place that felt as solid as any would, and feel confident saying Amanda was ill prepared. What portion is attributable to what Jackie Dreiling termed "Defective Character Disorder," to religious inculcation, to Jason's dominance and addictions, or to Amanda's narcissism, catalyzed by spite, can continue to be debated. There is no such thing as an immutable truth, much as our hearts might yearn for it and our justice systems demand it; there are only the stories we tell ourselves. But there are facts, and one—the one that started this story—is that Amanda tried to murder two of her children and did murder one, which tells us she was not prepared to navigate her own or her children's lives, and we know this because she threw her children off a bridge. We are right when we claim mothers do not do this out of the blue, that doing so is aberrant behavior. We may not when we are young know why we are certain of this—Eldon's friend Max did not make another best friend at school for several years after Eldon's murder because he was afraid that friend would die—but we know this as adults, which makes it all the more troubling, or troubling to me, when judges, attorneys, family, and strangers promote some version of "what Amanda Stott-Smith did will never be understood," to which I counter, with all due respect and because we do not know what we will find, that we can understand if we try.

POSTSCRIPT

On February 6, 2016, Trinity Smith and Gavin Beck were allowed to communicate via FaceTime. It was the first time they had seen or spoken to each other since the boat dedication in December 2010. Chelsea Beck and Christine Duncan, with whom Trinity was then living, arranged for the contact between the children. Jason Smith was not consulted.

In March 2016, Gavin Beck joined the US Navy, where as part of basic training he would learn how to survive in open water.

ACKNOWLEDGMENTS

When I was very young, my brother and I played a board game called Candy Land. In my recollection, pieces advanced along a winding path with the help of guides offering hints and totems. That I recently looked up this game and saw that's not how it works at all does not alter my sense that, during the years I worked on the story of Amanda and the children, others led the way. Some of these people walked with me for a long time. Others offered what they knew and disappeared. That anyone would speak about an issue as charged as the murder of a child by his mother seems to me an act of faith, and I am indebted to those who communicated with me, in some cases over a period of years:

April Anson, Sara and Ryan Barron, Chelsea and Gavin Beck, Pati Gallagher, Tiffany and Shanon Gray, Samantha Hammerly, Jen Johnson, Isaac LaGrone, Justin Montgomery, Thomas Parrish, Sabrina and Max Trembley, others who go unnamed, and those who asked not to be named. Whatever I am able to offer the story is thanks to them and the love and concern they carry for those who were lost.

Ken Hadley is wise and wry and patient. I thank him for letting me stick to him like a limpet during the run-up to Amanda's sentencing and for being a pal afterward.

What began as all-sorrowful conversations with Jackie Dreiling gave way to debating politics, going to lunch, and watching daytime TV. This might seem remarkable (and it is). It is also a result of becoming friends, if under most unlikely circumstances. Jackie, who died in 2016, told me one of the reasons she spoke with me was because "it's the only way I can leave any information for Trinity. Tell her how much I love her. And how much I miss not being able to see her grow up."

My appreciation to the agencies and organizations that provided records, including the Multnomah County Sheriff's Office, the Portland Police Bureau, the Tualatin Police Department, the Oregon Department of Corrections, Coffee Creek Correctional Facility, the Circuit Court for the State of Oregon, and the Counties of Clackamas, Lane, Multnomah, and Washington. Thanks to Matt Davis, then at the *Portland Mercury*, Kyle Iboshi at KGW-TV, and Amy Frazier at KOIN-TV. My thanks to Rene Denfeld, attorney Michael Rose, and Hank Stern for help in navigating various legal and governmental channels.

My thanks to readers of this manuscript in its various forms: Victoria Martin Del Campo, Charles Dubow, David Rensin (twice!), Nanci McCloskey, Ali Selim, Claire Anderson-Wheeler, Claire MF Rood, and the small groups at Queens University of Charlotte. To Steve De Jarnatt for the writing sojourn in Port Townsend, Hillary Johnson for her editor's eye and big brain, and Juliette Levy, who let me read her the entire manuscript aloud and fed me as I did so.

Matt Welch sent an email of encouragement during a dark time, a note so comprehensive and convincing I kept it on my bulletin board for four years (and referred to it as needed). Katherine Boo's friendship and generosity helped push me through to finish the book. Alexandria Marzano-Lesnevich and Robert Kolker were open handed in their introductions to agent and editor. All these writers floor me with their dedication to follow hard stories where they want to go. Read their work.

My thanks to the editors who gave me assignments as I worked on the book: Jeff Baker, Robert Messenger, Tom Beer, Emily White, Erik Lundegaard, Tom Christie, and, in perpetuity, Janet Duckworth.

Robert Guinsler at Sterling Lord Literistic took the manuscript over the transom and did so with enthusiasm and effectiveness. Barry Harbaugh at Little A bought the book and knew what to do with it. I am tremendously grateful to his editor's eye and sensibility. Angela Moody's cover design captured the book in one image, thank you. Also, to the fact-checking department, which clarified thousands of points, saved me from evident numbers dyslexia, and were able to snatch a near-finished draft from the jaws of a computer glitch.

My thanks to the home crew: Josh Gibby; Tim Sampson; Jonathan Tinn; my parents, Kathy Hayes and Richard Rommelmann; everyone at Ristretto Roasters; and Tafv's superstar crew, the wondrous young ones.

To Deborah Reed, beloved Lady Deborah, who from the day we met has made life better and better yet.

I am privileged to spend my life with the most calm, clear-eyed, and honorable people I know: my husband, Din Johnson—steady, strong, true—and my daughter, Tafv Sampson, shining light, seeker and bequeather of beauty, my very heart.

NOTE ON SOURCES

I am indebted to the following authors and how they put together their work. I looked to these books, as well as to an uncounted number of articles and essays, as I figured out how to write this story.

Boo, Katherine. *Behind the Beautiful Forevers.* New York: Random House, 2012.

Buss, David. *The Murderer Next Door.* New York: Penguin Press, 2005.

Capote, Truman. *In Cold Blood.* New York: Random House, 1965.

Carrère, Emmanuel. *The Adversary.* New York: Metropolitan Books, 2000.

Cleckley, Hervey. *The Mask of Sanity.* St. Louis, MO: The C.V. Mosby Company, 1941.

Cullen, Dave. *Columbine.* New York: Twelve, 2009.

Didion, Joan. *After Henry.* New York: Simon & Schuster, 1992.

Dow, David R. *The Autobiography of an Execution*. New York: Twelve, 2010.

Gilmore, Mikal. *Shot in the Heart*. New York: Doubleday, 1994.

Hare, Robert D. *Without Conscience*. New York: The Guildford Press, 1993.

Junger, Sebastian. *A Death in Belmont*. New York: W.W. Norton & Company, 2006.

Kipnis, Laura. *How to Become a Scandal*. New York: Metropolitan Books, 2010.

Kirn, Walter. *Blood Will Out*. New York: Liveright, 2014.

Kolker, Robert. *Lost Girls*. New York: HarperCollins, 2013.

Krakauer, John. *Under the Banner of Heaven*. New York: Anchor Books, 2004.

Lazar, Zachary. *Evening's Empire*. New York: Little, Brown and Company, 2009.

Lowry, Beverly. *Crossed Over*. New York: Knopf, 1992.

Mailer, Norman. *The Executioner's Song*. New York: Little, Brown and Company, 1979.

Malcolm, Janet. *Iphigenia in Forest Hills*. New Haven, CT: Yale University Press, 2011.

Malcolm, Janet. *The Journalist and the Murderer*. New York: Vintage Books, 1990.

McKee, Geoffrey R. *Why Mothers Kill*. New York: Oxford University Press, 2006.

Meyer, Cheryl L., and Michelle Oberman. *Mothers Who Kill Their Children*. New York: New York University Press, 2001.

Oberman, Michelle, and Cheryl L. Meyer. *When Mothers Kill: Interviews from Prison*. New York: New York University Press, 2008.

Olmi, Veronique. *Beside the Sea*. Translated by Adriana Hunter. Portland, OR: Tin House Books, 2012.

O'Malley, Suzanne. *Are You There Alone? The Unspeakable Crimes of Andrea Yates*. New York: Simon & Schuster, 2004.

Rule, Anne. *Small Sacrifices*. New York: Dutton, 1987.

Stout, Martha. *The Sociopath Next Door*. New York: Broadway Books, 2005.

Summerscale, Kate. *The Suspicions of Mr. Whicher*. London: Walker Books, 2008.

ABOUT THE AUTHOR

Photo © Tafv Sampson 2016

Nancy Rommelmann has written for the *LA Weekly*, the *Wall Street Journal*, and the *New York Times*, among other publications. She is the author of several previous works of nonfiction and fiction. She grew up in New York City and currently lives in Portland, Oregon. Find out more at nancyromm.com.